CONTENTS

ILLUSTRATIONS

Between pages 176–7 and 192–3

ix

PREFACE

THIS IS A STUDY of the movement of the Pre-Raphaelite imagination from 1848 to 1900. Its aims, distinct yet related, are to explore a type of art that enjoyed considerable minority esteem in the second half of the nineteenth century; and to trace some of the English origins of what is the most vocal, blatant, yet complex moment of that art—the 1890's.

That decade has been subjected to much exposition on the level of gossip or period charm—music halls, blue china or green carnations. Yet it still demands, as Dr Ian Fletcher has pleaded in *Victorian Studies*, more systematic study of its complexities. My own contribution is to note certain dominant characteristics of the 1890's and then to explore their provenance in the Pre-Raphaelite movement. Sometimes this study attends to the direct and obvious influence upon later artists and writers of such a central figure as Rossetti. More frequently, it conducts a circumspect inquiry into habits of mind, modes of imaginative energy, initiated by the early Pre-Raphaelites and invoked unconsciously by their followers to sustain fresh but related concerns. Whichever form of inheritance is involved, the Pre-Raphaelite imagination is clearly seen as the dominant means during the latter part of the nineteenth century of articulating a rich and involved consciousness to which the rest of Victorian culture was not usually hospitable. The first chapter is devoted to a fuller explanation of this 'continuity of admiration' and its place in the Victorian scene.

The remaining five chapters each discuss an important mode of Pre-Raphaelite imagination. First, the enthusiasm for what was seen as the picturesque and inspiratory Middle Ages, to which most Pre-Raphaelites looked for subject matter and even technical knowledge. Second, growing out of these mediaeval interests, their

xi

introspection and the fashion in which they chose to communicate their meditations and the shadowy depths of the psyche. Third, their celebration of the noumenous; the search for a dialect of symbolism subtle enough to convey their apprehension of a meaningful world beyond exterior description and rational habits of mind. Fourth, an account of one specific symbol invoked by almost all the Pre-Raphaelites—the famous image of a woman with large, staring eyes and masses of heavy hair (the illustrations in this volume document this chapter). Fifth, their attempt, often uneasy and hesitant, to accommodate themselves to a modern world of photography and scientific definition by means of realistic description, frequently of subject matter ignored by most other Victorians. There are, naturally, connections between these five topics, but they seem to represent distinct and important elements in the complex fabric of Pre-Raphaelitism. All were initiated by the first Pre-Raphaelite brothers and are equally integral parts of the imagination of the 1890's.

I insist upon a continuity from Pre-Raphaelite beginnings in 1848 to the end of the century for two reasons. Pre-Raphaelitism did not collapse with the Brotherhood; I share with William E. Fredeman's recent *Pre-Raphaelitism: A Bibliocritical Study* a sense of its larger boundaries. Professor Fredeman writes:

Critics and literary historians of the Victorian period have too often been inclined to simplify the term Pre-Raphaelite to denote only those aspects of Victorian romanticism centering on the Pre-Raphaelite Brotherhood. More accurately, the term includes three stages of a congeries of literary and artistic impulse which have been used loosely and interchangeably as synonyms: the Pre-Raphaelite Brotherhood, the Pre-Raphaelite Movement, and Pre-Raphaelitism. Actually, they are not mutually exclusive but sequential terms descriptive of a continuous, if not a unified, aesthetic force.

My own work traces this force from 1848 until the turn of the century. Equally, I am sceptical about isolating the last decade from the rest of Victorian art. Osbert Burdett, perhaps the period's most interesting early historian, noted in *The Beardsley Period* that the 1890's were not a definite period but a point of view.

Consequently, the patterns and attitudes of its mental economy
are likely to have their roots in previous artistic activities of the
century. I have tried to locate its point of view (Burdett is un-
necessarily simple to suggest only one viewpoint) among the
magazines of the period:

> intellectual marines
> Landing in little magazines
> Capture a trend.

These bear constant witness to the nourishment that their contributors derived from the Pre-Raphaelite imagination.

A further reason for invoking such magazines as *The Yellow
Book, The Savoy, The Dome, The Hobby Horse, The Albemarle,
The Pageant* and the books of the Rhymers' Club was that some
trends of the 1890's can there be seen in *detail*. For we are still liable
to be offered inert generalizations about the period, based upon
acquiescence to stock responses (*fin de siècle* and *aestheticism* are
two of the token phrases).

But in part also there has been too single-minded a concern
with the French taste of the 1890's, with the result that the native
traditions which informed the period have been neglected. It is
only recently, for example, that the Pre-Raphaelite contribution
to Art Nouveau has been adequately acknowledged and explored.
There have been frequent gestures towards the Pre-Raphaelite
influence in these matters: in 1903 Justin McCarthy saw the
aesthetic movement as 'a curious offshoot of pre-Raphaelitism',
and later in *Scrutiny* Dr Leavis noted the same pattern. But they
are no more than token gestures and it is perhaps time to explore
extensively these reaches of literary history.

It remains to acknowledge the encouragement and assistance I
have derived from a variety of individuals and institutions: in the
early stages of my work from Professor L. C. Knights and Dr B.
L. Joseph and from Professor A. J. Farmer of the Sorbonne; more
recently, from Professor Frank Kermode and from Dr Ian Fletcher,
whose considerable knowledge of this period has generously been
made available to me; from colleagues at York—Professor
Philip Brockbank, Dr C. A. Patrides, Dr James W. Harper, and

Dr Brian Morris. I would also like to acknowledge a longer standing obligation to the late F. L. Lucas, whose example and enthusiasm first led me into Victorian literature. I have necessarily incurred a large debt to the various libraries, museums, galleries and their staffs where my researches have been conducted, especially the libraries of Vassar College and the University of York and the Bancroft Pre-Raphaelite Collection of the Wilmington Society of the Fine Arts. I am grateful to the Shell Foundation for assistance in visiting various art galleries in the United States and to the University of York for similar, modest grants. The final, inexpressible debt, is to my wife.

LANGWITH COLLEGE
UNIVERSITY OF YORK

ACKNOWLEDGEMENTS

I am grateful to Mrs Rossetti Angeli for permission to quote from Rossetti's letters to Mrs Morris; to the Pierpont Morgan Library for permission to quote from Rossetti's letter to Mrs Cowper and from Swinburne's review of *The Well at the World's End*; to the Bancroft Collection for permission to quote from Rossetti's 'A Prayer'; and to the following publishers for permission to use material which has been quoted in my book: Macmillan & Co. for Yeats's prose and poetry; Faber and Faber for the lines from Ezra Pound, W. H. Auden and Howard Nemerov.

ABBREVIATIONS

The following abbreviations have been used in referring to nineties magazines:

A: *The Albemarle*
R.I: *Book of the Rhymers' Club*
R.II: *Second Book of the Rhymers' Club*
HH: *The (Century Guild) Hobby Horse*, old series, 1886–92
D: *The Dome*, new series, 1898–1900
P: *The Pageant*
S: *The Savoy*
YB: *The Yellow Book*

Unless otherwise stated, references to Dante Gabriel Rossetti's poems are to *The Collected Works*, 2 volumes (1886); to Christina Rossetti's, to *The Poetical Works* (1911); to Swinburne's, to *The Collected Poetical Works*, 6 volumes (Heinemann 1919); and to Arthur Symons's, to *Poems*, 2 volumes (1919).

CHAPTER ONE

The Pre-Raphaelite Movement

I propose to speak to you . . . of the Pre-Raphaelites. . . . There is all the more reason for my doing so because, as a matter of fact, their doctrines have been successful; they have impressed themselves upon the present generation, at any rate of the English people, and, I think, to a certain extent, have influenced also the artists of France.

—William Morris in 1891

It would be interesting to discuss the reasons for the appearance of pre-Raphaelitism as an anti-scientific movement and the reasons for its failure.

—Cleanth Brooks in 1939

I. 'A CONTINUITY OF ADMIRATION'

THE FORMATION of the Pre-Raphaelite Brotherhood in 1848 was ostensibly a youthful rebellion against the Royal Academy, in which schools its three most important members—William Holman Hunt, John Everett Millais, Dante Gabriel Rossetti—had first met. But this common antagonism to what they saw as stereotyped, meaningless and insincere art contained for only a short time the variety of artistic and spiritual impulses which were to energize the movement after the dissolution of the Brotherhood. Its illusionary unity broke down once the young artists, who had perhaps needed to find some courage in corporate action, grew more confident and independent, as their personalities matured.

Soon after the movement began the three, who had shared a mistrust of their tuition in the Academy schools enough to band themselves together to fight it, begin to reveal their own distinct, even conflicting imaginative interests. Hunt dedicates himself with lonely and single-minded integrity to religion and fidelity to nature. Millais, technically the best of the three, chooses to exercise his conception of truth to nature in ways that eventually lead him into the Victorian establishment. Rossetti, by far the most complex personality, continued to sustain a variety of interests in his writing as well as his painting and was to become the most influential of the Brotherhood. There had been four other members—William Michael Rossetti, Thomas Woolner, James Collinson, Frederic George Stephens. Drawn in probably to bolster confidence and provide an important sense of conspiracy, they never had active roles, with the exception of W. M. Rossetti who became the loyal, painstaking historian of the movement. The other three faded from the picture as soon as the divergent and stronger energies of the central figures emerged and destroyed the Brotherhood's unity.

The dissolution of an effective Brotherhood was not fatal to its ideas. On the contrary, Pre-Raphaelitism represented such an intricate protest against Victorian art and society that a less definite programme allowed more scope to each of the many notions which informed it originally. The variety of names they canvassed for their organization and of possible titles for their magazine suggests the complex ideas which nourished the movement besides its declared technical and painterly concerns.[1] The members themselves were never in the early stages fully aware of the variety and implications of their motives. Much was instinctive then; much was never even to be rationalized. Mediaeval and religious nostalgias seem to go alongside a missionary zeal to reform the age; social and intensely personal concerns both employ carefully described natural detail. The variety of influences upon these Pre-Raphaelites—Turner and Ruskin, Keats, Blake, Dante and the early Italian poets, Ford Madox Brown and the Nazarenes (a German school of 'Pre-Raphaelites'[2]), the Italian primitive painters,

[1] For the various notions they had about the Brotherhood see O. Doughty, *A Victorian Romantic: Dante Gabriel Rossetti* (1949), pp. 61–114; for list of possible titles for *The Germ* see *Rossetti's Letters to William Allingham* (1897), pp. 65–7.

[2] K. Andrews, *The Nazarenes: a brotherhood of German painters in Rome* (Oxford 1964).

the social idealism of Carlyle, the general Victorian ambience of Gothic revival and Oxford Movement—all exerted their pressures on these young artists. Although this complex of Victorian thought had common features, it is not surprising that with so much disparate inspiration the Pre-Raphaelite sense of direction was confused and that individual interests were obscured in the early stages by collective enthusiasms.

Despite the muddle and corporate failure of the group's aims and activities, a distinctly individual movement grew from those initial complexities. It was not merely

a group of young enthusiastic writers who issue a manifesto; who have or who pretend to have certain principles in common; whose work is likely to show a family resemblance; and who are banded together in championship of a common cause, or for sociability and mutual comfort, or at worst for purposes of collective self-advertisement,[1]

but who fell apart after that initial impetus had flagged. Rather the idea of a Pre-Raphaelite movement which I wish to emphasize implies a 'continuity of admiration', in which initial ideas are adjusted to individual talents, modified perhaps by each expression of them, but still maintaining some direct imaginative connection with the original inspirations and principles.

The lasting enthusiasm for the ideas which the Pre-Raphaelite Brotherhood promoted in 1848 is attested, not by the cohesion of the original *cénacle*, but by the new members constantly attaching themselves to it. Mainly because of Rossetti's personal magnetism a new 'Brotherhood', with its own magazine, started at Oxford in 1856.[2] This also contrived some corporate sense, for a while quite genuine, by painting on the walls of the Oxford Union. To this activity William Morris, Edward Burne-Jones and Arthur Hughes were drawn. Swinburne also attached himself, after reading the *Oxford and Cambridge Magazine*,[3] and later

[1] Both this passage and the phrase used later, 'continuity of admiration', are from T. S. Eliot's introduction to Joseph Chiari, *Symbolisme from Poe to Mallarmé: the Growth of a Myth* (1956), p. v.

[2] Rossetti referred to the later publication as 'the Oxford and Cambridge Germ' (*Ruskin, Rossetti and Pre-Raphaelitism* (1899), p. 135), and *The Germ* itself was acknowledged by its successor (*Oxford and Cambridge Magazine* for 1856, p. 60).

[3] See G. Lafourcade, *La Jeunesse de Swinburne (1837–1867)* (Paris 1928), I, 119.

through him both Walter Pater and Simeon Solomon are connected with the movement.

The inspiration and energy behind these continuing interests is certainly Rossetti. Morris dedicated his first volume of poetry to him in 1858 and Burne-Jones's early pictures emulated his mediaeval subjects. As Pater was to remark later to William Sharp, 'Rossetti is the most significant man among us. More torches will be lit at his flame . . . than perhaps even enthusiasts like you imagine.'[1] Although Holman Hunt always claimed that he alone persevered in 'our original doctrine of childlike submission to Nature'[2] and that by the 1880's he was the sole survivor of the first impetus, his is too simplified a notion of the Pre-Raphaelite imagination. Hunt's career, for one thing, suggests far more the impulse to accommodate his own predilections to central Victorian tastes that I shall discuss later,[3] an impulse which Rossetti and his followers did not share. But more importantly I do not think Hunt's imagination awoke in later artists the same rich response as Rossetti's. Arthur Hughes, for example, who helped with the Oxford Union decoration, obviously found more to admire in the sentimental colouring of Rossetti's work than in Hunt's austerely determined and single-minded application of his art to the service of Christ.[4] Hunt's failure to attract disciples was due in part to his long absences from England, which left him unable to share Rossetti's immense personal influence over younger artists.[5] Also, although Hunt admitted the essentially literary impulse of his own work,[6] he again did not share Rossetti's sustained activity in both painted and written art which broadened the range of his appeal. It is the breadth of what is, after all, a minor mode

[1] Quoted L. Rosenblatt, *L'Idée de l'Art pour l'Art dans la Littérature Anglaise pendant la Période Victorienne* (Paris 1931), p. 195n.

[2] *Pre-Raphaelitism and the Pre-Raphaelite Brotherhood* (1905), I, 132, and II, 332–4.

[3] See the second section of this chapter, pp. 15 ff.

[4] See Hunt, op. cit., I, 349, and II, 409.

[5] This can perhaps best be seen through his early letters, addressed to many artists and writers; they reveal the extraordinary warmth and spontaneity of his response to other people.

[6] Op. cit., I, 350, where he says that his symbolism was derived from figures which language had originally employed.

of the imagination that one notices in the Pre-Raphaelite move-ment. This breadth was a result both of the variety of arts eventu-ally invoked and of the movement's accommodation of new personalities and interests.

Two fresh and individual talents which the movement acquired along its course are Swinburne and Pater. Swinburne was almost always associated with the Pre-Raphaelites, and they with him. Apart from early friendships with them and certain pieces of his work after their fashion, the public identification of them might well have been brought about by such acts as his review of Rossetti's poems in 1870 or by W. M. Rossetti's defence of his *Poems and Ballads*.[1] W. M. Rossetti and Swinburne also col-laborated in 1868 on *Notes on the Royal Academy Exhibition*. Swinburne was of course included with Morris and Rossetti in Robert Buchanan's attack on the Fleshly School of poets.[2] By the 1890's Swinburne seems to have been accepted as part of the Pre-Raphaelite movement and a writer in *The Hobby Horse* singles out the same names as Buchanan to praise as 'geniuses' of the school (V, 119). Swinburne thus plays an important part in the continuity of admiration; associated with Pre-Raphaelitism, he yet brought to it new interests and enthusiasms which were more immediately acceptable to the affectations of the 1890's.

Walter Pater was another important link of this kind. His first volume, *Studies in the History of the Renaissance*, had many affini-ties with the poetic and pictorial art of Rossetti, Swinburne and Burne-Jones, as Symons was to suggest later in *The Savoy* (VIII, 34). Pater himself admitted a direct debt to Swinburne, who tells how Pater considered his own early essays in the *Fortnightly* 'as owing their inspiration entirely to the example of my [i.e. Swin-burne's] own work in the same line'.[3] It is to Pater as well as Swinburne and Morris that the hero of Richard Le Gallienne's *Book-Bills of Narcissus* acknowledges some of his profoundest debts.[4] In 1883 when F. W. H. Myers wrote on 'Rossetti and the

[1] This connection is noted by both N. St John-Stevas, *Obscenity and the Law* (1956), p. 64, and Gaunt, *The Aesthetic Adventure* (Penguin Book, 1957), p. 55.
[2] *The Contemporary Review*, XVIII (October 1871), pp. 334–50.
[3] Swinburne *Letters*, ed. C. Y. Lang (New Haven, 1959–62), II, 241.
[4] See chapters six and nine of the third edition.

Religion of Beauty' his allusion to Leonardo seems to link Rossetti with Pater's symbolic vision:

All the arts, in fact, are returning now to the spirit of Leonardo, to the sense that of all visible objects known to us the human face and form are the most complex and mysterious, to the desire to extract the utmost secret, the occult message, from all the phenomena of Life and Being.[1]

Indeed, it has been suggested that the Gioconda of Pater's imagination found its inspiration in Rossetti's art criticism,[2] just as Mario Praz traces in *The Romantic Agony* how Swinburne also may have influenced Pater. Pater himself was certainly interested in Rossetti. The essay on him in *Appreciations* first appeared in Ward's *English Poets* of 1883. More important still is his article on 'Aesthetic Poetry', written in 1868, printed in *Appreciations* twenty-one years later, but cancelled in later editions. This essay ends by naming Rossetti's as another example of that type of poetry he has been discussing in relation to Morris. Pater, like Swinburne, brings to his Pre-Raphaelite admiration his own particular interests and habits of mind, some of which, as I shall show, correspond to Rossetti's.

This Pre-Raphaelite movement continued to inspire new writers and artists, lending them a repertoire of basic themes and vocabularies in which to talk about them. By the 1890's the Pre-Raphaelite imagination was still a dominant attraction, rivalling that of the French arts, about which much noisy and distracting affectation was contrived. The Pre-Raphaelite example was, in fact, the most immediate and important to the 1880's and 1890's, as many people at the time readily acknowledged.

When Walter Hamilton published *The Aesthetic Movement in England* in 1882 he used the terms 'Aesthetic' and 'Pre-Raphaelite' interchangeably. He explains the intention of the book as an investigation of the origins of the aesthetic school; his chapters then cover the Pre-Raphaelites generally, their painting, *The Germ*,

---

[1] *Essays: Classical and Modern* (1921), p. 546.
[2] O. Doughty, 'Rossetti's Conception of the "Poetic" in Poetry and Painting', *Essays by Divers Hands*, XXVI (1953), p. 98.

Ruskin, and the Fleshly School controversy. Hamilton seems to have been moved to write with some seriousness on this topic by the success of *Patience*, where Swinburne and Wilde in particular were mocked. Hamilton takes Wilde as the aesthetic paradigm. This enables him to adduce further evidence on the Pre-Raphaelite continuity of admiration: he quotes, for example, from *Punch*'s review of Wilde's 1881 *Poems*—they were 'Swinburne and water, while here and there we note that the author has been reminiscent of Mr Rossetti'.[1] There is, of course, much support for Hamilton's and *Punch*'s emphasis. Wilde's early career and especially his London *début* were quite deliberately and unashamedly Pre-Raphaelite, though between 1875 when he saw a Bernardino Madonna in Italy 'which Morris and Rossetti would love'[2] and 1882, he had struck a fresh attitude when he told a correspondent that his departure from the Pre-Raphaelites marked a new era in the aesthetic movement.[3]

There were others besides Hamilton who acknowledged their generation's debt to the earlier Pre-Raphaelites. For Richard Le Gallienne, looking back to the 1890's, Rossetti seemed a figure of venerable authority; he 'still dwelt in mysterious sacrosanct seclusion, like some high priest behind the veil, in his old romantic house in Chelsea'.[4] George Moore thought *The Defence of Guenevere* the 'most perfect first volume of poems ever published by any man'.[5] Arthur Symons testifies that Rossetti provided 'a kind of leadership in art',[6] and among his collections of critical essays are several acute discussions of the Pre-Raphaelites. Symons was certainly seen by one magazine as a 'disciple of Paul Verlaine and less directly of Rossetti'.[7] William Archer, editing *Poets of*

[1] *The Aesthetic Movement*, p. 93. The connection of Wilde and Rossetti was probably made more conspicuous because in the same year that Wilde's *Poems* appeared Rossetti issued *Ballads and Sonnets* and a second, revised edition of his 1870 *Poems*.

[2] *Letters*, ed. Rupert Hart Davis (1962), p. 10.

[3] Ibid., p. 96.

[4] *The Romantic Nineties* (1925), p. 12.

[5] Quoted by Nancy Cunard, *Memories of George Moore* (1956), p. 106.

[6] *Figures of Several Centuries* (1916), p. 201; see also his essay on Rossetti in *Studies in Strange Souls* (1929).

[7] *The Spirit Lamp*, pp. 117–18.

the Younger Generation in 1902, confessed to a disproportionate love for Rossetti's and Morris's work and he makes a point of stressing the Pre-Raphaelite influence on the writings of those authors whom he prints.[1]

More persuasive because more resonant an example is provided by W. B. Yeats, who grew up 'in all things Pre-Raphaelite'.[2] His father had abandoned the law in 1867 and while at art school in London had met and formed a 'Brotherhood' with a group of other artists, one of whom—J. T. Nettleship—was friendly with Rossetti. William Butler Yeats's tastes in symbolic art would always acknowledge this Pre-Raphaelite influence on his family. In *The Bounty of Sweden* both Rossetti and Watts are listed with the 'great myth-makers and mask-makers'[3] and his literary-artistic pantheon inevitably mingles English Pre-Raphaelites with continental symbolists:

Wagner's dramas, Keats's odes, Blake's pictures and poems, Calvert's pictures, Rossetti's pictures, Villiers de l'Isle Adam's plays, and the black-and-white art of M. Hermann, Mr Beardsley and Mr Ricketts, and the lithographs of Mr Shannon, and the pictures of Mr Whistler, and the plays of M. Maeterlinck, and the poetry of Verlaine.[4]

The dominant role, too, that love poetry was to play in Yeats's poetic career as well as its language and symbology derive their shape if not their ultimate energies from images of Rossetti, Burne-Jones and Watts rather than from any French source.

Yeats and his circle were connected with several small magazines which were often generously and intelligently disposed towards Pre-Raphaelites. The group with whom he first made contact on his own, as opposed to his family's account, was what Augustus John termed 'the nest of decayed Pre-Raphaelites'[5] at

[1] Of Rossetti on Laurence Housman (p. 196), of Morris on William Watson (p. 500), of Rossetti on Watson (p. 502), and of the Pre-Raphaelites generally on Katherine Tynan Hinkson (p. 163).

[2] *Autobiographies* (1956), p. 114.

[3] Ibid., p. 550.

[4] *Essays and Introductions* (1961), p. 149.

[5] Quoted D. Gordon, I. Fletcher, *W. B. Yeats: Images of a Poet* (1961), p. 95. I am much indebted to this catalogue for my discussion of Yeats here.

the headquarters of the Century Guild in Fitzroy Street. Its magazine, *The Century Guild Hobby Horse*, champions the Pre-Raphaelites, devoting articles to Brown, to William Bell Scott and three to Rossetti; W. M. Rossetti, Scott and Morris all contributed; it published some Rossetti letters, a picture by Brown and two contributions from Christina Rossetti. Morris, who wrote for the final number, was virtually spiritual godfather of the magazine which maintained his interests both in the applied arts and in the association of all kinds of artist. All this compares with one article on recent French poetry by Lionel Johnson, contributions from Verlaine and Gustave Kahn and, more predictably, from Austin Dobson 'after Théodore de Banville'. Although *The Hobby Horse* was not blind to the fact that the Pre-Raphaelite school had 'run into so many vices' (V, 119), it generally looked more favourably on its English than on any French antecedents. It is from Herbert Horne, an editor of *The Hobby Horse*, that Sturge Moore says much of their detailed information about Rossetti derived.[1]

Another new review to which *The Hobby Horse* gave a hospitable welcome, was *The Dial*. It supported the Pre-Raphaelite dislike of Impressionism because of its mere transcription of the surface appearance of nature.[2] One of the editors of *The Dial*, who had also a large share in another magazine, *The Pageant*, was Charles Ricketts.[3] Ricketts was hailed by more than one of his contemporaries as an artist who prolonged the inspiration of Rossetti and it was doubtless under his aegis that *The Pageant* offered the hospitality of its pages to the Pre-Raphaelites—Watts, Rossetti and Burne-Jones are illustrated—as well as to Moreau and Puvis de Chavannes. An article on Ricketts himself begins—

Pre-Raphaelite!—the term is accepted, and a singularly individual movement of romanticism in literature and art must needs be content with the ill-formed adjective.[4]

---

[1] *W. B. Yeats and Sturge Moore; their correspondence 1901–1937*, ed. Ursula Bridge (New York 1953), p. 43.

[2] In an editorial note at the end of volume IV.

[3] His co-editor on *The Dial* was C. H. Shannon, who was also, with Gleeson White, editor of *The Pageant*.

[4] The author is Gleeson White, in the volume for 1896, p. 79.

The writer calls the Pre-Raphaelites 'a great school', notes that anything uncongenial to contemporary taste is dubbed 'impartially "Pre-Raphaelite" or "Impressionist"' and sees a renaissance of the Pre-Raphaelite idea by the 1890's after its relapse during the 1870's.

A most interesting example of Pre-Raphaelitism in *The Pageant* and of its meeting with French symbolism is the reproduction of Rossetti's *Monna Rosa*, accompanied by a poem on the picture by Paul Verlaine.[1] His verses make a colour symphony of the painting:

> Sur fond blanc dans le soir
> Teinté d'or vert et noir

and

> La grâce d'une feuille
> Verte comme le soir
> Noir et or du boudoir.

The figure is 'En bandeaux d'or liquide, En robe d'or fluide', while the Japanese pot spreads into this exquisite atmosphere 'Un flot mélodieux / Selon le rhythme juste.' Perhaps the most significant fact is that Rossetti's painting provides a very congenial stimulus to Verlaine's peculiar inspiration without being at all obviously distorted by it. This suggests that for the 1890's there was perhaps an important similarity in the Pre-Raphaelite and French symbolist imaginations, which could be easily blended in the eclectic minds of these later writers.

The Dome was another periodical where Pre-Raphaelite interests outweigh the French. Compared with one poem by Vielé-Griffin and an essay on Moreau, there are articles on Rossetti's painting, a re-print of his 'Hand and Soul', a review of Burne-Jones's work, praise of Watts, a story of the Blessed Damozel is used as a symbol of all that is opposed to Philistinism and another where a group of young artists 'were sworn Pre-Raphaelites'. *The Dome* also published three sonnetts for pictures by Gordon Bottomley, of which one on Giorgione's *Chamber Concert*

[1] In the volume for 1896.

has distinct echoes of Rossetti and another is on Botticelli's *Virgin and Child*. These leave little room for doubting Bottomley's own 'quite willing' acceptance of the label of the last Pre-Raphaelite.[1]

Hostile or sympathetic writers alike in the 1890's note how Pre-Raphaelitism survives either degenerately or as an energizing force for fresh writers and artists. Harry Quilter, writing on 'The New Renaissance: or, the Gospel of Intensity', explained that

though pre-Raphaelitism, in its pure and original form, has passed away, its dead carcase is still left with us, and is a source of corruption.[2]

He evinces obvious admiration for the earlier movement—'new phases of thought and feeling had been laid open to artists'—but deplores its adverse effects on everything from dress to morals. Eight years later in *The Hobby Horse* Arthur Galton similarly noted the end of the Pre-Raphaelite movement. But the very magazine in which he is writing illustrates his other claim that 'what used to be called the Pre-Raphaelite school had a distinct and imperative call'.[3] Answers to that call throughout the 1880's and 1890's bear witness to the continuing attractiveness of the Pre-Raphaelite mode of imagination. Even *The Savoy*, more committed to the French enthusiasms and affectations, testifies to that legacy.[4]

Besides the conscious declarations of Pre-Raphaelite inspiration we have found in these little magazines, there is also a great deal of original work, at worst in bare imitation of the Pre-Raphaelites and at best inspired responsibly by them. Whereas French influences and imitations are clearly and quickly apparent, a corollary perhaps of the deliberate air with which they were cultivated, the Pre-Raphaelite continuity of admiration does not strike us so

---

[1] In a letter to my grandfather Gordon Bottomley 'quite willingly' accepts the description as the last of the Pre-Raphaelites. In a further letter he acknowledges that Charles Ricketts 'had more influence on me than any other man alive'.

[2] *MacMillan's Magazine*, XLII (September 1880), p. 392.

[3] III, p. 7. See above for *The Hobby Horse*'s Pre-Raphaelite enthusiasms.

[4] For instance, Symons wrote an article on Millais, and O. G. Destrée another on windows and paintings by Pre-Raphaelites in St Martin's Church at Scarborough—both in volume VI; Shaw talks of Morris and Burne-Jones in 'On Going to Church' (I).

glaringly. Because this inheritance was accepted more automatically or subconsciously and with none of the compulsive baiting of Mrs Grundy which accompanied some Francophilia, it was usually more absorbed into writers' imaginations and so less conspicuous. In contrast to the French enthusiasms, which seem rather like a young man's deliberate adoption of aggressive attitudes, the Pre-Raphaelite influences are more like a child's early assimilation of the behaviour patterns and intellectual interests that inform his immediate environment. Indeed, one of the writers for *The Dome* explained why he was Pre-Raphaelite in exactly those terms:

> It was bound to be so, for those ideas were still chiefly in vogue in my formative years: new books by Morris and Swinburne were still coming out, Walter Crane still dominated childhood.[1]

The instinct of both Harry Quilter and Arthur Galton was to isolate the Pre-Raphaelite *school* in the first twenty years of its existence and to lament its subsequent demise. Our own more elevated historical perspective accepts less rigid and more intricate patterns. Pre-Raphaelitism not only continued to shape imaginations, but in many ways it anticipated the work of the French symbolists who were in vogue by the 1890's. Many of Symons's remarks on French literature, for instance, may equally be applied to Rossetti's introspective poetry.[2] I think that critics have too readily accepted the prominent Francophilia as the major element of the 1890's and have neglected the extent to which English art anticipated and so could absorb the foreign importations. As Gide reminds us, 'influence creates nothing; it awakens something'. If French arts influenced the last decades of the nineteenth century in England they did so only because by that time there had evolved a sympathetic and comparable *native* tradition.[3]

---

[1] From the letter to my grandfather cited in note 1, p. 11 above. Compare Lionel Johnson's enthusiasm for Christina Rossetti and Swinburne while still at school (see Ezra Pound, *Literary Essays* (1954), pp. 368–9).

[2] E.g., his stress on Baudelaire's self-analysis, the 'perverse self-scrutinizing troubled art of sensation and nerves' ('Henley's Poetry', *Fortnightly* (August 1892), p. 184). See also the opening of chapter four.

[3] The French influences on the English arts of the late nineteenth century have been extensively charted and I do not think there is much need to recapitulate

The French enthusiasms of the 1890's were eagerly broadcast and the writings of the enthusiasts are full of extravagant praises for France. Paris haunted Dowson 'like a regret' (*S.* II, 176); Wilde learnt to write English prose by studying the prose of France; Harland, whose *nostalgie du Boul' Miche* is shared by many contemporaries, invited Le Gallienne to come and sup with dear old Verlaine and breakfast with the Muses in a Paris where 'everybody has the Artistic Temperament'.[1] *The Yellow Book* obviously endorsed Dauphin Maunier's reaction to a London dissenting chapel—

> Mieux vaut, bonne ou male,
> La mort à Paris
> Que la vie au prix
> De cette morale! (V, 103)

Most prominent English writers and artists were in Paris for some time, often during their formative years. George Moore spent ten years there from 1872; Whistler rented a studio and continued, after his return to England, to send pictures to the Salon d'Académie (in 1860 and 1861) and the Salon des Refusés (1863). Henry James, Wilde, Symons, Sickert, Dowson, Harland, Yeats, all made their pilgrimage to the French Capital. Symons writes of visits to Mallarmé's Tuesday *soirées* in the Rue de Rome or to the Goncourts where he found the cult of beauty and personal nuance.[2] Such 'collecting' of literary figures was a popular pastime; Edmund Gosse poked gentle fun at the vogue for catching symbolists and decadents as if with a butterfly net in their café haunts (*S.* II). Certain of these 'catches' were brought to England (Verlaine and Zola in 1893, Mallarmé the next year) to be fêted by the select few. Toulouse Lautrec also visited London and

---

[1] Respectively *Letters of Oscar Wilde*, p. 233, and Le Gallienne, *The Romantic Nineties*, pp. 237–8.

[2] On Mallarmé see the chapter in *The Symbolist Movement*; on the Goncourts, *The Savoy*, V, 85 ff. See also Henry Davray's account of Mallarmé's English visitors, among them Symons, Moore, Dowson, Gray, Crackanthorpe, in 'Mallarmé as I knew him', *Horizon*, May 1943.

---

them here. The books and articles which treat of this aspect of the period are marked with an asterisk in the bibliography at the end of this book.

painted a portrait of Oscar Wilde, who had himself spent some time in Paris in the rôle of *flâneur*.

The vogue might well have been said to have started with Swinburne, who was writing to Baudelaire in the late sixties and later to Mallarmé between 1875 and 1876.[1] But both he and Whistler, who were among the first to make any impression in introducing ideas from France, were working against considerable antipathy. A mistrust of French art can be clearly seen in contemporary reviews, which frequently denounce French immorality: *Blackwoods* talked of the 'profoundly vicious tendency' of French novels; the *Saturday Review* thought *Salammbô* a 'foulest fungus'; the *Edinburgh Review* wrote of 'the corrupted school of French art and French poetry'.[2] Although these prejudices became less strident from the 1870's onwards, much of even the well-informed and serious interest in France continued to be a gesture of defiance towards the anti-French tone of the reviews and the Germanic partialities of Victorian society.

Havelock Ellis remarked that the name of Zola was 'like an anarchist's bomb' (*S.* I, 67) and it is impossible not to believe that similar bombs were tossed around with zest. It is perhaps difficult today to realize the effect upon Victorian minds of *The Yellow Book*'s championing Stendhal's 'unabashed egotism', the relativity of his moral position, his role as rebel;[3] or of Moore's *Confessions*, originally written in French for the *Revue Independente* of 1885, with its account of his settling down in a flat in the Rue de la Tour des Dames with a python and a Persian cat. Beardsley, with his acute attention to current taste, made his three musicians

---

[1] For his relations with Baudelaire, see Lafourcade, *La Jeunesse de Swinburne*, I, 200 ff., and for his letters to Baudelaire and Mallarmé see *The Swinburne Letters*, I and III.

[2] Louise Rosenblatt discusses this prejudice of the English press and my own references are taken from her larger selection, op. cit., pp. 27 ff. Swinburne parodied this contemporary distaste for French literature in two articles, submitted to the *Spectator*, in which he condemned the immoralities of some imaginary writers, Felicien Cossu and Ernest Clouët. See *New Writing by Swinburne or Miscellanea Nova et Curiosa, Being a Medley of Poems, Critical Essays, Hoaxes and Burlesques*, ed. C. Y. Lang (Syracuse, N.Y. 1964).

[3] Norman Hapgood, 'Henri Beyle', IV.

mock the woods with Siegfried's horn,
And fill the air with Gluck, and fill the tweeded
 tourist's soul with scorn . . .
The tourist gives a furious glance,
Red as his guide-book grows, moves on, and offers up
 a prayer for France.[1]

Provocations such as these were frequent attitudes of a period that deliberately chose as its colours the mauve and yellow of the French novel, or gave French titles to its pictures and poems. But it is not only these colours and titles that are rather superficial gestures; the French affectations generally seem to have been on the surface, concealing other less deliberately exploited legacies and other, maybe less conscious, influences. Subsequent chapters will be concerned, in part, with tracing these unconscious debts.

The 1890's, sensitive to their place at the close of a century, were self-consciously concerned with the past:

We were the last romantics—chose for theme
Traditional sanctity and loveliness.[2]

They were, equally, like Monsieur Verog, alert to the historical chemistry that produced them,

Among the pickled foetuses and bottled bones,
Engaged in perfecting the catalogue.[3]

They shared with Walter Pater a keen interest in tracing traditions and 'the way in which various phases of thought and sentiment maintain themselves, through successive modifications'.[4] The Pre-Raphaelite imagination and its absorption into the complicated mental economy of late nineteenth-century culture is one such tradition.

II. THE VICTORIAN CONTEXT

Many discussions of Pre-Raphaelitism, rather than showing how central Pre-Raphaelite interests merge with other Victorian concerns, feel impelled to define its limits, isolating those writers that

[1] *The Eighteen-Nineties. A Period Anthology*, chosen by Martin Secker (1948), pp. 1–2.
[2] W. B. Yeats, *Collected Poems* (1952), p. 240.
[3] Ezra Pound, *Personae* (1952), p. 202. [4] *Appreciations* (1913), p. 244.

come within its territory or establishing the point at which a particular painter's work ceases to be Pre-Raphaelite. This impulse shares the perplexity of Forster's young missionary, who was forced to decide at which point in the chain of being admission to heaven was denied: his justification was that if we do not exclude something we shall be left with nothing. But at the risk of destroying any exact notions of the nature of Pre-Raphaelitism I would suggest some of its affinities with the surrounding artistic and philosophical landscape.

Although the Pre-Raphaelite Brotherhood was established as a rebellion against Victorian art, it soon manifested interests and anxieties that link it intricately to the movements of mind and art in the period. The Pre-Raphaelite imagination, as I have sketched its progress, may have established for its artists an authentic and self-reliant citadel. But their sense of its authenticity was determined at least unconsciously by recognition of how insufficient contemporary epistemologies were and how awkward were some of the strategems by which art adjusted to them. Equally, many Victorian artists with no formal Pre-Raphaelite connections cherished visions of that citadel even as they chose to travel roads that took them far from its shelter. Many artists and writers who did contribute to the continuity of the Pre-Raphaelite imagination from 1848 to 1900 were attracted by its honouring of areas of spirit to which Victorian culture seemed hostile. The basic conflict for all Victorians, Pre-Raphaelite and non Pre-Raphaelite, was focused by Tennyson in 'The Palace of Art' and the final irresolution of that poem should be a reminder, if any is needed, of the artistic difficulties which faced the age.

Many of the major Victorian poets and sages sought to accommodate their individual inclinations to the taste of their time. Tennyson, for example, was in crucial matters at odds with his age, locating his enthusiasms and authority in resources of individual being rather than in the existing social order. His early poetry may be seen as a dialogue between an inner, timeless and fixed core of apprehension and an outer, public world of activism

[1] See for example E. D. H. Johnson, *The Alien Vision of Victorian Poetry* (Hamden, Connecticut 1963) who discusses this aspect of the three major poets.

and energy. Ulysses' idealism leads him to reject the dull pragmatic world of Telemachus, who is

> centred in the sphere
> Of common duties, decent not to fail
> In offices of tenderness, and pay
> Meet adoration to my household gods.

Yet Tennyson is forced to offer Ulysses' sustaining idealism in
the practical language of the quest's activity, while the idealism
is located beyond the actual descriptions of the poem—

> that untravell'd world, whose margin fades
> For ever and for ever when I move.

Tennyson's career seems a constant experiment with various
modes of accommodating private insights, without materially
falsifying them, to contemporary currents of thought. He tries to
translate the visions that he cherished and the vagueness often
endemic to them (he said his trances were 'utterly beyond words'[1])
into a language of public sensation and public symbol. *In Memoriam* is less remarkable for—as Yeats saw it[2]—Tennyson's brooding over scientific opinion as for his use of scientific metaphors
to articulate his own faith. As a young man he may have voted
against a motion that 'an intelligible first cause is deducible from
the phenomena of the Universe',[3] but he later proceeds less cate-
gorically in *In Memoriam*. Not only is the climax of the poem a
unification of scientific and religious language, but the concept of
geological evolution becomes an exact and exhilarating analogue
of Tennyson's own confidence in spiritual progress.[4]

Carlyle is another Victorian figure who tries to convey idealist
notions to a sceptical and pragmatic age by presenting them in
the age's own language: his famous sections on Work in *Past
and Present* begin by using an acceptable industrial concept, but
end by transforming it into a spiritual activity unconnected with

[1] Quoted ibid., p. 35.
[2] *Essays and Introductions*, p. 163.
[3] *Tennyson. A Memoir, By His Son* (1897), I, 44n.
[4] See in this respect John D. Rosenberg, 'The Two Kingdoms of *In Memoriam*',
J.E.G.P., LVIII (1959), pp. 228 ff.

notions of labour as Dickens's Mr Bounderby would accept them.[1] Similarly Tennyson's Ulysses conveys his idealism in a language almost more appropriate to Coketown than to his voyage beyond the sunset:

> How dull it is to pause, to make an end,
> To rust unburnish'd, not to shine in use . . .
> Some work of noble note, may yet be done . . .

A central anxiety among major Victorian writers was to communicate with an age often hostile to or ignorant of their ideas: Mill writes to Carlyle in 1832—

my word is partly intelligible to many more persons than yours is, because mine is presented in the logical and mechanical form which partakes most of this age and country, yours in the artistical and poetical.[2]

Carlyle himself was to explain nine years later in *Heroes and Hero-Worship* that their age had produced a new type of hero—the Man of Letters—precisely to engage with this problem of articulation. He first alludes to Fichte's concept of a 'Divine Idea of the World' and then continues:

To the mass of men no such Divine Idea is recognisable in the world; they live merely, says Fichte, among the superficialities, practicalities and shows of the world, not dreaming that there is anything divine under them. But the Man of Letters is sent hither specially that he may discern for himself, and make manifest to us, this same Divine Idea; in every new generation it will manifest itself in a new dialect: and he is there for the purpose of doing that.[3]

It is as much as anything a search for new dialects to communicate with a hostile or indifferent age that characterizes much major Victorian writing. The seminal tract here is undoubtedly *Signs of the Times* of 1829.

In urging upon his countrymen a wisdom and poetry which

---

[1] John Holloway, in *The Victorian Sage* (1953), pp. 44 ff., discusses Carlyle's handling of 'work', but without my own emphasis on accommodation.

[2] Quoted John M. Robson, 'J. S. Mill's Theory of Poetry', *Toronto Quarterly* XXIX, p. 428.

[3] *Heroes and Hero-Worship* (World's Classics), p. 205.

should recognize the invisible, Carlyle supplies writers with the basic diagnosis of the age and a vocabulary to express it:

The truth is, men have lost their belief in the Invisible, and believe, and hope, and work only in the Visible; or, to speak it in other words: This is not a religious age. Only the material, the immediately practical, not the divine and spiritual, is important to us. . . .

To speak a little pedantically, there is a science of Dynamics in man's fortunes and nature, as well as of Mechanics. There is a science which treats of, and practically addresses, the primary, unmodified forces and energies of man, the mysterious springs of Love, and Fear, and Wonder, of Enthusiasm, Poetry, Religion, all which have a truly vital and *infinite* character; as well as a science which practically addresses the finite, modified developments of these.[1]

The habit of internal perfection, of individual resourcefulness, of confidence in a boundless Invisible world and in mystic and ideal aims have all been surrendered by his age or, which seems just as bad, modified or accommodated to its inclinations. Even at the most paltry level, the wonder and delight of a firework display is reduced to a diagnosis of its 'saltpetre, pasteboard and catgut',[2] just as a later writer was, satirically, to reduce the horse to 'Quadruped. Graminivorous. Forty teeth . . .'[3] Arnold was to maintain this hostility to mechanism (*Estote ergo vos perfecti*) and to reiterate Carlyle's need for what he called in a letter to Clough 'an Idea of the world in order not to be prevailed over by the world's multitudinousness'.[4] He celebrates in his lectures on Celtic literature a body of work which, whatever his scholarly competence in the matter, offers him a metaphor for dynamism, a 'passionate, turbulent, indomitable reaction against the despotism of fact'.[5] So, too, Oxford is hailed as another image of the necessary wisdom:

And yet, steeped in sentiment as she lies, spreading her gardens to the moonlight, and whispering from her towers the last enchantments of

---

[1] *Critical and Miscellaneous Essays* (1872), II, 245 and 240-1.

[2] Ibid., p. 238.   [3] *Hard Times*, chapter 1.

[4] *The Letters of Matthew Arnold to Arthur Hugh Clough*, edited with an introductory study by H. F. Lowry (Oxford 1932), p. 97.

[5] *The Complete Prose Works of Matthew Arnold*, ed. R. H. Super (Ann Arbor 1962), III, 372.

the Middle Age, who will deny that Oxford, by her ineffable charm, keeps ever calling us nearer to the true goal of all of us, to the ideal, to perfection,—to beauty, in a word, which is only truth seen from another side?—nearer, perhaps, than all the science of Tübingen.[1]

There the University (already for Arnold the home of lost causes?) is strenuously opposed to the theological school which was notorious for what Arnold's recent editor calls 'its powerful scientific development of Rationalism'.[2]

The challenge and threats to their traditional romantic mythologies and ideas were felt by all Victorians, though they each chose to explain them by different oppositions, different metaphors. For Carlyle on one occasion it is dynamism and mechanism; for Arnold, Oxford and Tübingen or Hellenism and Hebraism; for Burne-Jones, 'the more materialistic science becomes, the more angels shall I paint'.[3] Just as individual formulations of these antagonisms differed, so did the 'strategems of the spirit'[4] by which each grappled with the conflicts. Many Victorians attempted explanations of their idealisms in terms which their audiences would find congenial or familiar; or like Dickens concentrated on diagnosing and dramatizing deficiencies instead of celebrating sustaining idealisms.

Generally the Pre-Raphaelite imagination was disinclined to accommodate its insights and divine ideas of the world to a wider public and uncongenial age. Pater and Swinburne, for example, constantly praise the life of inaction in direct opposition, as it were, to Tennyson's Ulysses. Later Oscar Wilde, with his keen sense of Victorian anxieties, seems to parody any attempts to accommodate private insights to public awareness by wittily arguing that sin is an 'essential element of progress'.[5] Perhaps

---

[1] *The Complete Prose Works of Matthew Arnold*, ed. R. H. Super (Ann Arbor 1962), III, p. 290.

[2] Ibid., p. 485.

[3] Quoted J. H. Buckley, *The Victorian Temper* (Cambridge, Mass., 1951), p. 164.

[4] The phrase is J. Hillis Miller's from *The Disappearance of God* (1963), p. 359. His study is a fascinating and brilliant account of such strategems in five nineteenth-century writers.

[5] *The Works of Oscar Wilde*, edited, with an introduction, by G. F. Maine (1949), p. 962.

the most forceful and, finally, influential Pre-Raphaelite attempt
at treaty with the age was Morris's Firm, which Rossetti at any
rate obviously considered a daring exercise, an exciting departure
from private modes of existence.[1] But in fact the Firm moved
into Victorian life very much on its own, Pre-Raphaelite terms,
refusing any accommodation to contemporary taste. Behind much
of Morris's work as designer as behind all of his writing lies a
central Pre-Raphaelite wish to ignore the 'mechanisms' of the
Victorian world. As he writes in *The Earthly Paradise*:

> Forget six counties overhung with smoke,
> Forget the snorting steam and piston stroke,
> Forget the spreading of the hideous town.[2]

The hollowness of such gestures was often self-defeating, though
perhaps less amusing than that form of accommodation to which
Auden draws attention, the naming of locomotives after knights
in Malory. Turning away from the world had perhaps the best
intentions, for to accommodate idealisms to contemporary culture
was often to compromise them irreparably, as some of Tennyson's
work unhappily demonstrates. But on the other hand a reluctance
to accommodate meant that ideas gained no strength from being
tested in an alien world or against an alien vocabulary. Arnold,
more strenuous than the Pre-Raphaelites, rejoiced at the opportunity of '*getting at* the English public . . . exercising the power
of persuasion, of charm'.[3] Often he was only persuading deaf
Hebraic ears of Hellenic idealisms which were already Utopian
nostalgias. But the astringency and point they derived from being
directed at an uncongenial public are invaluable to Arnold. In
contrast, the Pre-Raphaelite imagination disengages itself from
contemporary culture to work out its own inner visions, retreat-
ing further and further from contact with an active life and a public vocabulary. Its privacy is both a measure of its integrity and

---

[1] *Letters of Dante Gabriel Rossetti*, edited O. Doughty and J. R. Wahl (1965–
8), II, 393. More about 'The Firm', which was of course a commercial success,
may be found in Paul Thompson, *The Work of William Morris* (1967), an excellent, detailed introduction to all aspects of Morris's career.

[2] *Collected Works* (1910–15), III, 3.

[3] Quoted J. Holloway, *The Victorian Sage*, p. 202.

a reason for its insufficiency. For, although Wilde could claim that withdrawal was the very mark of elect spirits,[1] their isolation precluded adequate awareness of opposing positions.

Rossetti's career represents the most ardent Pre-Raphaelite stand against negotiation with his age. The scepticism that he felt about Carlyle's and Tennyson's metaphors from work or activism may be guessed from his thoughts on Brown's attempt in *Work* to celebrate this central Victorian enthusiasm:

Brown gets on slowly but surely with his *Work*, which will certainly be, in many respects, his finest picture; but I am beginning to doubt more and more, I confess, whether that excessive elaboration is rightly bestowed on the materials of a modern subject—things so familiar to the eye that they can really be rendered thoroughly (I fancy) with much less labour; and things moreover which are often far from beautiful in themselves.[2]

With a very few exceptions Rossetti's own work is a deliberate rejection of the real for the ideal.[3] When he comes to illustrate Moxon's edition of Tennyson he deliberately evades the dialogue of responsibilities in 'The Palace of Art', choosing instead to glorify Arthur:

> mythic Uther's deeply-wounded son
> In some fair space of sloping greens
> Lay, dozing in the vale of Avalon,
> And watched by weeping queens.

He chooses 'The Vision of Sin' for another illustration, because it allows him to 'allegorize on one's own hook on the subject'. Rossetti ignored most public events and claimed typically that he would retain a youthful piece written *de rigueur* on the Duke of Wellington only as 'a monument of the universal influence of public frenzy even on the most apathetic';[4] it was Rossetti's influence that Swinburne claimed prevented him from speaking out

---

[1] *The Works*, p. 973.

[2] Letters, I ,335. There is an interesting analysis of *Work* by Michael Kitson in *The Listener* for 9 September 1965.

[3] William Michael Rossetti on two occasions (*Rossetti Papers 1862–1870* (1903), pp. 456 and 468) urges his brother to express 'an actual love, rather than an ideal amatory proclivity'; however, Dante Gabriel seems not to have heeded him.   [4] *Letters*, I, 133.

sooner than he did on Italian nationalism.[1] As Rossetti grew older this attitude was maintained with increasing rigour and conviction, despite momentary attempts to compensate with modern subjects like *Found* and 'Jenny'. He even refused to exhibit after the early 1850's, waiting for interested purchasers to approach him privately or through the agency of friends. (Though for one so aloof from the world Rossetti reveals, in his letters especially, a very human interest in his earnings, perhaps facetiously disguising this interest from himself and his correspondents by references to 'tin').

His enthusiasm, expressed so early, for the 'pure religious sentiment and ecstatic poetry'[2] of the art he saw in the Hospital of St John at Bruges, exercised itself into a deepening introspection and private symbolism. That Memling would have spoken to and for his own age did not occur to Rossetti who valued him for qualities inaccessible, as it seemed, to the Victorian age. Pre-Raphaelite mediaeval interests, what Pater identifies as an inverted homesickness,[3] were one means of access to themes and especially vocabularies which they were denied in their own time. If the main Victorian process was that which John Stuart Mill noticed—'the idea of comparing one's own age with former ages'[4] —the Pre-Raphaelites seemed to evade this dialogue with the past in favour of a direct assumption of its themes and dialects. As an undergraduate Tennyson found it miserable 'not to be able to consolidate our gossamer dreams into reality';[5] his subsequent career as a poet is often devoted to giving to dreams and ideals the solid definition of Victorian reality. In contrast, the Pre-Raphaelite imagination authorized the reality of the dreams themselves. Where they dreamed of the past they simply translated it into actual terms, as in Rossetti's ballads or Morris's romances. Rossetti's sketch, *Before the Battle*, conveys the astonishing confidence of a vision which believes absolutely in the actuality of its dream and an artist who is apparently oblivious of other realities.

[1] Swinburne *Letters*, I, 195–6.
[2] *Letters*, I, 84.
[3] In 'Postscript' to *Appreciations*.
[4] *Essays on Politics and Culture* (Doubleday Anchor Book 1963), p. 1.
[5] *Memoir by His Son* (1897), I, 34.

Again it is worth stressing how this represents a severe limitation of the Pre-Raphaelite imagination. The painter, Watts, envied the easy access to 'beauty' of former artists:

with the language of beauty in full resonance around him, art was not difficult to the painter and sculptor of old as it is with us.[1]

But this beauty is a traditional concept, the celebration of which made Yeats see himself and his circle as the last romantics. The aesthetics of beauty were elsewhere undergoing revision: in the imaginations of Dickens, Baudelaire, Francis Thompson, Sickert or Whistler Morris's hated smoke, steam, pistons and urban sprawls were acquiring new and beautiful resonance. The conservatism of Pre-Raphaelite aesthetics required them, as Watts also explained, to 'return to extinct forms of speech if [they] would speak as the great ones have spoken'. But the Pre-Raphaelite resumption of extinct speech is often too absolute and indiscriminate; it preserves none of, say, Browning's awareness of the metaphoric function of the past:

> you saw me gather men and women,
> Live or dead or fashioned by my fancy,
> Enter each and all, and use their service.[2]

Even Tennyson's Arthurian material is taken up for its artifice, its metaphoric function. The Pre-Raphaelite return to the past, on the other hand, sometimes lacks this artistic objectivity, satisfying spiritual rather than artistic needs. As I suggest in the chapters that follow it is only when the Pre-Raphaelites learn the *uses* of their nostalgia that their art flourishes.

If Rossetti represents the most deliberate withdrawal from negotiation with his contemporary world, then Holman Hunt is perhaps the most eager of the Brotherhood to accommodate himself to Victorian problems.[3] The bulk of his painting is designed to communicate what he saw as religious truths to an age conspicuous for its disappointments and hesitations of faith. He explained

---

[1] Quoted Arthur Symons, *Studies in Seven Arts* (1906), p. 105.
[2] *The Poetical Works of Robert Browning* (1887), V, 318.
[3] I exclude Millais, because he seems to slip out of Pre-Raphaelitism into the Victorian 'establishment' rather than try to accommodate the one to the other.

his visit to the Near East to paint Biblical subjects in their authentic, appropriate settings as a 'wish to use my powers to make *more tangible* Jesus Christ's history and teaching'.[1] That is surely a characteristic Victorian impulse to insist upon Christ's real, physical, even historical existence. Yet this pragmatic and historicist instinct in Hunt is balanced by a romantic, Pre-Raphaelite concern for imaginative vision: he objects to Renan's *Vie de Jésus* for its lack of imagination into Christ's rôle as proclaimer of truth and love.[2] And this attitude probably controls his best work, where—as in *The Light of the World*, for example—he offers imaginative renditions of his dynamisms instead of those painstakingly factual accounts of Christ's life, like *The Finding of Christ in the Temple*.

A similar interest in making Christ's life more tangible informs two other pictures from the early years of the Brotherhood. Millais's *Christ in the House of His Parents* tries to actualize the distant and scarcely conceivable, while Rossetti was preoccupied with a similar conflict of motives in the *Girlhood of Mary Virgin*, which he saw as an attempt to make his topic 'more probable and at the same time less commonplace'.[3] The nostalgia for the incredible, the distant and the irreducible mysteries which the second part of Rossetti's phrase betrays is more at the centre of Pre-Raphaelite art than either a moral or a literalist inclination. But in the heterogeneous motives of the early Pre-Raphaelites both had an insecure place. The Journal of the P.R.B., kept by William Michael Rossetti between 1849 and 1853, notes that Coventry Patmore, a close friend of the group, thinks a poem by Rossetti lacked 'moral dignity', with which all the others agreed.[4] Madox Brown's diary records his friendship with William Cave Thomas who, Rossetti informs us, was the author of some 'very thoughtful books on the Theory of Fine Art, as co-ordinate with Science and Morals'.[5] *The Germ* included a contribution from John Orchard in the form of a dialogue about art, in which the

---

[1] *Pre-Raphaelitism and the Pre-Raphaelite Brotherhood*, I, 349; my italics.
[2] Ibid., I, 409.
[3] *Letters*, I, 48.
[4] *Pre-Raphaelite Diaries and Letters* (1900), p. 230.
[5] Ibid., p. 67n.

character with which we can most obviously associate the author invokes pre-Raphael art as an example for the modern artist of how he must 'teach the world through sense or through thought' (p. 159).

But the motives which sustained Pre-Raphaelite imagination, giving it a purpose and life beyond its indiscriminate beginnings, were the celebration and articulation of what Carlyle, already quoted, termed the Invisible. This was in direct conflict with what he saw as its antimonies—the material and the immediately practical. A writer on Pre-Raphaelitism later in the century welcomed, with what degree of irony remains uncertain, their nostalgia for the invisible: 'the reappearance of the dragon in poetry, and in the face of a sceptical age, is an event which all readers of poetry should welcome.'[1] We can ourselves welcome more serious Pre-Raphaelite achievements than the sponsoring of dragons. For the best of their work explores those dynamisms which Carlyle identified in 1829. Their introspection treats of the 'primary, unmodified forces and energies of man'; a similar, but often more spiritual and symbolist imagination penetrates 'the mysterious springs of Love, and Fear, and Wonder, of Enthusiasm, Poetry, Religion'. These are handled within a safe world of imaginative privacy where an interest in the invisible is not challenged.

Many of the major Victorians defined the self in terms of its dialogue with society. Arnold rebukes Wordsworth, Obermann and Lucretius for their retreat from such an exchange, although elsewhere he evinces a genuine nostalgia for the Scholar Gipsy's self-dedication:

> For early didst thou leave the world, with powers
> Fresh, *undiverted to the world without*,
> Firm to their mark, not spent on other things.[2]

That is not Arnold's last word even within the particular poem, but it was to be exactly and fully the insistence of much Pre-

---

[1] 'The Latest Development of Literary Poetry', *The Quarterly Review*, 132 (1872), p. 79.

[2] My italics. On Wordsworth and Lucretius see the *Complete Prose Works* III, 121 and I, 33 respectively; on Obermann, 'Obermann Once More'.

Raphaelitism, which chose to establish its authentic self by inward rather than outward dialogues. It lent itself with increasing ease to a rapt and uncritical absorption. Wilde captures this intensity in his superb parable of 'The Disciple':

'But was Narcissus beautiful?' said the pool.
'Who should know better than you?' answered the Oreads. 'Us did he ever pass by, but you he sought for, and would lie on your banks and look down at you, and in the mirror of your waters he would mirror his own beauty.'
And the pool answered, 'But I loved Narcissus because, as he lay on my banks and looked down at me, in the mirror of his eyes I saw my own beauty mirrored.'[1]

It is a further extension of these introspective anxieties that with some of the Pre-Raphaelites the doppelganger myth—that primitive horror of loss of identity—should acquire new life. The third chapter of this book chronicles other elements of their introspection. It is a rich world, sustaining for the best their faith in the efficacy of the imagination, redeeming the atrophy that Empedocles experienced upon the barren summit of Etna.

But a reliance upon introspective modes of imagination— 'une reprise par l'âme de ses propres profondeurs'[2]—still sets each artist the problem of finding an adequate language in which to articulate what a contemporary called 'a soul's delight in its own extended sphere of vision.'[3] Hence the Pre-Raphaelites' atavistic search through various 'mythologies' for viable vocabularies, of which but a small proportion are successful. The difficulty was that only the most compelling of personal experiences could fill out these borrowed garments and make them something of their own. Rossetti could use with this force metaphors from Dante; Pater is most valuable in *The Renaissance* when his personal visions can find a language in the arts he discusses with such a studied, but misleading objectivity.

---

[1] *The Works*, p. 844.
[2] Charles Morice, *La Doctrine Symboliste* (*Documents*), ed. Guy Michaud (Paris 1947), p. 65.
[3] Robert Browning, 'An Essay On Shelley', reprinted in *The Avon Booklet* (1904), I, 5.

Much Pre-Raphaelite symbolism may also be read as the search for a vocabulary in which to treat of their perception of the Invisible. The noumenous abstractions by which Carlyle designated his dynamisms—Love, Wonder, Fear—need explication in phenomenal idiom, above all in a pragmatic age which can only credit such notions when translated into a familiar language. As Mill complained of Bentham:

He had a phrase, expressive of the view he took of all moral speculations to which his method had not been applied, or (which he considered the same thing) not founded on a recognition of utility as the moral standard; this phrase was 'vague generalities'. Whatever presented itself to him in such a shape, he dismissed as unworthy of notice, or dwelt upon only to denounce as absurd. He did not heed, or rather the nature of his mind prevented it from occurring to him, that those generalities contained the whole unanalysed experience of the human race.[1]

To these same areas of experience the Pre-Raphaelites appealed. And Mill's emphasis is relevant to our assessment of their success or failure; for I think they often tried to symbolize much that was unanalysed and to gesture too imprecisely towards resonant but undefined areas of the human spirit. In this they may be seen to avoid the stringent process of symbolism about which Puvis de Chavannes theorized:

Pour toutes les idées *claires*, il existe une pensée plastique qui les traduit. . . . La pensée . . . je la roule jusqu'à ce qu'elle soit *elucidée* à mes yeux et qu'elle apparaisse avec *toute la netteté possible*. Alors je cherche un spectacle qui la traduisse avec *exactitude*.[2]

This translation of idea into plastic fact is an exact and thoughtful art; it was often beyond the Pre-Raphaelite imagination (as it may, in passing, be noted that it was sometimes beyond the practice of Puvis de Chavannes himself). For despite Rossetti's insistence on poetry's fundamental brainwork, the Pre-Raphaelites

[1] *Mill on Bentham and Coleridge*, with an introduction by F. R. Leavis (1962), p. 59.
[2] Quoted S. T. Madsen, *Sources of Art Nouveau* (Oslo 1956), p. 246, my italics.

tend to respond intuitively and emotionally to the resources and depths of human experience which their symbolism chooses to celebrate.

Psychology was to provide a vocabulary of greater precision later in the century, and in many ways it superseded symbolism; obviously many contributors to the magazines of the 1890's had begun to appreciate its usefulness. But at the start of the Pre-Raphaelite movement the articulation of invisible ideas and passions depended on other, less adequate vocabularies. We may find Hunt's *Awakened Conscience* amusing because its mode of presenting the inner movement of soul is so richly and factually a social vision of upholstery and interior decor. Hunt probably intended just such use of quotidien, physical matter, as the best means of conveying the interior drama. Similarly, Rossetti's physically oppressive women are attempts, as he put it, to make the symbolism inherent in the fact. We sometimes smile, because, as with Holman Hunt, the facts are rarely commensurate with what is symbolized. Those faint personifications of Simeon Solomon or G. F. Watts's dull allegories of Hope, Psyche or Love Triumphant are also inadequate attempts to body forth in visual spectacle the dominant images of a spiritual drama.

The Pre-Raphaelites admired William Blake's symbolism because he had evolved a dialect for his visions, which was a source of envy to them as well as a sanction for their own private attempts. In other ways, too, he seemed their champion. Both Burne-Jones and Yeats confessed that with Blake their spirits revived after too much rationalism and materialism.[1] Smetham called him the 'great Idealist', W. B. Scott linked him with the New Spiritualism, and Swinburne saw him as the enemy of the merely factual and of that 'obstinate adherence to one external opinion which closes and hardens the spirit'.[2] The Pre-Raphaelite imagination constantly sought to evade such constrictions of the spirit and by the end of the century, when it found eloquent and

[1] See *Memorials of Edward Burne-Jones* (1904), II, 319, and Yeats in *The Works of William Blake* (1893), I, 26.

[2] Respectively, Gilchrist's *Life of Blake* (2nd ed., 1880), II, 311; *William Blake. Etchings from his Works* (1878), p. 4; *William Blake. A Critical Essay* (2nd ed., 1868), p. 188.

informed theorists in Yeats and Symons, symbolism was hailed precisely as 'the only escape from our many imprisonments'.[1]

In one curious and important way Pre-Raphaelite symbolism did accommodate itself to Victorian mechanisms. Although it offered access to wisdom as distinct from knowledge,[2] and to authentic worlds beyond the constrictions of mere phenomena, it was often forced to employ the factual details of the world to communicate its visions. The early Pre-Raphaelites especially were students of phenomena and they share with other Victorians this interest in the authority of factual description; W. B. Scott even claimed that photography and Pre-Raphaelitism were distinguished by the same response to indiscriminate detail. Both their excursions into realistic, modern subjects and their concern to translate symbolic vision into factual idiom show a certain willingness to grapple with the intractable material of the physical world. They thus pay some deference to a central Victorian concern. Browning and Ruskin, for example, both saw in the intricacies of nature intimations of divine genius:

> God's work—paint any one, and count it crime
> To let a truth slip.[3]

And Ruskin in the forest at Fontainebleau, sketching the small aspen tree, realized 'with wonder increasing every instant' that its beautiful lines ' "composed" themselves, by finer laws than any known of men'.[4] While The Pre-Raphaelites were, with the exception of Hunt and Christina Rossetti, less deliberately religious than either Browning or Ruskin, they share the same confidence that through the visible world the invisible is best apprehended. By itself the external world seems to bore them: Rossetti left *Found* unfinished, while it is the excessive interest in indiscriminate detail that makes him mistrust Brown's *Work*. But

[1] Symons, *The Symbolist Movement in Literature* (Dutton Everyman Paperback, 1958), p. 74.

[2] This was a favourite Victorian distinction: Disraeli saw that the 'fallacy of the great Utilitarian scheme consists in confounding wisdom with knowledge'; Tennyson, 'Knowledge comes, but wisdom lingers'.

[3] *The Poetical Works of Robert Browning*, V, 244.

[4] *Praeterita*, with an introduction by Kenneth Clark (1949), p. 285.

where externals are redolent of more than their circumstantial detail, as in his poem, 'The Woodspurge', he delights in their emblematic virtue. And where no obvious symbols present themselves he is at pains to read the phenomenal accidents of his experience as cyphers of the inarticulate. As Pater wrote of Giorgione, Rossetti responds to any

profoundly significant and animated instants . . . into which, however, all the motives, all the interests and effects of a long history, have condensed themselves.[1]

It comes then as no surprise that it is to a Pre-Raphaelite that Newman appeals in his *Apologia* when, explaining scriptural symbolism, he talks of the 'exterior world, physical and historical' as 'but the outward manifestation of realities greater than itself'.[2]

At the end of the century W. B. Yeats formulated certain conclusions about the Pre-Raphaelite movement and these he absorbs into his highly stylized account of late romanticism. Despite his need to organize literary history into heightened dramatic patterns ('The Tragic Generation'), his insights are valuable. He is typically Pre-Raphaelite in his rejection of any attempts to engage with his contemporaries or accommodate his insights to theirs; this is perhaps what lies behind his famous apophthegm that only rhetoric results from our quarrel with others, while poetry must come from quarrelling with ourselves. He thought the poetry of Tennyson and Browning had tried too conscientiously 'to absorb into itself the science and politics, the philosophy and morality of its time'.[3] In reaction he announced a new poetry, which would 'speak out of some personal or spiritual passion in words and types and metaphors that draw one's imagination as far as possible from the complexities of modern life and thought' (p. 191). He realizes not only the direction these

---

[1] *The Renaissance* (1899), p. 156.
[2] *Apologia Pro Vita Sua* (Fontana Books, 1959), p. 115n. The reference is to Morris's 'Nature is a Parable'.
[3] *Essays and Introductions*, p. 190. All further references in this section, unless otherwise stated, are to this collection.

new visions would take, but also sees their crucial difficulty is the discovery of vocabulary.

Yeats confessed that Huxley and Tindall had destroyed the simple-minded religion of his youth.[1] It was a feeling he shared with contemporaries like Hardy, whose poem on 'The Oxen' expresses a nostalgia for the Christmas legend, which his poem wistfully celebrates, of the oxen kneeling in their stalls on the eve of Christ's nativity—'So fair a fancy few would weave / In these years'.[2] In an effort to preserve something for the fancy or imagination from the encroachments of science, Yeats ardently endorsed literature's distinctness from 'explanatory and scientific writing' (p. 195). Literature is beginning to 'be interested in many things which positive science, the interpreter of external law, has always denied' (pp. 191–2). Or again, he claims some British participation in the European revolt against the 'externality' which a time of scientific and political thought has brought into literature.[3]

Yeats is the most vocal and theoretic voice of the Pre-Raphaelite imagination. His confidence in an anti-scientific movement is a restrospective formulation; what Carlyle predicts, Yeats celebrates as history. Although he acknowledges the Pre-Raphaelite contribution to the movement, his construction of literary mythology requires more emphasis upon the endeavours of his own generation. It also assumes a more severe distinction than we would now accept between authentic new voices and the compromised integrities of major Victorians. The chapters that follow explore the Pre-Raphaelite contribution to the movement which Yeats persuasively champions. They also assume a more intricate Pre-Raphaelite relationship with the Victorian world than Yeats's mythology could allow.

---

[1] *Autobiographies*, p. 101.
[2] *Collected Poems*, p. 439.
[3] *Essays and Introductions*, p. 189. A similar operation to rescue literature from science is mounted by the New Critics in America, especially by John Crowe Ransom, and I have discussed this in an article on the New Criticism in *The Critical Survey*, II, 201–10.

CHAPTER TWO

Embroideries of Myth:
Mediaevalism

What we have lost is a world of fine fabling—Hurd (1762)

your convention must be your own, and not borrowed from
other times and people; or, at the least, . . . you must make it
your own by thoroughly understanding both the nature and
the art you are dealing with

—William Morris

I

ONE OF THE MOST ELOQUENT explorations of Pre-Raphaelite
interest in mythology is W. B. Yeats's essay of 1897, 'The Celtic
Element in Literature'. He declares that

literature dwindles to a mere chronicle of circumstances, or passionless fantasies, and passionless meditations, unless it is constantly
flooded with the passions and beliefs of ancient times;

and in a note dated 1924 he adds 'as an alternative that the supernatural may at any moment create new myths'.[1] He celebrates,
with numerous examples, the passion of folk literature

whose like is not in modern literature and music and art, except
where it has come by some straight or crooked way out of ancient
times.[2]

Much later in his career he perhaps realized that an absorption in
mythologies had often tempted the Pre-Raphaelite movement
into picturesque and decorative visions, which were neither their

[1] *Essays and Introductions*, p. 185.   [2] Ibid., p. 180.

most successful nor most important mode of imagination. In the
process of his self-education he learnt to discard the poetic clothes
borrowed in his youth from other times and people:

> I made my song a coat
> Covered with embroideries
> Out of old mythologies
> From heel to throat . . .
>
> Song, let them take it,
> For there's more enterprise
> In walking naked.[1]

His new nakedness represented, of course, not artless simplicity
but a differently studied, artificial patterning of his experience.

From the beginnings many Pre-Raphaelites patterned their
experience upon a variety of mythologies, derived from Arthurian
romance, Irish folklore, Greek myth, Scandinavian saga, from
Malory, Froissart and Villon, or from Shakespeare and early
Italian poetry. For we should understand their notion of 'mythologies' in a broad sense as richly coloured images of a historical
or legendary past that serve also as metaphors for the life of the
human spirit. Yeats says something similar in his essay on Celtic
literature:

And so it is that all the august sorrowful persons of literature, Cassan-
dra and Helen and Deirdre, and Lear and Tristan, have come out of
legends and are indeed but the images of the primitive imagination
mirrored in the little looking-glass of the modern and classic
imagination.[2]

Sometimes the Pre-Raphaelites chose subjects from myths like the
San Grail or Perseus. Or they invoked actual events from
chronicles or early literatures and reworked them in such a way
that they became myths or metaphors for a kind of life which they
believed their own age could not provide. Rossetti translated *La
Vita Nuova* because Dante offered him a romantic and resonant
image of love, to which, incidentally, he subsequently fitted his

---

[1] *Collected Poems*, p. 142.
[2] Op. cit., p. 182.

actual experience.[1] Swinburne, similarly, was provided by Villon with a mouthpiece for visions of eroticism which his own voice could not express.[2]

At its least strenuous this taste for mediaeval subjects and décor was an escape into congenially picturesque worlds, an excuse for exotic effects and easy atmospherics, for what a writer in the 1856 *Maga̧ine* called 'strange and wild songs'. For instance, Morris's

> Black grew his tower
> As we rode down lower
> Black from the barren hill;
> And our horses strode
> Up the winding road
> To the gateway dim and still;[3]

or Rossetti's watercolour, *The Wedding of St George and the Princess Sabra*, which James Smetham describes as

a golden dim dream. Love 'credulous all gold', gold armour, a sense of secret enclosure in 'palace chambers far apart'; but quaint chambers in quaint palaces where angels creep in through sliding panel doors . . .[4]

Quaint indeed. Rossetti's attention in the picture is devoted mostly to the rich clothes and upholstery, into which exotic patterns the central event and its characters are absorbed. In the same way the tapestry on the back wall in Millais's *Lorenzo and Isabella* is as minutely wrought as Isabella's dress in the foreground, and Burne-Jones takes infinite and ultimately distracting pains over the gilt carvings in the setting of his *King Cophetua and the Beggar Maid*.

[1] See William Gaunt's account of his relationship with Elizabeth Siddal in *The Pre-Raphaelite Tragedy* (1942) and a rather more imaginative, but nevertheless very suggestive, reading of his personality by David Larg, *Trial By Virgins. Fragment of a Biography* (1933).

[2] See *New Writings By Swinburne or Miscellanea Nova et Curiosa, Being a Medley of Poems, Critical Essays, Hoaxes and Burlesques*, ed. C. Y. Lang, pp. 13–14 and, for editorial comment, pp. 183–7.

[3] 'Winter Weather', *Oxford and Cambridge Maga̧ine*, pp. 62–4.

[4] Quoted Ironside, *Pre-Raphaelite Painters* (1948), p. 34, where the watercolour is also reproduced. A similar work to Rossetti's in this respect is Burne-Jones's drawing of 'Sir Galahad'.

These mediaeval tastes could be as uncritical and arbitrary as the details of the artwork were unselective. Rossetti confesses that 'these chivalric, Froissartian themes are quite a passion of mine'.[1] They offered him, as presumably did his readings in Poe, Malory, Scott, *The Arabian Nights* and his sister Christina's in Keighley's *Fairy Mythology*, images of existence constantly sustained by great passion and significant activity. What was frequently ignored was that these images were often literary intensifications, Sidney's golden world, and not the brazen conditions of everyday life. It was, in fact, not an appeal from nineteenth-century to mediaeval existence, but from Victorian daily life to older artifacts. But confusions between art and life were ignored and a hunger for 'romance' satisfied, as one of Morris's early mediaeval *epiphanies* discloses:

How well I remember as a boy my first acquaintance with a room hung with faded greenery at Queen Elizabeth's Lodge, by Chingford Hatch, in Epping Forest . . . , and the impression of romance that it made upon me; a feeling that always comes back on me when I read, as I often do, Sir Walter Scott's Antiquary, and come to the description of the green room at Monkbarns, amongst which the novelist has with such exquisite cunning of art imbedded the fresh and glittering verses of the summer poet Chaucer; yes, that was more than upholstery, believe me.[2]

In pursuit of such impressions of romance to colour their drab world, the Pre-Raphaelites often neglected to ask how their borrowings could serve their art, how their own personal concerns could find appropriate images in what they borrowed. Yeats wanted literature flooded with the 'passions and *beliefs*' of ancient times; but modes of belief had changed. The enthusiasm of Rossetti or Brown for tri-panelled pictures ignored how irrelevant the form was; Dante's use of and delight in mystical numbers becomes vague decoration in

> She had three lilies in her hand
> And the stars in her hair were seven.

[1] *Ruskin, Rossetti and Pre-Raphaelitism*, p. 198.
[2] *Collected Works* (1910–15), XXII, p. 254.

The difficulty in discussing this mediaevalism is that it is tangled from the start with other elements of the Pre-Raphaelite inspiration. Among the titles Rossetti suggests for *The Germ* are *The Chalice*, *The Spur* and *The Casket*.[1] If the second two announce his general fondness for all things mediaeval, the first—together with his suggestion of 'Early Christians' as a title for their group —reveals his nostalgia for their religious inspiration. On his Belgian trip he records the attraction he felt towards the 'pure religious sentiment' of Memling.[2]

But the nostalgia which these mid-century Victorians could feel for the confident religious beliefs they saw celebrated in pictures by Memling, Cimabue or Giotto was also entangled with the impression of sincerity that they derived from the same artists. What we nowadays call the Italian primitives sanctioned the Pre-Raphaelite concern to express their own insights. It even sanctioned naïve technique, and we may justly suspect that at times they equated poor technical skill with artistic sincerity. The early Italian painters, especially seen through the inadequate engravings by Lasinio of the Campo Santo at Pisa, seemed not only quaint but also eminently sincere. They were certainly preferable to the studied and, because technically assured, transparently insincere imitations of Raphael by his less talented followers. Holman Hunt, writing of the Brotherhood's inspiration from the Lasinio engravings, emphasized that they showed 'no trace of decline, no conventionality, no arrogance', but were entirely simple and sincere.[3]

When Ruskin wrote to *The Times* in defence of the Pre-Raphaelites he accused the paper's art critic of supposing they intended a return to archaic *art* instead of archaic *honesty*.[4] The

---

[1] *Letters of Dante Gabriel Rossetti to William Allingham*, pp. 65-7.

[2] *Pre-Raphaelite Diaries and Letters*, p. 13. Collinson, a sincere Catholic, obviously felt the original Brotherhood had some religious inspiration, for he left when, in the July of 1850, he could no longer feel assured that his fellow Brethren were not 'bringing the sanctity of God's saints into ridicule' (ibid., p. 275).

[3] 'The Pre-Raphaelite Brotherhood: A Fight For Art', *The Contemporary Review*, 1883 (in three parts, April, May and June); the quotation is from the first, p. 480.

[4] *Collected Works* (1903-12), XII, p. 322. Ruskin also expressed no desire to encourage them in their Romanist and Tractarian tendencies.

art critic's misapprehension is not altogether unjustified. *The Germ* printed on its cover a sonnet by William Michael Rossetti which he later explained as meaning that 'a writer ought to think out his subject honestly and personally, not imitatively, and ought to express it with directness and precision'.[1] The paradox is that the sonnet is printed in an aggressively Gothic type which makes it difficult to read. And, although the main point of Rossetti's story, 'Hand and Soul', which is another reaffirmation of the artist's integrity and independence, is clearly presented, he is nevertheless tempted by the mediaeval décor, especially the feuds between Marotoli and Gherghiotti and the faintly archaic idiom in which Chiaro's soul addresses him.

As much of this book will show, some of the most successful parts of the Pre-Raphaelite imagination derive ultimately from its original, confused mediaevalism. But the point to emphasize, I think, is that in 1848 the Pre-Raphaelites were too immature and divided in their aims to distinguish what was useful to each of them. They all needed time to learn how to adapt, as Morris insisted they should,[2] the earlier conventions. This chapter will describe some of the possibilities they each explored, as well as illustrate the ease with which later members of the movement succumbed to the lures of the romantic décor.

II

The slight amount of mediaeval inspiration in *The Germ* perhaps indicates the hesitations and divided aims of the Brotherhood. (Later in 1856 the *Oxford and Cambridge Magazine*, though hardly single-minded in its contents, has more assurance and coherence and a more dominant 'mediaeval' emphasis.) In *The Germ* there are four engravings with some slight mythological motif; some decorative verses by Woolner, which Patmore complained 'were a trifle too much in earnest in the passionate parts';[3] Orchard's thin ballad, 'On a Whit-Sunday morn in the month of May',

---

[1] See his notes to the facsimile reprint of *The Germ*, p. 16.
[2] See motto at the head of this chapter, from *Works*, XXII, p. 107.
[3] See W. M. Rossetti's notes to facsimile edition of *The Germ*, p. 16.

which is set in a mildly sentimental Middle Ages; Bell Scott's 'Morning Sleep' in which he dreams of Merlin, and some sonnets for old pictures by Rossetti. Otherwise the poetry is as timeless as it is colourless. The most forceful pieces are Madox Brown's article on the painting of historical subjects, F. G. Stephen's on 'The Purpose and Tendency of Early Italian Art' and Orchard's 'Dialogue'. Alternatively there were two strong advocations of modern subjects by Tupper and Stephens; the latter (under the pseudonym of 'Laura Savage') feels that the poetry of the industrial scene has more mystery than is supposed and has been too much neglected (p. 170). W. M. Rossetti contributed a sonnet on the Hungarian Insurrection and Walter Deverell a 'Modern Idyll'. The final impression of *The Germ* is less the atavistic bent of the Brotherhood's imagination than its concern with the nature of art and the necessity for good contemplation, even if the actual quality of the work in it is meagre.

But the writers for the *Oxford and Cambridge Magazine* are obviously more inhibited by their contemporary settings and more liable to take refuge in earlier worlds. Setting *The Druid and the Maiden* in pre-Christian Brittany, its author explains this by saying that even now 'the nineteenth century—that paragon of progress—has not polluted its hills and vales ... (Brittany) is useless, manufactureless' (p. 676). The dilemma for this and other writers is summed up, probably unconsciously, by the author of *A Few Words Concerning Plato and Bacon*. He criticizes contemporary poverty and social misery, yet, at the same time, complacently reflects that the nineteenth century was turning more and more towards Art, because 'our safety lies in imitating ... that Past which ... we have too much despised and neglected' (p. 190). But while Emerson had talked of drawing out of the past 'genuine life for the present', these writers usually seem to forget their contemporary scene totally for a closed, literary world of their own fabrication. Rarely do they offer any other justification than to admit the unreality of their stories by setting them within a framework of dreams. 'The Druid and the Maiden' is the vision of a Victorian visitor to Brittany; 'A Dream' is less subtle, beginning, 'I dreamed once that ...' In 'Lindenborg Pool' (pp. 530–4) a nineteenth-century author dreams he becomes a thirteenth-century priest; quoting ecclesiastical Latin, he proceeds Janus-like through the story:

I watched him in my proper nineteenth-century character, with insatiable curiosity and intense amusement; but as a quiet priest of a long-past age, with contempt and disgust enough, not unmixed with fear and anxiety.

Well might another author argue that the 'age is retrospective. It builds the sepulchres of our fathers' (p. 212). None of the authors engaged in that retrospection seemed to entertain any doubts about their work. These were voiced by other contributors: one talks of 'these chaotic middle ages' (p. 732); another insists that 'we shall go far wrong if we suppose that what was best in the sixteenth century is therefore best in the nineteenth' (p. 134); a series of articles on Carlyle continually champion the Middle Ages as an era of order, faith, work, duty, loveliness, and worship.

Yet it is this latter enthusiasm which seems to dominate the *Magazine*, enough to earn a rebuke from another contributor: 'and those who . . . would strive to conjure up images of the Middle Ages, as they pore, in some quaint Gothic nook, over the stirring chronicles of olden days, must learn to . . . go down to the busy city, to mingle with the common herd' (p. 564). There is a medi-aeval setting or motif in ten out of the seventeen stories and in eight of seventeen poems. Since it was a slightly more mature production than *The Germ*, less youthfully irresponsible, with a tone no longer of open revolt, such indications would seem more surely indicative of the editors' decided aims. Its tendency to dream of the Middle Ages has already been noticed; even the modern tale, 'Frank's Sealed Letter', has its old romances and quaint panelling. Yet with an increase of such enthusiasms came little preoccupation with any responsible or imaginative use of them. The narrator of 'A Story of the North' nods asleep over a book minutely and lovingly described:

dark green and purple and melancholy gold lay upon the page and round about the writing; very sad and pensive was the colouring; and in among the flowers and interlacings of delicate branches, long-leaved branches, showed a castle tower grey against a sky of windy blue, and a lady leaned therefrom in the tower-window, resting her white forehead on her right hand, and playing dreamily with her left among the leaves, and an agony of long expectation sealed itself upon her face. (p. 82)

The Blessed Damozel, losing any emotional reality she ever had, reappears to decorate the turret window; the whole passage is an attempt to elicit emotion from something which is incapable of supporting it (neither is gold, I would have thought, a particularly melancholy colour). Elsewhere the reviewer of *Hiawatha* knows the reader will delight in 'the early unskilled numbers of those true poets of the people, whose names are countless and unknown ... those legends so old and yet so young' (p. 45). A reviewer recommended that all art, whether an accurate picture of the past or not, should point some moral learnt from history (pp. 1–2); nevertheless at the same time he indulges in quaintly archaic expressions which show little awareness of what is relevant for his own age. Anything archaic wins full praise; Rossetti's picture of Dante's vision of Beatrice is 'of course intensely mediaeval' (p. 82).

Not all the mediaevalism in the *Magazine* is as blatantly decorative as 'The Dream', with its knight of the 'long brown hair, interwoven with threads of gold' and the lady 'with golden hair and white raiment'. Even 'A Story of the North' has a certain terseness, when, for instance, the Nordic women sing 'magic runes above the body of the dead, that his spirit might have rest in its journey to the gods'. This ability to narrate tautly and feelingly is apparent also in Morris's 'The Hollow Land', a tale of mediaeval feud and fight which fades off into a vaguely symbolic vision of the landscape which gives the story its title.[1]

Three further pieces by Morris are notable for their serious concern and affection for the art of the Middle Ages and significant

---

[1] As I have said, the Pre-Raphaelites could learn to use their mediaevalism, and 'The Hollow Land' shows Morris beginning to do so. Consequently examples of their successes, like Morris's symbolist landscapes or Rossetti's use of metaphors from Dante for his own introspection, are discussed in subsequent chapters. For an example of Victorian mediaevalism used rather than relished for its mood and decoration see my forthcoming discussion of Tennyson's *Idylls of the King* in *Victorian Poetry (Stratford-upon-Avon Studies)*.

in relation to his practical activities as craftsman and designer. They are 'The Story of an Unknown Church', 'A Night in a Cathedral' and 'The Churches of Northern France: Shadows of Amiens'. The first is a story told by a master mason, an exercise in nostalgia, in which Morris obviously participates with enthusiasm. It seems worth considering for its controlled impressionism of style and for the mason's vision of his friend Amyot, which is made more than merely decorative, I think, by Morris's compelling handling of the shifting images of the dream, and for the loving concern for details of natural beauty which had obviously provided the mason with models for his carvings of 'flowers and strange beasts'. The second is the reverie of a man who professes no knowledge of architectural technicalities, but it ends with a re-imagining of Amiens cathedral during its construction.

The third, and perhaps the best, is a factual essay, which is perhaps its strength. Morris communicates considerable enthusiasm and his interest and love for mediaeval art and architecture are immediately apparent: indeed, he apologizes for using 'beautiful' so frequently. The essay contains detailed descriptions, especially of the carvings—those in the choir tell the story of Joseph in a 'gloriously quaint, straightforward manner'; there is also in the essay a sense of the atmosphere of the building, of the 'twined mystery of the great flamboyant rose window', that is as good as in some of Ruskin's well-known passages. (The general debt to Ruskin is obvious, even in Morris's story of 'Svend and the Brethren' where the carvings are grand, although roughly cut, 'because the hand of the carver had followed his loving heart'.) Morris's farewell to Amiens, if somewhat over-rhetorical, is as controlled and visionary as, say, Ruskin's passage on St Mark's:

Farewell to the sweep of the arches, up from the bronze bishops lying at the west end, up to the belt of solemn windows, where, through the painted glass, the light comes solemnly. Farewell to the cavernous porches of the west front, so grey under the fading August sun, grey with the wind-storms, grey with the rain-storms, grey with the beat of many days' sun, from sunrise to sunset; showing white sometimes, too, when the sun strikes it strongly; snowy-white, sometimes, when the moon is on it, and the shadows growing blacker; but grey now, fretted into deeper grey, fretted into black by the mitres of the bishops, by the solemn covered heads of the prophets, by the company of the risen, and the long robes of the judgement angels, by hell-mouth and its flames gaping there, and the devils that feed it; by the saved souls and the crowning angels; by the presence of the Judge, and by the roses growing above them all for ever.

Farewell to the spire, gilt all over with gold once, and shining out there, very gloriously; dull and grey now, alas; but still it catches, through its interlacement of arches, the intensest blue of the blue summer sky; and, sometimes at night you may see the stars shining through it. (p. 109)

He redeems this mediaevalism from the tendency towards effete decoration and irresponsible gambolling in the paradise of an imagined Middle Ages by his grasp of detail, his sense and obvious knowledge of the mediaeval arts and his imaginative projection into their actual ambience.

The poetry of his first volume, *The Defence of Guenevere*, is also at its best when he can use those abilities; such lines as—

> Edward the king is dead; at Westminster
> The carvers smooth the curls of his long beard—[1]

combine both his sense of detail and his very real feeling for the sculpture described. The extraordinary power with which these first attempts at poetry actualize the mediaeval world that Morris's dreams inhabit is aided by a stammering, often abrupt rhythm. Easy melodies would lull the poetry into a falsely poetic trance: as it is the speech rhythms beneath the metre give their own realistic support to Morris's visual concreteness. He was a superb descriptive writer, whose love of the phenomenal world is displayed extensively, but rarely prolixly, in his writing:

> There I pluck'd a faint wild rose,
> Hard by where the linden grows,
> Sighing over silver rows
>   Of the lilies tall.
> I laid the flower across his mouth;
> The sparkling drops seem'd good for drouth;
> He smiled, turn'd round towards the south,
>   Held up a golden tress.

[1] From 'Sir Philip Harpdon's End', *Works*, I, 37.

43

Here the detailed account by Sir Galahad (from 'The Chapel in Lyoness') holds the attention.

Morris writes about the approach to Kelmscott and his vision of the utopia in chapter thirty of *News from Nowhere*:

> I thought of all the beautiful grey villages, from the river to the plain and the plain to the uplands, which I could picture to myself so well, all peopled now with this happy and lovely folk, who had cast away riches and attained to wealth.

He *could* picture them to himself so well. Though his idealism at times seems naïve, the impossibility of his various ideal worlds is balanced by the very probability of his visual pictures. It is equally true, as one of his critics has pointed out, that although he seems to 'have caught the trick of the chronicles, and sights, sounds and smells are magnified by his very nearness' to them, the final meaning of events blurs.[1] This ultimate lack of definition is mainly because his later work is no longer helped by the interesting rhythmic activity that sustained much of *The Defence of Guenevere*.

Another fashion in which Morris's cosmic homesickness manifests itself is his translations from Icelandic saga. It is a topic dealt with elsewhere by more competent authorities,[2] but some consideration of it here can help to illuminate Pre-Raphaelite mediaevalism. Morris, like many writers in the century from Wordsworth and Coleridge onwards, found in earlier, 'primitive' literatures not only romantic subjects but more importantly a diction and imagery which carried associations of great emotion and resonant experience. Shakespeare, Dante, ballads and romances, Scandinavian saga—all seemed to provide a vocabulary which avoided literary sophistication. Rossetti read through 'all manner of old romaunts [*sic*] to pitch upon stunning words for poetry'.[3] It was, of course, a superficial exercise and for all the

[1] M. R. Greenan, *William Morris Mediaevalist and Revolutionary* (New York 1945), p. 98; this quotation concludes a long and thorough discussion of the relation of the *Dream of John Ball* to historical fact.

[2] See D. M. Hoare, *The Works of Morris and Yeats in Relation to Early Saga Literature* (Cambridge 1937) and K. Litzenberg, *The Victorians and the Vikings: a bibliographical essay on Anglo-Norse literary relations* (Ann Arbor 1947).

[3] *Letters*, I, 55.

stunning words—*mead, countrie, chaunted, damoysel*—the experience invoked was most often decoratively superficial. Perhaps only G. M. Hopkins was successful in learning from older poetry, and he worked up through his ideas to find a style both capable of saying what he wanted in the nineteenth century and still 'poetic'. The more usual results were Swinburne's 'auld' Scots style for a ballad like 'Keilder Side'[1] or Morris's opening to *The Water of the Wondrous Isles*:

Whilom, as tells the tale, was a walled cheaping-town hight Utterlay, which was builded in a bight of the land a little off the great highway which went from over the mountains to the sea.

Morris's search for words nearest to the actual and literal form of Icelandic produced weird archaisms and semi-biblical language: 'And yet withal it misliked them both' or 'Then they tilted over a wain in most seemly wise'[2] are both highly misleading versions of what could better be put as 'Yet neither was pleased' and 'They put a canopy over a splendid carriage'.

This concern solely for the verbal texture is most striking in his versions of Homer. The Greek epics supplied another metaphor or myth of human experience, analogous to those of Scandinavia, in which Morris could find what Yeats was to call 'passion whose like is not in modern literature'.[3] He turns the Greek into quasi mediaeval, sham archaic style:[4]

Antinoüs, art thou angry with the shapen word of my voice?
This thing, if of Zeus it were given, I should take it and rejoice;
Or of all that befalleth manfolk dost thou deem it the evillest thing?
For look you, I deem it no evil to become a lord and a king,
For in wealth his house is waxen and most glorious doth he grow.
But many a King of Achaeans meseems there is e'en now

[1] Just as Wilde was later to use Scots vocabulary, with less excuse, in his 'Ballade de Marguerite'!

[2] These examples together with the Icelandic originals are given by Hoare, p. 54.

[3] Op. cit., p. 180.

[4] R. A. Knox has drawn attention to Morris's translation of the hero's traditional description 'destroyer of cities' as 'Burgbane' ('On English Translation', The Romanes Lecture for 1957 (Oxford), p. 20). My own example comes from the end of Book One of *The Odyssey*.

In Ithaca the seagirt, both young and old; and one
Amidst these may chance on the lordship since Odysseus' days are
    done.
But o'er this my house and my war-thralls will I verily be the king,
E'en they that Odysseus gat me in his gainful warfaring.

In contrast, even the heroic idiom of Pope's version seems
straightforward and unobtrusive:

> Those toils (Telemachus serene replies)
> Have charms, with all their weight, t'allure the wise.
> Fast by the throne obsequious fame resides,
> And wealth incessant rolls her golden tides.
> Nor let Antinous rage, if strong desire
> Of wealth and fame a youthful bosom fire;
> Elect by Jove, his delegate of sway,
> With joyous pride the summons I'd obey.
> Whene'er Ulysses roams the realm of night,
> Should factious power dispute my lineal right,
> Some other Greeks a fairer claim may plead;
> To your pretence their title would precede.
> At least, the sceptre lost, I still shou'd reign
> Sole o'er my vassals, and domestic train.

There is, admittedly, little to choose between 'domestic train' and
'war thralls'; but placing Pope beside Morris reveals how the
latter's concern for linguistic usage seems to have destroyed his
ear for other important tones and manners; just as crucially, too,
Morris blurs the meaning of the passage far more than Pope by
his substitution of a vague aura of quaint antiquity.

    Similarly, his treatment of the Scandinavian material ignores
essentials in favour of surface rhythms and moods. The speed and
compression of the originals are forgotten in 'The Fostering of
Aslang' or 'The Lovers of Gudrun', where the verse, partly because so facile, seems limp. In the latter the tragedy is softened
with the result that though the heroine's life is supposedly spent
'amidst mad love and crime'[1] the final effect is more pensive pathos.
The startling exception to this concern for mere mood is *Sigurd
the Volsung* (1876). The long, surging lines, contained by the

---

[1] *Works*, V, p. 392.

rhymed couplets and the subtle presence of alliteration, carry the poem firmly along and allow much strongly felt and dramatized passion to be accommodated within the epic. It becomes by the end a powerful Victorian myth of a long-lost, lamented capacity for real emotion.

This nostalgia which Morris identifies with Icelandic saga is suggested in his poem, 'Iceland First Seen'.[1] He celebrates the austere landscape, 'Dreadful with grinding of ice, and record of scarce hidden fire'. But it is typical of the faults we have noticed in his treatment of Icelandic material that immediately afterwards he sees this land as the home of 'the tale of the Northland of old and the undying glory of *dreams*' (my italics). In the wishful thinking of the final stanza he apostrophizes Iceland, crowns her with lilies, and asks to talk with her of 'thy sweetness of old'.

III

Rossetti's earliest excursions into balladry with translations of Burger's *Lenore* and Auë's *Henry the Leper* suffer from his inability to absorb the emotions and ideas of the original into his own imagination; he has still insufficient knowledge of older literature and his technical skills are not as assured as they were to become. His version of *Lenore* is too sophisticated in its double-stanza form and false, pseudo-poetic language, while a certain prudery leads him into such a mistranslation as 'That the bride and bridegroom's sweet rest be unbroken' for 'Eh wir zu Bett uns legen'.[2] Meaningless Catholic touches are introduced by rendering 'Vaterunser' as 'Ave Marie'. His version of *Henry the Leper* also poetizes instead of keeping to the hard, dramatic realism of the primitive story; and he omits the passage where Henry looks through the door chink to see the naked virgin.

Similar distortions and misunderstandings occur in his version of Villon's 'Ballade pour prier Nostre Dame'. The hard, concrete

---

[1] *Works*, IX, pp. 125–6.

[2] Similarly in his version of Ciullo D'Alcamo's dialogue the original reference to their going straight to bed becomes the less pointed: '(I) will give thee entrance presently.' And he excluded 'Dennis Strand' from publication in his later volumes because it dealt 'trivially with a base amour'.

French is dissolved into weakness—'suis pécheresse' becomes 'mine undeserving', the pact with Satan, 'bounden service'. Archaisms run throughout; 'pitiful', added to the third strophe, introduces a note of sentimentality, and Rossetti shows himself incapable of conveying Villon's real sense of sin[1] and appreciating the strict theological point at the end of the second strophe.[2] His two other translations from Villon, the Rondeau to death and the 'Ballade des dames du temps jadis', are somewhat more successful, despite continued archaisms, mistranslations, attempts to prettify and to avoid Villon's directness.[3] His Italian translations are the most successful of all, doubtless because he is able to identify his own imagination with the spirit of the originals and because they offered him a mode of contemplation highly sympathetic to his own experience.[4]

Graham Hough has said that Rossetti's best work is in his ballads, yet adds that these are sheer pastiche.[5] But I think that Rossetti's mediaevalism is made more than pastiche by his belief in damnation and eternal pain, by the communication of his own guilt and remorse which give some real intensity to his ballads.[6] There is more to this work than Arnold's remark that the Middle Ages had 'poetically the greatest charm and refreshment for me'.[7] Rossetti's use of mediaeval objects does not charm or refresh. Rather he would have agreed with Stendhal about those 'siècles

[1] Compare Rossetti's 'Thou of whom all must ask it even as I; / And that which faith desires, that let it see. / For in this faith I choose to live and die' (II, p. 464) with Villon's 'A qui pecheurs doivent tous recourir, / Comblez de foy, sans fainte ne paresse: / En ceste foy je vueil vivre et mourir'.

[2] Compare Rossetti's 'Oh help me, lest in vain for me should pass / (Sweet Virgin that shalt have no less thereby!) / The blessed Host and sacring of the Mass. / Even in this faith I choose to live and die' (II, p. 463) with Villon's 'Preservez moy de faire jamais ce, / Vierge portant, sans rompture encourir, / Le sacrement qu'on celebre à la messe: / En ceste foy je vueil vivre et mourir'.

[3] For instance, 'Pour qui chastré fut et puis moyne' becomes 'Lost manhood and put priesthood on'.

[4] They have, accordingly, been discussed in the more relevant context of the following chapter.

[5] *The Last Romantics* (1947), p. 71.

[6] This point is made by F. L. Lucas in his introduction to his anthology of Rossetti's writings (Cambridge 1933), p. xxvi.

[7] Quoted by H. A. Beers, *A History of English Romanticism in the 19th Century* (1926), p. 274n.

de passion où les âmes pouvaient se livrer franchement à la plus haute exaltation, quant les passions qui font la possibilité comme les sujets des beaux arts existaient'.[1] Rossetti saw in these past centuries the possiblity of greater passion than his own allowed him, and he was able to identify his own emotions with them and infuse them often with genuine feeling.

In the ballad stories he chooses he presents convincing psychological explorations of the tormented minds of his three heroines, Sister Helen, Rose Mary and the bride of 'The Bride's Prelude'. The most successful means he uses of demonstrating the anguish of their minds is to use the setting to reflect a suitable atmosphere for the state of mind and, by extension, to seem to *be* that state of mind. To realize how adept Rossetti is, the examples that follow have only to be contrasted with Morris in 'King Arthur's Tomb', where, as Guenevere walks towards Launcelot, the downs behind her became as 'lumps of sin'.

'The Bride's Prelude' conveys a mood of listlessness, thundery heat which closely parallels the stifling guilt of Aloyse:

> . . . the stir
> Of thought made noonday heavier. (II, 36)

The depiction of mental stress is accompanied by explicit natural description which is highly effective. When Rose Mary's mother tells her of the ambush, Rossetti images her swoon:

> Deep the flood and heavy the shock
> When sea meets sea in the riven rock . . .
>
> In the hair dark-waved the face lay white
> As the moon lies in the lap of night;
> And as night through which no moon may dart
> Lies on a pool in the woods apart,
> So lay the swoon on the weary heart. (II, 117–18)

and he takes up the sea image at the start of the third section when she recovers, 'A swoon that breaks is the whelming wave.' His poetry benefits from his keen eye more intelligently than his painting did from his visual fidelity to details of nature. The queen

[1] Quoted by Pater, *Appreciations*, p. 216.

in 'The Staff and Scrip' 'heard the arras stir' and the poise of her body was like water-reeds; or in 'The Bride's Prelude'

> The room lay still in dusty glare
> Having no sound through it
> Except the chirp of a caged bird
> That came and ceased; and if she stirred
> Amelotte's raiment could be heard. (II, 40)

Rossetti's interest in the tensions of the human mind in these ballads is perhaps revealed by his alteration of a line in 'Sister Helen'; 'But Keith of Ewern's sadder still' became 'But he and I are sadder still', with the result that Helen is less of a witch and more human. This ballad is a most effective picture of a tormented and evil mind, especially in the contrast with the young child's innocent questions; the tension of the continual dialogue and the slow emergence through it of the facts make one more aware, I think, of some real oppression and guilt than of the mediaevalism of its inspiration.

These effects are helped considerably by his capture of some authentic ballad notes. 'Stratton Water' introduces its hero briskly and without explanation, like Sir Patrick Spens; the situation is explained in swift dialogue; there is the hypnotizing effect of incremental repetition and the brutal presentation of the lovers' past. In 'The White Ship' he uses the supernatural element without falsity:

> 'Tis said that afar—a shrill strange sigh—
> The King's ships heard it and knew not why. (II, 140)

He can also manage the supreme concentration of the ballad:

> The first of all the rout was sound,
> The next was dust and flame,
> And then the horses shook the ground:
> And in the thick of them
> A still band came. (II, 79)

Or its abrupt and telling juxtaposition:

> And once she woke with a clear mind
> That letters writ to calm

> Her soul lay in the scrip; to find
> Only a torpid balm
> And dust of palm. (II, 81)

Yet the prolonged movement into a fifth line can dissipate the concentration and make the stanza seem occasionally self-indulgent. Refrains are occasionally well used, and he is capable of absorbing narration, if perhaps not for a *whole* poem. 'The Staff and Scrip' opens well, and the woman prophesying in 'The King's Tragedy' and the antiphonal question and answer of 'Sister Helen' raise both out of the merely imitative.

Swinburne, although not as accomplished, I think, as Rossetti, can also rise above pastiche in a ballad like 'Duriesdyke'.[1] He succumbs at the start to a pattern of mere mood and Scots dialect, too diffuse to let events emerge crisply. But when the narrative begins to dominate the verbal ingenuity 'Duriesdyke' is more exciting:

> The ship drove hard upon the wind,
> I wot it drove full mightily;
> But the fair gold sides upon the ship
> They were bursten with the sea.
>
> 'O I am sae fain for you, Lord John,
> Gin ye be no sae fain
> How shall I bear wi' my body,
> It is sae full of pain?'
>
> 'O I am sae fain of your body,
> Ye are no sae fain of me;
> But the sails are riven wi' the wind
> And the sides are full of sea.'
>
> O when she saw the sails riven
> The sair pain bowed her back;
> But when she saw the sides bursten
> I wat her very heart brak.
>
> The wind waxed in the sea between,
> The rain waxed in the land;

---

[1] *New Writings*, pp. 5–6.

> Lord John was happit wi' saut sea-faem,
>   Lady Maisry wi' sea-sand;
> And the little bairn between them twa
>   That was to her right hand.

The ballad techniques are well used, settings contribute, as in Rossetti, to the depiction of mental and physical states and the emotions of the characters communicate some power through the dispassionate tones of the narrator. But in comparison with Rossetti Swinburne inclines more easily towards pastiche and appears less interested in the ballad as a vehicle for his own emotion.

IV

The number of coats covered with mythological embroideries that were worn in the 1890's reveals the continuing homesickness of the wearers. Davidson readily acknowledges this in his 'Fleet Street Eclogue', for to

> wonder worlds of old romance
> Our aching thoughts for solace run: (*YB*. V, 301)

while the question which opens Douglas Ainslie's 'Chrysoreas' seems to have expected an enthusiastic response—

> Now who with me will leave for a while
> this age of Mammon, vulgar, vile,
> and glide twelve sleeping ages hence? (*D*. VI, 175)

But escape to a 'spell-bound forest, a charmèd place' (*S*. V, 28) has little of the imaginative purpose or success of earlier Pre-Raphaelites and rightly justified the severity of the anonymous wit who castigated the fatuousness and decorative feebleness of much later 'mediaeval' work:

> Long ladies, knights, and earles and choris-
>   ters in the most appropriate drapery,
> Samite and silk and spotless napery,
> Sunflowers and apple blossoms and orris,
> Behold the work of William Morris.[1]

---

[1] Quoted John Press, *The Chequer'd Shade* (1958), p. 79.

Early in the Pre-Raphaelite movement, it will be remembered, contributors to the *Oxford and Cambridge Magazine* had stimulated their imaginations with Thorpe's *Northern Mythology* or old manuscripts,[1] just as the original Brothers had relied upon engravings of the Campo Santo, upon Dante, Malory or the Memling triptych seen on a trip to Belgium. By the 1890's, although stronger stimulants like drugs, harlots and visits to Dieppe and Paris had to be invoked, the mediaeval enthusiasms still provide many contributions to the magazines. But the dangers inherent in such work are now more pronounced. They were dangers into which the movement had fallen much earlier, despite some occasional successes.

At best Pre-Raphaelitism discovered in mythologies viable metaphors for its own interests and impulses, somewhat as Keats avoids pastiche in 'La Belle Dame Sans Merci' by using the ballad form and situation to dramatize a personal despair and sadness. But such imaginative processes also tempted less strenuous artists or artists in less strenuous moments into facile, decorative visions with little human interest. Morris himself, of course, rightly recognized the decorative possibilities in the mediaeval vogue; the most exciting feature of his career is devoted to adapting mediaeval décor and applied art for his own society.[2] But he also continued to produce literary work which could not survive entirely on this decorative ability. In *The Defence of Guenevere* a few characters are not suffocated by this tendency: Guenevere herself and the heroine of 'The Haystack in the Floods' ('a long way out she thrust her chin') survive as personae capable of communicating emotion. But others are more like tapestry figures whose passions are finally blurred by Morris's exquisite manipulation of the décor. Perhaps the best example of this is his picture, *La Belle Iseult*: the lady is seen in the pensive act of fastening her belt; but the thoughts that preoccupy her, the emotional predicament she is presumably in, these do not succeed in communicating

---

[1] See 'A Story of the North', where the author is set dreaming by his persual of an illuminated book, and 'Lindenborg Pool', which is inspired by Thorpe's volume.

[2] See infra, section V.

themselves and the canvas remains little more than a decorative and thinly emotional excursion into mediaevalism. Similarly, Rossetti's fascination for the decorative effects of the refrain in 'Sister Helen' sometimes refuses to allow the bald statements of the narrative to make their own effects:

> 'And lonely her bridegroom's soul hath flown,
> Little brother!'
> (O Mother, Mary Mother
> The lonely ghost, between Hell and Heaven.)

By the 1890's such decorative and vaguely sentimental inclinations of the early Pre-Raphaelite imagination are the dominant impression.

The main solace of mediaeval themes continues to be the scope offered for more resonant passions than the nineteenth century seemed to allow. McChesney's 'At Old Italian Casements' are slight, atmospheric sketches of fierce passion and bloodshed (*YB*, XIII). Similarly in *The Pageant* (a significant title too, in this context) the only excuse for two meagre mediaeval pieces is their reliance upon wickedness and revenge.[1] In the tradition of 'Norse saga' that Morris had started, Nigel Tourneur's 'Haegon the King' opens—'All day long the din of battle echoed in the waste land by the sea' (*D*. IV). Many of these writers may have thought that the passions they presented had a relevance for their own day merely by being passions common to all humanity. Oscar Wilde, for example, considered that plays dealing with bygone times had the peculiar charm of combining 'in one exquisite presentation the passions of the living with the picturesque that is dead'.[2] Yet such psychological justifications are hardly supported by much of the writing that explores the past. Frederic's 'The Truce of the Bishop' (*YB*, VII) mounts to its climax of massacre and supernatural activities; Gilchrist's 'The Crimson Weaver' (*YB*, VI) tells of ancient evil and blood sacrifice in 'the Castle of the Ebony Dwarf, where a young queen reposed in the innermost casket of the seventh crystal cabinet'. This story is further decorated by the

[1] Volume for 1896, W. Delaplaine Scull's 'Alfric' and 'On the Shadows'.
[2] *Reviews* (Methuen Collected Works), p. 8.

macabre symbolism of the 'bleeding heart whence a crimson cord unravelled into many threads'. This same penchant for mixing the passionate and the macabre occurs in Gordon Bottomley's 'La Belle Isoud in a Lazar-Cote' (*D*. III), a monologue which reveals a 'dim-grown bliss' amid decay, and compares the dead face to a 'rotting rain-pool'.

W. B. Yeats's early work also betrays a fondness for such violent events and passions, like the 'passion-dimmed eyes'[1] and the severed head that sings from the bushes in 'The Binding of the Hair' (*S*. I). The 'loveliness / That has long faded' from the world is evoked in a way that stresses its emotional excitement as well as its decorative qualities:

> The jewelled crowns that kings have hurled
> In shadowy pools, when armies fled;
> The love-tales wrought with silken thread
> By dreaming ladies upon cloth
> That has made fat the murderous moth. (*S*. III)

Maurice Hewlett emerges from such shadows and unashamedly confesses his reasons for entertaining the reader of *The Forest Lovers* without bothering to veil it all in dreams:

My story will take you into times and spaces alike rude and uncivil. Blood will be spilt, virgins suffer distresses; the horn will sound through woodland glades; dogs, wolves, deer, and men, Beauty and the Beasts, will tumble each other, seeking life or death with their proper tools. There should be mad work, not devoid of entertainment. When you read the word *Explicit*, if you have laboured so far, you will know something of Morgraunt Forest and the Countess Isabel; the Abbot of Holy Thorn will have postured and schemed (with you behind the arras); you will have wandered with Isoult and will know why she was called La Desirous, with Prosper le Gai . . . (p. 1)

It is only a short step from that to exploiting this décor for its own charm rather than its passions, as in Patten Wilson's drawing of a dragon breathing fierily at a knight and a lady who crouch,

---

[1] 'He Reproves the Curlew', *Collected Poems*, p. 69.

rather improbably, in crystal balls.[1] Macabre horrors or explorations of extreme states of mind, as in Housman's 'The Troubling of the Waters',[2] give way to a picture-book fairyland which may be enjoyed by anyone unwilling to support adult emotions, let alone adult responsibilities. In the fifth volume of *The Yellow Book* Maurice Baring praises Anatole France's *Abeille* for not striving after modernity: it is 'a real fairy tale, where there are stately *grandes dames*, trusty squires, perfidious water-nymphs, industrious dwarfs, and disobedient children ... a genuine fairy tale ... which only the elect who believe in fairies can feel and appreciate, whether they find it is *The Odyssey* [*sic*] or in Hans Andersen' (p. 268).

The continual reliance upon dreams and reverie reflects this uncritical, child-like absorption—like Makower's piece in *The Yellow Book* (XI) where an old man dreams of his own childhood's dreams of mediaeval knights and castles: two removes from life! In such work the two tendencies which Huysmans noticed—'un retour aux âges consumés' and 'un élancement vers la fantastique et vers le rêve'—are combined. Yeats, too, is often like his own 'Man who dreamed of fairyland' (*R*. I, 7–9), seeming as enthusiastic about the *little people* as Kenneth Grahame's little boy about his knights in 'The Roman Road' (*YB*, II).

For Arthur Symons a gothic church was 'a nest of dreams' (*S*. I, 92), a remark which appears merely a rationalization upon such a piece as 'The Story of an Unknown Church' in the *Oxford and Cambridge Magazine*. And Yeats described how in Pre-Raphaelite art he saw 'wonderful, and happy people, moving through the scenery of my dreams'.[3] It is not only significant that he acknowledges his dreams, but ironically just that he should

---

[1] *YB*. XI. This curious motif of a crystal ball seems to have been rather popular: cf. 'The Crimson Weaver' (*YB*. VI) and Frederick Shields's 'The Vision of Britomart' (*The Hobby Horse*, IV). The motif is taken perhaps from *The Faerie Queene*, III, 2.

[2] *The Dome*, II: in this Housman is closer to Rossetti's best mediaeval work than to his contemporaries. His illustration to his story also shows traces of Rossetti's influence, for Eyloff has the thick neck, massed hair and prominent chin of the Pre-Raphaelite woman.

[3] *Essays* (1924), p. 429.

choose the word 'scenery', with its double meaning of landscape *and* of canvas painted for theatrical illusion. For in much of his early work there is this latter sort: when he tosses the bell branch of 'Dedication of Irish Tales' (*R*. I), the sound of which makes all who hear it 'dream a little while'; or when 'weary of the world's empires' (*S*. II, 109) he listens too intently to peasant visionaries, to old sages, to the 'Good People' who are thousands of years old (*R*. I, 71), and to the sentimental supernaturalism of

> He sat and played in a dream
> Of her long dim hair. (*R*. II, 38)

Occasionally in a turn of phrase or the force of a moment's imagination there is evidence of a great poet; and when his work in this vein is compared with that of less assured writers like Ernest Rhys,[1] Yeats's superiority is evident. But he dreams too readily among Pre-Raphaelite scenery which has lost all the intensity of Rossetti's sullen spirit or Morris's grasp of actualities. Later in his career Yeats may have used Irish culture as a basis for a new, personally sustained mythology, but his early work makes of it an end in itself.

This decorative facility is most obviously betrayed in magazine illustrations. The 'Vision' of William T. Horton (*S*. II), which illustrates the text, 'Strait is the gate', shows a zig-zagging causeway leading to a Heavenly City of ramparts and pinnacles, while the angel with the fiery sword is a knight in armour. The image of the causeway and castellated town he uses again in the fourth volume. The massive blacks and plain white areas give these a certain compelling power, but the repetition of the quaint causeway is tiresome and seems mainly decorative.[2] In Patten Wilson's drawings the illustrative function is lost quite literally under strokes of the pen: the intricate and minutely detailed 'Rustem Firing the First Shot' (*YB*. IV) becomes less a scene illustrated than a pattern of black lines amongst which one deciphers objects

---

[1] See his 'Howel the Red' (*R*. II), decorated in a highly ineffectual way with a vocabulary of Celtic names and such weird archaisms as 'they gave their hearts to Death' or 'stirred the strain'; or 'The Wedding of Pale Bronwen' (*R*. I).

[2] Further confirmed by yet another drawing by him of a mediaeval rampart in *The Dome*, V.

after careful, close study. His 'Penelope' (*YB*. VI) seems mainly an excuse for a detailed exposition of the lilies in the pool, and the embroidery of her dress, a clearly Morris-inspired pattern of natural foliage which distracts, however, by the irrelevant care over detail. That was a clear legacy from Pre-Raphaelite painting, but is even more enfeebled by its use in a picture that seems as a whole to serve no other function but that of decoration. The sketch, 'A Pleasaunce' [*sic*], by Fred Hyland (*S*. VII) shows a lady gathering roses in a walled garden; but the study is entirely betrayed by the dramatic and totally unrealistic sweep of her scarf and the drawing remains merely a variation in black and white upon a pseudo-mediaeval theme. When artists made less imaginative use of the blacks and whites and were less proficient draughtsmen, the results are of exceptional iconographical dullness.[1]

There were, of course, critical voices raised in protest against these unimaginative exercises in mediaeval mythologies. Even Rossetti had seemed disturbed on a few occasions by his own enthusiasms, remarking once that his sketch, 'Before the Battle' was 'ultra-mediaeval', having been composed 'when I was peculiarly nourishing myself with such impressions'.[2] On another occasion in 1874 when he sent two translations of the nineteenth-century poet Tommaseo to the *Athenaeum* he felt impelled to apologize for their not being at all contemporaneous.[3] By the 1890's the mediaeval cult is as sharply rebuked as it is feebly practised. *The Hobby Horse* complained that Morris's style in *The House of the Wolfings* was too archaic and unnatural in its vocabulary and turns of expression (IV, facing p. 80). Le Gallienne condemns, although with a certain wistful reluctance, the futility of any return to the past, whether to 'mediaeval France, to Elizabethan, Caroline, or at latest Queen Anne England' (*YB*. VI, 313).

---

[1] See, for example, the Norse 'Idyll' by MacDougal (*YB*. II), the drawing by Evelyn Holden (*YB*. IX), Rutland's 'Lady of Shalott' and 'Tristram and Iseult' (*YB*. IX).

[2] *Ruskin, Rossetti and Pre-Raphaelitism*, p. 298. A judicious self-criticism, for the drawing is a most extraordinary kaleidoscope of colour and pageantry, a nourishment of his decorative vision but, as such, strangely compelling.

[3] Note in *Collected Works*, II, p. 518.

Ella D'Arcy directs a well-merited gibe at mediaeval revivalists (*YB*. V, 38). In *The Savoy* (VII. 76) Verhaeren is praised for discarding the facile lures of romance.

Yet another fashion in which the vogue is criticized is through irony, though the satiric tones are rarely secure and slide easily into self-indulgence. Evelyn Sharp's story, 'The Restless River', (*YB*. XII) seems at first a straightforward fairy tale, but gradually there becomes noticeable a certain irony, an irony which is at the expense of the tale and *genre* themselves. It is a fairy story where the fairies do not function or appear, where the Prince is given a fairy god*father* who 'arrived on foot . . . and walked in at the front door, instead of coming down with a bang, in a cloud of blue smoke'; everything in the story is 'decidedly original' on account of the exceptional Queen of Nonamia whose totally mundane enthusiasm for the practical issues of life makes her a veritable Victorian *femme de ménage*, with no nonsense, and certainly not the sort of person to tolerate living in a fairy story.

Kenneth Grahame's 'The Headswoman' (*YB*. III) also seems to satirize itself, by tones and remarks which are completely alien to the setting and characters. The story concerns the sixteenth-century town of St Radegonde where the hereditary post of executioner has fallen to a beautiful girl of eighteen. Grahame uses this for some gentle and pleasant enough ironies at the expense of suffragettes and the emancipation of the 'new woman'. Jeanne, the girl, is very touchy on the subject of woman's place and the adjective she most dreads is 'unladylike'; her cousin (a bad case of the aesthetic young man whose laboured composition of sonnets interferes with his legal duties) is severely lectured when he dares to suggest that women are not temperamentally suited to be executioners. Grahame is not content with this. He maintains throughout the story a gently ironic manner towards the mediaeval setting: 'It was a bland sunny morning of a mediaeval May— an old-style May of the most typical quality.' A condemned criminal remarks that it is a real pleasure to be handled by Jeanne, who knows her work so well and whose motto on the job is 'quality, not quantity'. And the young dandy of a local seigneur who finds his way by mistake to the scaffold takes a truly Wildean attitude to it all and with his head on the block remarks upon the admirable view it gives him of the river valley.

Vernon Lee's 'Prince Albert and the Snake Lady' is the most interesting example of this ironic use of the *genre*. It is a story decorated with such mediaeval trappings as a ballad-monger, tattered gothic tapestries, the flowers and beasts depicted in which are described as carefully as those of Morris's sculptor in 'The Story of the Unknown Church', and, above all, the Castle of the Sparkling Waters. But this 'terrible place' to which the Prince is exiled has lost all its ferocity and stern appearance and is 'reduced to its outer circuit of walls, enclosing vineyards and orange-gardens instead of moats and yards and towers', and to the large gate tower 'where, now, the peasants keep stores and cattle'. At this point the keen edge of the whimsical irony is certainly felt, and what at first has troubled a reader by its slight sense of self-mockery is at last made explicit. The whole 'mediaeval' atmosphere down to the Prince's refusal to marry some beautiful princess and his mournful death, is presented in solemn tones which are totally out of key with the fantastic events described: the political machinations of Dwarf, Jesuit and Jester; the Duke Balthasar Maria building a grotto or producing 'the ballet called Daphne Transformed' in which he dances the 'part of Phoebus Apollo to the infinite delight and glory of his subjects'; the Duke 'Humming the well-known air, "Thyrsis was a shepherdboy" of which the ducal fiddlers instantly struck up the ritornel'.

The irony of this last tale is more secure than the whimsy of either Evelyn Sharp or Grahame, both of whose stories betray an incipient fondness for the mediaeval material they are mocking. But in 'Prince Albert and the Snake Lady', as in Beardsley's 'Under the Hill', to which it is probably indebted,[1] the irony is tautly controlled. Both wittily rebuke the decorative tendencies of Pre-Raphaelite mythologies with a grotesquely minute parody. Where Beardsley is superior is not only in the economy of his satire, but

[1] Vernon Lee's story appeared in *The Yellow Book* (X) in July 1896. 'Under the Hill' appeared in the January and April numbers of *The Savoy* earlier the same year. Lee's décor is especially similar to Beardsley's, including topographical details of the castles and the aesthetical antics of the Duke.

also in his more intelligent and perceptive response to the Pre-Raphaelite imagination. For he is sensitive to the impulses which produced Pre-Raphaelite art and literature and is well-informed, too, about their inspiration. So that he seems simultaneously to celebrate their visions and to ridicule their pretensions.[1]

'Under the Hill' responds, first, to the Pre-Raphaelite delight in mythic metaphors of passion by invoking the legend of Venus and Tannhauser, at the same time wittily rejecting the vicarious-ness of much Pre-Raphaelite passion:

Those who have seen Helen only in the Vatican, in the Louvre, in the Uffizi, or in the British Museum, can have no idea how very beautiful and sweet she looked. Not at all like the lady in 'Lemprière'.

Beardsley also draws upon *The Romance of the Rose* ('beautiful, but all too brief') for its opulent anatomical imagery[2] and to mingle it in the waking thoughts of Abbé Franfreluche with other mockeries of Pre-Raphaelite mediaevalism, like romantic land-scapes and madonnas with 'high egg-shaped creamy foreheads and well-crimped silken hair'. Beardsley is equally alert to their religious nostalgia and to their sometimes unconscious flirtation with Catholicism, which Ruskin had originally rebuked. The 'Hill' or Venusberg of the story combines religious ritual and amorous passion, as Rossetti's Italian-inspired poetry did; Beardsley succeeds in mocking the false intensities without al-together relinquishing his own nostalgia for modes of passion his own century denied him.

But the satire is also directed at the indiscriminate eclecticism into which the Pre-Raphaelite movement's search for mythologies led. Beardsley makes this point most obviously by brilliantly

---

[1] See chapter five for a discussion of his similarly dual response to the Pre-Raphaelite image of woman. This double response in 'Under the Hill' is noted by Annette Lavers, ' "Aubrey Beardsley, Man of Letters" ', *Romantic Mythologies*, ed. Ian Fletcher (1967). But her scholarly account of the context of Beardsley's reading and interests in which we should place the tale does not make sufficient allowance, I believe, for his Pre-Raphaelite allusions, nor does her reading of either version of the story pay much critical attention to the workings and effect of the satire.

[2] This point is made by Stanley Weintraub in his introduction to *The Savoy. Nineties Experiment* (University Park, Pennsylvania 1966), p. xxvii.

rendering the Venus and Tannhauser legend in a rococo, eighteenth-century décor ('little mutinies of cravat and ruffle'); fairies from enchanted woods mingle at Helen's Vespers with beaux and Pierrots in a Venusberg that is itself contrived out of many mythologies from Morris's romances, Ruskin and Swinburne, to Wilde's Salomé:

In the middle (of the terrace) was a huge bronze fountain with three basins. From the first rose a many-breasted dragon and four little loves mounted upon swans, and each love was furnished with a bow and arrow. Two of them that faced the monster seemed to recoil in fear ...

Huge moths, so richly winged they must have banqueted upon tapestries and royal stuffs, slept on the pillars that flanked either side of the gateway ... The pillars were fashioned in some pale stone and rose up like hymns in the praise of pleasure, for from cap to base, each one was carved with loving sculptures, showing such a cunning invention and such a curious knowledge, that Franfreluche lingered not a little in reviewing them. They surpassed all that Japan has ever pictured from her maisons vertes, all that was ever painted in the cool bath-rooms of Cardinal La Motte, and even outdid the astonishing illustrations to Jones's 'Nursery Numbers'.

The accompanying drawings, especially that of the servitors at the banquet, are equally a parody of the decorative declensions we have traced in Pre-Raphaelite mediaevalism. Both the mass of their details, which almost obscure the subject, and the narrative which is apparently 'without consequence, without cohesion, without unity'[1] mimic the extraordinary, but finally bewildering, richness of Rossetti's *Before the Battle* and *St George's Wedding* or Burne-Jones's *Sir Galahad*, examples of Pre-Raphaelite mediaevalism which sanctioned much duller and pointless decoration among their followers. Yet there underlies Beardsley's sharp eye for the absurdities of the mediaeval enthusiasms a sympathy for this return to the past, which is perhaps revealed in his exquisite care and inventiveness. Like Pope and the dunces, he is reluctantly forced to celebrate what he is also determined to repudiate.

[1] Quoted, Stanley Weintraub in his introduction *The Savoy. Nineties Experiment* p. xxviii.

V

The Pre-Raphaelite nostalgia for the past which often exercised itself in decorative fantasy did, however, discover one legitimate and exciting use for this facility. The career of William Morris as designer and craftsman, although much praised, has not been explicitly related to the movement's mediaeval enthusiasms.[1] Yet his ideas in this field stem almost wholly from his continuous love and detailed absorption in the past. The general theory he preached about design was that it should be suitable for its function and for the process by which it was produced and that designers would find their best inspiration in natural beauty. The second emphasis saw its precedent in the design and art of the Middle Ages; the first appealed to what Pevsner has called 'decorative honesty'[2] and represents a similar impulse in Morris to the Brotherhood's plea for archaic honesty and the examples of this they discovered in early Italian painting.

It is possible, I think, to see a clear comparison between the P.R.B. of 1848 and Morris's Company of 1861. When Morris told art students that their designs should be distinct and without vagueness and 'always, form before colour, and outline, silhouette, before modelling',[3] he was demanding a return to the essentials of honest design and a rejection of much that had been presented so proudly thirty years before at the Great Exhibition; it was the same type of reaction that led the original P.R.B. to reject the jaded formulae of Academy art. Morris's demands for good design are distinctly analagous to the early pleas for good contemplation and 'archaic honesty': he told his students that they were

only to be limited in the quantity and quality of such work (ornament) by artistic considerations as to how much or what kind of work really suited the wares.[4]

[1] A recent book by Paul Thompson, *The Work of William Morris* (1967), has now noted Morris's constant debt to mediaeval examples in his own work as a designer.
[2] N. Pevsner, *Pioneers of the Modern Movement* (1956), p. 61.
[3] *Works*, XXII, p. 168. All references in this discussion of Morris as a designer are to this volume, unless otherwise stated.
[4] *Selected Writings* (Nonesuch Press, 1934), p. 653.

Such functional ornamentation had its precedent in earlier work of the mediaeval craftsman where

it is often difficult to distinguish where the mere utilitarian part of his work ended and the ornament began.[1]

Morris was not alone in his plea for reform; nor must the Victorian furnishings against which his own tastes were directed be typified by those prestige pieces in the Great Exhibition of 1851.[2] But many of his ideas for good furniture seem, deliberately or accidentally, to be criticisms of precisely the gross and florid items shown in the Exhibition. Many displayed a grotesque pride in the ingeniousness that knew no limits. Imitations of one material in another, notably *papier-mâché*; or the prominence of the *trompe-d'oeil*, like an inkstand in the form of a deer and trees, which Ouida found 'did not look at all what it was, it was lovely'.[3] A more macabre manifestation of this was the taxidermist's display of stuffed animals in the 'attitudes, habits, and occupations of rational creatures'.[4] Equally disturbing were the uses of anachronistic styles to produce an Engine in the Gothic taste or the Rococo upright pianoforte;[5] or the thoroughness with which outline was broken and blurred, with which every available surface was decorated in the flat or relief; or the indiscriminate admiration of novel and tricky gadgets from a Life-preserving Portmanteau to a Patent Double Grand Piano for four performers at a time.[6]

Against such monstrous eccentricities Morris reacted forcibly. He condemned as the 'last resource of the decrepitude of art' the tendency to 'make stone look like ironwork, or wood like silk, or pottery like stone' (p. 169), urging that materials be used as their nature directs. Ornament and decoration are not produced to serve their viewers as an excuse for some parlour guessing game of 'How was it done?' (p. 182); they must rather serve as a demonstration of how all articles 'must be evolved in a natural and un-

[1] *Works*, XXIII, p. 113.
[2] Both points are made by Paul Thompson, op. cit., pp. 138 and 67.
[3] Quoted Pevsner, *High Victorian Design* (1951), p. 87.
[4] Ibid., p. 112 and figs. 87 and 88.
[5] Ibid., figs. 7 and 44.   [6] Ibid., figs. 20 and 23.

forced manner from the material that is dealt with' (p. 240). Thus Morris advised against making wall-paper look as if it were hand-painted (p. 260), when it is obvious by its very nature that it cannot be so produced. Pottery should be conveniently shaped for the purpose it has to fulfil and only be decorated with designs suitable for such objects (pp. 243–7), and he reserves his special scorn for such pieces as the bedroom ewer and basin wrought in ferns and convolvulus (p. 367). Lines of furniture should not be disrupted or 'blotched over with idiotic sham ornament' (p. 333); it was equally ridiculous to imitate in furniture manufacture 'the minor vices of the Borgias, or the degraded and nightmare whims of the *blasé* and bankrupt French aristocracy of Louis the Fifteenth's time' (p. 261). With a recurring pattern for a *flat* surface it must be remembered that the surface to be decorated *is* flat and such relief as there is must be suggested by colours and shades of colours (pp. 183 and 187). Carpet designs especially must be flat (p. 195); accordingly Morris's 'Hammersmith' rug[1] presents a restful and sensible (because two-dimensional) surface upon which to tread. Finally, simple combinations of colour and abstract form were infinitely superior to the High Victorian delight in distinct meaning and narrative in their décor (p. 209).

Against the scientific naturalism of Victorian design Morris reacted, at least in his theory, by warning designers against trying to 'outdo Nature's green tints on our walls'(p. 99); their work should be 'suggestive of such facts, and not descriptive' (p. 209). Otherwise it would be more logical to nail on the wall a few cut flowers, a branch or even a butterfly (p. 178). In practice, Morris frequently contradicted his theories by his own designs. Many of them are firmly naturalistic and it is not always true, as Pevsner claims, that his 'designs are paraphrases of natural growth. His observation of tree and flower was as close and intense as that of any English landscape painter. But his genius lies in the conversion of these observed data into perfectly fitting surface patterns[2].' I

[1] Illustrated in Crow, *William Morris Designer* (1934), p. 81; compare with carpets from the Great Exhibition, *High Victorian Design*, figs. 73 and 74. However, Paul Thompson, op. cit., p. 103, offers several examples of much more naturalistic carpets.

[2] *The Englishness of English Art* (1956), p. 90.

think his work as a designer was sometimes the result of com-
promising his instinct for paraphrase and for formalistic *'suggestions* of gardens and fields' (p. 195, my italics) by his mediaeval
nostalgia. This latter instinct inspired his furnishings, textiles and
wallpapers in two ways. First, he went to mediaeval examples for
details of his own work and techniques: Pevsner has rightly
analysed the 'valuable imitation, inspired by fifteenth-century
delicacy' which produced the 'Honeysuckle' chintz;[1] in 1865–6
Morris's Company paid for an analysis of the methods used in the
mediaeval decoration of roofs and screens in Norfolk and Suffolk
churches.[2] But, second, Morris was inspired by his sense that for
mediaeval men the 'unspoiled countryside came up to their very
doors'[3] and his determination that Victorian man should recapture
something of that glorious closeness of nature:

Is it not better to be reminded, however simply, . . . of the wild-woods
and their streams, with . . . dogs panting beside them; or of the
swallows sweeping above the garden boughs toward the house-eaves
where their nestlings are, while the sun breaks through the clouds on
them; or of the many-flowered summer meadows of Picardy? Is not
all this better than having to count day after day a few sham-real
boughs and flowers casting sham-real shadows on your walls with
little hint of anything beyond Covent Garden in them? (p. 178)

This advice on pattern-designing has the same romantic and
nostalgic tones as his prose romances, for most of his design work
is a practical extension of his utopian visions.[4] But perhaps his
visionary nostalgia prompted too rigorous a naturalism, that his
instinct as designer should have controlled more often. Such a
tension in his work would explain the contradictions between his
pronouncements on design and his own, mediaevally inspired,
practice. In his 'Story of the Unknown Church' he makes the
mason describe with loving care the surrounding landscape, which
obviously inspires the details of his carving. Morris was surely
remembering such a 'mediaeval' example when he said that

---

[1] *Pioneers*, pp. 58–60.
[2] See Paul Thompson, op. cit., p. 69.
[3] Quoted *ibid.*, p. 224.
[4] I have noted elsewhere how descriptions in his prose anticipate the characteristic qualities of his designs: see chapter four, p. 134.

designers must 'know plenty about the natural forms you are conventionalizing' (p. 107). He was also reminding Victorians that England provided far more suitable natural detail for their designs than the Egyptian scarab or Indian lotus. Mediaeval carvers had recreated versions of what their own eyes had seen. Morris echoes the original Brotherhood's appeal to the close observation of nature identified with artists before Raphael.

Mediaeval examples were similarly invoked in the later extension of Morris's craftsmanship, his production of books at the Kelmscott Press.[1] He had made a considerable collection of early printed books and he sought his inspiration in these and in other manuscript sources. From mediaeval and Italian humanist calligraphy and from Roman typefaces of the great fifteenth-century Venetian printers he adapted his own types, which recall, as do his designs and his prose romances, the flowing curves of gothic art.[2] His researches into materials were equally patient and energetic; he went, for instance, to Hanover for an ink that was as black as his models, to a Bolognese paper of about 1473 and to the Vatican for as much of the ideal vellum as he could purchase.

The pervasion of these interests and the fashion in which Morris energized fresh activities in the applied arts are illustrated in most of the magazines at the end of the century.[3] *The Century Guild Hobby Horse* was the most consistent and enthusiastic exponent of his ideas. In its editorial preface to Volume IV (1889) it affirmed its interest in all arts and architecture, especially what Morris had called the 'lesser arts'; among its contents is Mackmurdo's article on the 'Arbitrary Conditions of Art' which echoes many of William Morris's central beliefs. May Morris writes on embroidery, Pollard on title-pages and on Geoffrey Troy, an early printer and engraver; there are articles on Ford Madox Brown's

[1] See Morris's 'Aims in Founding the Kelmscott Press', reprinted in H. Halliday Sparling, *The Kelmscott Press and William Morris Master-Craftsman* (1924), pp. 135 ff.

[2] See Crow, op. cit., p. 199, for Morris's notes on a proof for one of his types.

[3] Morris was not, of course, alone in prosecuting these interests: the designs of E. W. Godwin, Ricketts's Vale Press, Mackmurdo and *The Hobby Horse* were all involved. Morris's work has been discussed here because it is the most obvious example of the Pre-Raphaelite movement's participation and its use of mediaeval inspiration.

stained-glass windows and on mediaeval architecture. And the man who inspired so many of these pages himself contributed on 'The Influence of Building materials upon Architecture'.

The Dome (V) published a design for a smoke room by Joseph Crouch and Edmund Butler and a note emphasizes that 'the furniture (is) produced by simplicity of design and honesty of construction' (p. 229). In *The Pageant* Charles Ricketts has a note on 'Original Wood Engraving' and Pollard another which is illustrated by original woodcuts of the Florentine Rappresentazioni. In the designs for backs of playing cards by Aymer Vallance (*YB*. II) it is possible to recognize the influence of Morris's ideas: the birds and animals are represented formalistically with only a very slight indication of the third dimension; the natural details are conventionalized and their curves graceful and pleasing without extravagance.

Morris's interest and concern in book production were also maintained. Dent was the first publisher to employ an artist, in this case Beardsley, as an illustrator, and until recently their Everyman Library had end papers and title pages in the Kelmscott fashion. Joseph Pennell had an article in *The Savoy* (I), 'A Golden Decade in English Art', on book illustration, which is a well-documented, factual account written in an attempt to 'point out the great value and importance' of illustrations of the 1860's which are 'as important as *those of the fifteenth century*' (my italics). Pennell does not make any attempt to distinguish a Pre-Raphaelite group of illustrators, and the names of Millais, Burne-Jones, Rossetti and Morris occur among others like Leighton, Tenniel or Houghton; while of the three illustrations reproduced only the second with its carefully wrought flowers and glimpses of a mediaeval town or the detailed naturalism of the first might be said to be in the Pre-Raphaelite tradition. But Pennell's article is an interesting example of how a concern for illustration had been fostered by workers, of whom Morris and the Pre-Raphaelites generally were the most energetic; Pennell's concern to have artists' work well engraved is typical of Morris's anxiety over craftsmanship's need to be related closely to art.

More specifically, the sixth number of *The Savoy* carried an article by Oliver Georges Destrée on 'The stained-glass windows and decorative paintings' executed by Rossetti, Burne-Jones, Ford Madox Brown, William Morris and Webb for the church of St Martin's-on-the-hill, Scarborough. (Previously two of Rossetti's cartoons for windows had appeared in *The Hobby Horse* for 1886.) Destrée is enthusiastic about all aspects of Pre-Raphaelitism, the 'most remarkable school of painting of this century'; he is constantly noting the mediaeval antecedents of their decorative work, while at the same time conscious of how they have been adapted. He reserves special praise for the Rossetti panels on the small wooden altar and for the 'renaissance' of the art of stained-glass by Morris's Company.

But perhaps most interesting is an article by G. Bernard Shaw entitled 'On Going to Church' (*S. I*). It begins as a mildly satiric homily upon the virtues of abstaining from drugs and stimulants, suggesting in their place the worth of going to church; although we later learn that it is not for the services. The church which this professedly atheist writer says he may be found in is one 'old enough or young enough to be fit for its purpose'; it will be one devoid of snobbery, and with that word Shaw seems to imply all that Morris did with the word 'luxury . . . the supplanter, the changeling of Art'.[1] In an appeal to the Master Builder Shaw demands that he work in enduring stone and that the church be made by hand. To these sentiments which are highly reminiscent of Morris, Shaw soon seems to add his master's style and tone:

when an enlightened country parson wants an unpretending tub to thump, with a few pretty panels in it and a pleasant shape generally, he will, with a little perseverance, soon enough find a craftsman who has picked up the thread of the tradition of his craft from the time when that craft was fine art. (p. 18)

Compare that with Morris's address to Birmingham students in which he lamented that 'the long chain of tradition which was

[1] *Works*, XXIII, p. 195. Further compare Morris—'the middle classes of our civilization have embraced luxury instead of art' (p. 148)—with Shaw on the church of SS. Annunziata in Florence, which he says has been carefully and expensively restored—'there you will see the worship of glory and the self-sufficiency of intellect giving way to the display of wealth and elegance as a guarantee of social importance'.

unbroken till the end of the Middle Ages has been snapped' (p. 432). Shaw makes explicit reference to the way in which Morris and Burne-Jones tried to learn from early masters and he ends by claiming that 'churches fit for their proper use can still be built by men who follow the craft of Orcagna instead of the profession of Mr Pecksniff'.

Although we may be a little disconcerted by Shaw's mildly ironic tones, his attitude to applied art was still serious and well-intentioned. But his humorous tendency to regard church-going as an aesthetic, Paterian experience has in it the seeds of attitudes which other, less intelligent men would readily adopt. George Moore, always sensitive to contemporary fashions, explores this declension in the hero of a rather too solemn tale in *Celibates*.[1] John Norton attempts to 'reconstruct the ascetic life of the Middle Ages', but his ignorance of material life easily leads him to be seduced by gothic cathedrals and Gregorian chant. Notions that Morris might have found congenial—the high-pitched roof of the converted billiard-room, the fifteenth-century window in the chapel, the chairs copied from a picture by Dürer, the denunciation of Victorian padded upholstery—mingle indiscriminately with gestures Morris would have found silly and pointless. Although one character remarks, as he lays his hand upon an imitation mediaeval bell-pull, 'How Birmingham the whole place does look' (p. 263), it is not particularly clear how much Moore wishes to criticize Norton's activities. For he is allowed by the author to indulge unreproved in too much nostalgic atavism—he would love to have gone on crusades which 'were once as real in life as tennis parties are today' (p. 274), and he sees Kitty as a woman from Botticelli or Mantegna, 'sexless . . . as the women of the first Italian painters' (p. 323).

Oscar Wilde's is the most absurd example of such affectations. Throughout his criticism and reviews[2] and his lectures on art and

[1] *Celibates* appeared in 1895; the mediaeval touch occurred earlier in Moore's *A Mere Accident* and *Mike Fletcher*. References to *Celibates* are to the New York edition of 1919.

[2] The volume of *Reviews* in the Methuen edition of his *Works* shows him reviewing books on lace-making, tapestry, book ornament and binding, in all of which Morris's main arguments are echoed.

handicraft he parades the borrowed ideas of Ruskin and Morris. What is, incidentally, interesting about these borrowed attitudes is that they reveal how much mediaeval enthusiasms, specifically the vogue of arts and crafts, were firmly established as part of the eclectic patterns of 1890's aestheticism. For the lectures on design that Wilde delivered in the United States were little more than advance publicity for *Patience*, a means of letting the American public see a real-life example of the objects of Gilbert's satire.

The most important lecture he gave was 'The English Renaissance of Art'.[1] The *renaissance* in question was an inclusive movement beginning with Keats and moving via Tennyson to the Pre-Raphaelite Brotherhood, which had wished for profounder spiritual and more *decorative* values in art. In his equation of these two we have a rationalization of the decline into decorative mediaevalism which has been charted in this chapter. Wilde contrasts the artisan of a gothic cathedral with the modern salesman who has no hand in making what he sells. Industry without art is barbarism:

Hewers of wood and drawers of water there must be always among us. Our modern machinery has not much lightened the labour of man after all; but at least let the pitcher that stands by the well be beautiful and surely the labour of the day will be lightened: let the wood be made receptive of some lovely form, some gracious design, and there will come no longer discontent but joy to the toiler. For what is decoration but the worker's expression of joy in his work?

Morris's ideas, parrotted with a mixture of nonchalance and intensity, are weakened by sacrificing content to presentation: *pitchers at wells* is an anachronism of which Morris would not have been guilty, a poetic fancy that Wilde might have used in a fairy tale. The obvious and absurd discrepancy is that apart from

[1] He lectured also on 'Art and the Handicraftsman' and 'The Practical Application of the Principles of the Aesthetic Theory to Exterior and Interior House Decoration, with Observations upon Dress and Personal Ornaments'. Parts of this second lecture could almost have been set up intentionally to provide a source for Lady Jane's speculation in *Patience* on a new uniform for the Dragoons which would be Early English with touches of Florentine, Venetian, Spanish and Japanese!

his rumoured pushing of the wheelbarrow for Ruskin at the Hinksey road-making and his visits to the South Kensington Museum to meet 'the handicraftsman, the wood-worker, the glass-blower and the worker in metals'[1] Wilde never practised these essentially functional arts. There is a bitter irony in his final contact with handicraft. He tells Robert Ross that in his chalet at Berneval the only beautiful work of art he possesses is an old *vierge en bois sculpté* from a fisherman's boat.[2]

Fortunately Wilde's pretensions did not materially hinder the revolution in design to which the Pre-Raphaelites contributed. In his literary exploration of mythologies Morris, like most other Pre-Raphaelites, was always liable to produce decorative visions of a golden age. But in his designs those visions are provided with a contemporary purpose where their decorative inclinations are at last exactly relevant. Similarly, the Pre-Raphaelite imagination could harness its mediaevalist enthusiasms to more purposeful, because personal, art and some examples of this achievement are considered in the following chapters.

[1] Wilde boasts of both incidents in his American lectures.
[2] *Letters*, p. 623.

CHAPTER THREE

'The Narrow Chamber of the Individual Mind'

Here is a fine saying of Keats's in one of the letters: 'I value more the privilege of seeing great things in loneliness than the fame of a prophet.'

> I shut myself within my soul,
> And the shapes come eddying forth.
>
> —Rossetti

THE ROMANTIC MOVEMENT cherished as its central dogma the supremacy and all-importance of the individual, his inner experience and imagination. As Coleridge puts it in the *Biographia Literaria*:

> We are to seek therefore for some absolute truth capable of communicating to other positions a certainty, which it has not itself borrowed; a truth self-grounded, unconditional and known by its own light. . . .
> This principle, and so characterized, manifests itself in the SUM or I AM; which I shall hereafter indiscriminately express by the words spirit, self, and self-consciousness. . . .
> For to us, self-consciousness is not a kind of *being*, but a kind of *knowing*, and that too the highest and farthest that exists for *us*. . . .[1]

The early Romantics held this belief so faithfully that they were able to offer it as the absolute value in all imaginative experience and, consequently, to believe in imagination as the 'reconciling

[1] Chapter 12, theses III, VI and X.

73

and mediatory power' in all human endeavours.[1] Later writers seemed less able to subscribe wholeheartedly to such beliefs, and we get the spectacle of Tennyson grappling in *In Memoriam* with both his own personal agonies and the general intellectual problems which absorbed his society. Or, as with Arnold, the poet's certitude is the meagre one of Empedocles, truth to 'our own only true, deep buried selves'. The vital principle of Coleridge has retreated underground in Arnold's poetry. The river of life flows through subterranean caverns, now not only measureless to man, but unseen and inaccessible:

> from time to time, vague and forlorn,
> From the soul's subterranean depth upborne
> As from an infinitely distant land,
> Come airs, and floating echoes, and convey
> A melancholy into all our day.[2]

As a public and general vivifying force man's essential spirit or self is useless—'vague' and 'melancholy'.

Arnold found it such a forlorn prospect because he still wished to believe with the early Romantics that the individual's experience and imaginative powers were forces for the general good. But writers who were not discouraged by the impossibility of poetic legislation of the world found their buried lives less forlorn and still accepted the value of the imaginative recreation of their self-awareness and self-consciousness. The Pre-Raphaelites, some of them unburdened with the conflicts of the Great Victorians, were one group in whose art Coleridge's great principle still managed to thrive. But its survival was not without a real and dangerous curtailment of its strength. Coleridge wished for the absolute truth to communicate a certainty to *other positions* and to inspire *all* human enterprises. But the Pre-Raphaelites celebrated their moments of heightened self-consciousness for *their own sakes*. Their insights had only a limited relevance to the realities of life around them and the tendency of the movement between 1848

---

[1] The phrase is Coleridge's from *The Statesman's Manual*; see *Political Tracts of Wordsworth, Coleridge and Shelley*, ed. R. J. White (Cambridge 1953), p. 24.
[2] 'The Buried Life', ll. 72–6.

and 1900 was to constitute these momentary visions of personality as the sole reality of which they needed to be aware. The danger is implicit in Rossetti, confirmed and acknowledged by Pater and actively courted by writers in the magazines at the end of the century.[1]

I

From Rossetti's early contact with Italian poetry grew two modes of introspection, closely connected, but still distinct. One took its initial inspiration from the Sicilian poets and the *dolce stil nuovo*; the other from Dante's *La Vita Nuova*. The one mainly concerned the poet's ideal love for a beautiful woman; the other allowed him to explore the *selva oscura* of his own soul. The first was largely an imitative phase in Rossetti's imagination, growing out of an enthusiasm for the Italian poetry rather than out of his own experience. The latter, on the other hand, produced in *The House of Life* a work where the feeling and expression of Dante seem to have proved an exciting correlative to his own state of mind.

We must not underestimate the enormous impression on Rossetti's young mind of his early connections, via his father's studies, with Italy's late mediaeval and early Renaissance poets. Of these the example of Dante was certainly the most powerful.[2] But he was unable to accept his father's interpretation of Dante's works. Gabriele Rossetti's direct application of masonic ideas to Dante led him to see *La Vita Nuova*, for example, as wholly allegorical and Beatrice, who had in his opinion never existed, as a

[1] A recent book which has come to my attention since this chapter was written and which offers a similar analysis of introspective poetry during this period is Barbara Charlesworth's *Dark Passages, The Decadent Consciousness in Victorian Literature* (Madison and Milwaukee 1965).

[2] In the preface to his translations Rossetti wrote: 'the first associations I have are connected with my father's devoted studies . . . Thus, in those early days, all around me partook of the influence of the great Florentine: till, from viewing it as a natural element, I also, growing older, was drawn within the circle' (II, p. xv). See also Christina's remark: 'Perhaps it is enough to be half an Italian, but certainly it is enough to be a Rossetti, to render Dante a fascinating centre of thought' (*Family Letters of Christina Rossetti* (1908), p. 184).

mere symbol in Dante's masonic cryptogram.[1] The whole tone and quality of such criticism, which by concentrating on the political entirely ignores the personal and imaginative aspects, were uncongenial to Dante Gabriel; he wrote of his father's studies 'which, *from his own point of view*, have done so much towards the general investigation of Dante's writings'.[2] Thus, although drawn to the early Italian poets by the family enthusiasm for them, Rossetti was intensely dissatisfied with and repelled by his father's analysis of Dante. This reaction led to what Dorothy Sayers calls 'the Pre-Raphaelite stress upon the Vita Nuova and the Beatrician image of love'.[3]

Although it was Dante who offered Rossetti the most forceful image of love in the figure of Beatrice, he could have derived it from several of the other Italian poets. It is there in its earliest and most charming form in Guido Guinicelli's 'Canzone: of the Gentle Heart', which Rossetti translates beautifully, and in its latest form in Guido Cavalcanti. This school of amatory poetry was characterized by a mystique of 'love as inseparable from the noble heart and the contemplation of a beautiful woman as a way for man towards the contemplation of divinity'.[4] In *La Vita Nuova*, for instance, Dante sees Beatrice as the very limits of blessedness, while his ballata upon gazing at Beatrice contains the essence of this idea: 'Mirerol tanto fiso, / Ch'io diverrò beato, lei guardando'; or in the canzone where he beseeches death for the life of Beatrice:

> Tu disfai la beltà ch'elle possiede,
> La qual tanto di ben più ch'altra luce,
> Quanto conven, che cosa che n'adduce
> Lume di cielo in creatura degna.[5]

---

[1] An analysis of the father's ideas may be found in R. E. Vincent, *Gabriele Rossetti in England* (Oxford 1936).

[2] *Works*, II, p. xv, my italics. W. M. Rossetti confirms his brother's reaction to their father's scholarship in *Ruskin, Rossetti, and Pre-Raphaelitism*, p. 262.

[3] *Introductory Papers on Dante* (New York 1954), p. xvi.

[4] *Lyric Poetry of the Italian Renaissance*, ed. L. R. Lind (New Haven 1954), p.50n.

[5] Neither quotation is now attributed to Dante, as Rossetti thought. The editors of the Società Dantesca Italiana's *Opere di Dante* list them under 'Rime Spurie'. Full texts of them may be found in *Le Opere di Dante Alighieri*, ed. E. Moore (Oxford 1924), p. 182a.

The adoration of the poet's lady was a metaphysical attitude informed by strong religious ideas; it was derived from the Provençal troubadour tradition in which the early Sicilian poets had written.

It is difficult to decide how much of this Italian amatory tradition Rossetti really understood.[1] In Guido Orlandi's work he finds a love-song 'which proves to be beside the purpose of poetry, filled with metaphysical jargon . . .' (II, 15); and he criticizes Cavalcanti for 'causing the perversity of a logician to prevail in much of his amorous poetry' (II, 5). These remarks suggest both a certain impatience with the metaphysical nature of some of the Italian originals and a leaning towards poetry ruled by the heart and not the brain. His actual translations also reveal that his desire to turn a good poem in the original into another good one in English led him to make his versions after a highly Romantic image of poetry. Thus Pugliese's stanza becomes more heavy and soulful in Rossetti's version—

> Oi Deo, perchè m'ái posto in tale iranza?
> ch'io son smaruto, non so ove mi sia,
> che m'ai levata la dolze speranza.
> Partit'ai la più dolze compagnia.

> O God, why hast thou made my grief so deep?
> Why set me in the dark to grope and pine?
> Why parted me from her companionship
> And crushed the hope which was a gift of thine?
>
> (II, 304)

And such a line as 'Chè soverchianza—m'ha vinto e stancato' becomes 'I am oppress'd with languor and foredone' (II, 347). The second line of his translations of Dante's 'Gli occhi dolenti per pietà del core' contains the added idea of languish, not in the original. In the first canzone of Bonaggiunta Urbiciani, Rossetti writes of love 'languished for' (II, 311); the third line of his version of Cino da Pistoia's 'A Trance of Love' includes the

---

[1] In this connection see Ann Paolucci, 'Ezra Pound and D. G. Rossetti as translators of Guido Cavalcanti', *Romantic Review*, LI (December 1960), pp. 256–67.

phrase 'painful languor' (II, 171); the first sonnet of *La Vita Nuova* introduces the significant words 'sweet pain' into the first line (II, 33)—all of these without the authority of the original.

Obviously Rossetti's imagination has transfigured these poems in such a way that it is perhaps beside the point to assess their value merely as translations. They represent more of an original creation, in which Rossetti's own self-consciousness begins to find expression. Yet his own self-awareness was not fully alert and sure of itself by the time he was making the translations and very obviously he allowed the Italian poetry to condition or even create his feelings and ideas rather than be a vehicle for them.

'The Blessed Damozel', first written during 1847 in the very middle of his most sustained work on the translations, reveals the confusion which resulted from the impact made by the Italian poetry on an impressionable imagination which had not as yet established its own identity. The poem's theme seems to have been inspired generally by *La Vita Nuova* and more particularly by Jacopo da Lentino's sonnet 'Of his Lady in Heaven' and perhaps Pugliesi's 'Canzone of his Dead Lady'.[1] But while Rossetti seems to appreciate the ideal nature of their loves, his own Damozel achieves the rather puzzling situation of being a spirit in Heaven consumed by distinctly earthly passions.

Rossetti starts well enough and emphasizes the pure spirituality he wishes to impute to the lady who has 'a white rose of Mary's gift / For service meetly worn', although the image is rather superficial. But the disturbing elements appear immediately: first, with the artificial simile of her hair and its insistence upon ripeness; then, in the fourth stanza, with Rossetti's emphasis upon her physical presence—'Surely she leaned o'er me—her hair / Fell all about my face.' The very bar of heaven is warmed by the pressure of her bosom. And by the middle of the poem, when she speaks, the spirituality Rossetti may have wished to emulate from the

---

[1] We know that 'The Blessed Damozel' was a result of Rossetti's being provoked by Poe's 'The Raven' to reverse its theme of a lover's grief on earth and 'give utterance to the yearning of the loved one in heaven' (see *Family Letters and a Memoir*, I, 107). I believe that his Italian reading provided him with a suitable vehicle for this attempt.

dolce stil nuovo has been forgotten. The love which the Damozel desires would surely be found blasphemous by Christians; for although the shrine the lovers will frequent is 'Occult, withheld, untrod', their conduct smacks too severely of earth to be imaginable in even a poetic heaven. The Damozel demands

> Only to live as once on earth
> With Love,—only to be,
> As then awhile, for ever new
> Together, I and he;

that could presumably be taken as a continuation of the ideal, beatific love, yet its context as well as the approval which the Holy Mother will apparently accord their heavenly conduct only serve to emphasize its ineptness. In making the Damozel serve as a *persona* for his own notions of love Rossetti has failed imaginatively to reconcile the Christian images learnt from the Italians and his own highly romantic ideas.

The original version of the poem published in *The Germ* had a few passages more appropriate to the theme,[1] later omitted. Rossetti also made additions which seem to sustain the Dantesque element of his poem. The ethereal nature of the Damozel's voice, for instance, was introduced by adding the two stanzas beginning 'The sun was gone now . . .'; while three stanzas later he introduced, if a little coyly, the more explicit religious imagery of 'And see our prayers, granted melt / Each like a little cloud'. Finally, in the stanza beginning 'Alas! we two, we two, thou sayst . . .', he insisted upon the unworthiness of her lover to rise to Heaven and be her equal, an alteration which eliminated the vain sighs of 'Alas for lonely Heaven! Alas / For life wrung out alone!' These alterations would indicate that Rossetti certainly appreciated the nature of his difficulty. Yet, on the other hand, the omission of such a stanza as the following from later versions is sufficient indication of his inability to cope with it:

> Yea, verily; when he is come
> We will do thus and thus;

---

[1] For instance, the suitably Dantesque passage beginning 'But in those tracts, with her it was / The peace of utter light . . .'

> Till then my vigil seems quite strange
> And almost fabulous;
> We two will live at once, one life;
> And peace shall be with us.

The vigil, the ultimate peace, even the biblical phrasing, might have steadied the poem. But in rejecting his father's image of an allegorical Beatrice, Rossetti went too far in the direction of a warm, personal one, so that the Blessed Damozel assumes the appearance of the sensuous 'donna della finestra'.

The *dolce stil nuovo* offered him scope for an exploration of his own self. It was a poetry which saw earthly love as a mutual recognition of twin souls, which used a woman as the soul's symbol, and which believed in an absolute reality beyond sense and intellect where the soul is reunited with God.[1] The poet's response to such beliefs, indeed the mere articulation of love within such conventions, would inevitably illuminate his own self-awareness. Rossetti's translations repeatedly reveal this introspective element:

> I think that I shall die; yea, death begins;
> Though 'tis no set-down sickness that I have,
> Nor are my pains set down.
> But to wear raiment seems a burden since
> This came, nor ever any food I crave;
> Not any cure is known
> To me, nor unto whom
> I might commend my case:
> This evil therefore stays
> Still where it is, and hope can find no room. (II, 256)

> Even so Love rends apart
> My spirit and my heart,
> Lady, in loving thee;
> Till when I see thee now,
> Life beats within my brow
> And would be gone from me. (II, 313)

[1] See O. Doughty, 'Rossetti's Conception of the "Poetic" in Poetry and Painting', *Essays by Divers Hands*, XXVI (1953), for a discussion of Rossetti's use of Platonic ideas.

> Mine inmost being then feels throughly quit
> Of anguish, and all evil keeps afar.
> Love also gathers to such power in me
> That my sighs speak, each one a grievous thing,
> Always soliciting
> My lady's salutation piteously. (II, 75–6)

> With sighs my bosom always laboureth
> In thinking, as I do continually,
> Of her for whom my heart now breaks apace;
> And very often when I think of death,
> Such a great inward longing comes to me
> That it will change the colour of my face;
> And, if the idea settles in its place,
> All my limbs shake as with an ague-fit:
> Till, starting up in wild bewilderment,
> I do become so shent
> That I go forth, lest folk misdoubt of it. (II, 80–1)

> Vanquished and weary was my soul in me,
> And my heart gasped after its much lament,
> When sleep at length the painful languor sent.
> And, as I slept (and wept incessantly),—
> Through the keen fixedness of memory
> Which I had cherished ere my tears were spent,
> I passed to a new trance of wonderment;
> Wherein a visible spirit I could see,
> Which caught me up, and bore me to a place
> Where my most gentle lady was alone. (II, 171)

It is to this aspect of the Italian poetry that Rossetti was drawn and which he found responded to his own imaginative needs. It contained subject matter and attitudes which seemed analogous to or actually formed a part of what he saw as his own emotional experience.[1]

'The Blessed Damozel' represents an early attempt to utilize the introspective tendencies of the Italian poems without departing

[1] Similarly, as Graham Hough suggests, when Rossetti paints the Annunciation 'he is depicting something that has really been a content of his own soul' (*The Last Romantics*, p. 54).

too far from their substance or general quality. Perhaps his considerable reworking of the poem is an indication of Rossetti's dissatisfaction with that uneasy compromise.[1] Later poems retain obvious traces of the Italian influence, yet show a more confident and independent use of the love mystique as a mode of introspection.

The House of Life borrows several motifs from the Italian poetry, although they do not seem particularly central to the sonnet sequence. Ostensibly it *does* concern 'Love's sworn suit service, / With whom cold hearts are counted castaway' (XIV), but the love which is 'light at night and shade at noon' (XXII) seems less interesting to Rossetti than the exploration of his soul, which arises from it. Nevertheless the poet relies upon many of the attitudes and devices of the amatory convention. The insignificance of a man without the sustaining rays of his lady's love is presented in 'Life-in-Love' (XXXVI), for through her presence the lady 'yields thee life that vivifies / What else were Sorrow's servant and death's thrall.' The poet displays the conventional humility before his lady:

> I graceless, joyless, lacking absolutely
> All gifts that with thy queenship best behove. (XXXII)

The merging of man's love for a woman with his knowledge of the Divine, which Dante experienced in his love for Beatrice, comes rather crudely in the fifth sonnet:

> Lady, I fain would tell how evermore
> Thy soul I know not from thy body, nor
> Thee from myself, neither our love from God.

And throughout those parts of the sequence which celebrate his successful love Rossetti draws upon religious imagery: his lady's breath is felt 'to be the inmost incense of his (Love's) sanctuary' (III); her face is the altar of the poet's eyes (IV) or the shrine of Love (X); Love weeps for the 'sacred hour' of supreme surrender (VII); the allegorical figure of Love has an 'aureole' (LII); and the poet's heart takes sanctuary in the shrine of Love (XXXI).

---

[1] See '*The Blessed Damozel*'; *the unpublished manuscript, texts and collation* with an introduction by P. F. Baum (Chapel Hill 1937).

Much of this remains mere decoration, but it is intended to give a heightened colour to these moments of Rossetti's emotional existence. As momentary and fugitive visions they are precious, but the intensity which this older imagery imparts to them makes them even more valuable. Yet they are still threatened, as are all his instants of resonant insight, by the passing of time. Fortunately for his poetry he is unable to secure permanently for his love the sanctuary which the opening sonnet describes:

> Love's throne was not with these; but far above
> All passionate wind of welcome and farewell
> He sat in breathless bowers . . .

Soon his most characteristic and successful note, a lament for the passing of time, sounds in 'The Song of the Bower' and 'A Little While', where the bowers seem, if not less decorative and unreal, at least conducive to 'welcome and farewell'; the latter's sense of imminent dissolution and the former's of impotent longing give them a personal forcefulness which survives the conventions they employ. Similarly 'The Portrait' continues to make use of certain Italianate properties, yet at the same time Rossetti manages to convey an exquisite nostalgia in a piece whose introspection is scarcely affected by the borrowed conventions:

> Last night at last I could have slept,
>   And yet delayed my sleep till dawn,
> Still wandering. Then it was I wept:
>   For unawares I came upon
> Those glades where once she walked with me:
> And as I stood there suddenly,
>   All wan with traversing the night,
>   Upon the desolate verge of light
> Yearned loud the iron-bosomed sea. (I, 242)

He is less successful in 'Love's Nocturn', where the celebration of his spirit's uncertainties is occasionally too diffuse and cloying; but here again the Italianate imagery does not prevent him from achieving quite a compelling sense of love's dominance over his existence and the constant threat to it from change:

But for mine own sleep, it lies
  In one gracious form's control,
Fair with honorable eyes,
  Lamps of a translucent soul:
  O their glance is loftiest dole,
    Sweet and wise,
  Wherein Love descries his goal.

Reft of her, my dreams are all
  Clammy trance that fears the sky:
Changing footpaths shift and fall;
  From polluted coverts nigh,
  Miserable phantoms sigh;
    Quakes the pall,
And the funeral goes by. (I, 289)

But if Rossetti's poems inspired by the *dolce stil nuovo* utilize their conventions as a means and mouthpiece for his own real emotions, this cannot be said of later writers who still drew upon this source of inspiration.

Oscar Wilde in a graciously patronizing interview accorded to a journalist from the *Echo de Paris* in 1891 explained that there was

dans votre histoire littéraire une époque qui me ravit tout particulièrement. C'est l'époque des Cours d'amour. La poésie sensuelle et mystique des troubadours est délicieuse. Elle a exercé une grande influence sur les Préraphaelites, sur Dante Rossetti, sur Swinburne et sur moi-même.[1]

But in neither Swinburne nor Wilde does this influence elicit any particularly compelling introspection. All the external trappings of the allegory of love are employed and Wilde even lards his work with a few Dantesque phrases, but nothing particularly rewarding emerges. A pose has been adopted, and poses are by their very nature a camouflage for real emotion.

Swinburne reports[2] how once in the Oxford Union Burne-

---

[1] Jacques Daurelle, 'Un poète anglais à Paris', *Echo de Paris* (6 December 1891).
[2] *The Swinburne Letters*, I, pp. 17–18.

Jones and himself defended their idea of Heaven as a 'rose-garden full of stunners' (i.e. beautiful women). He says that they spoke of 'kisses in paradise, and expounded our ideas on the celestial development of that necessity of Life'. Continuing about Morris's forthcoming marriage to that 'wonderful and most perfect stunner', Swinburne thinks the idea is insane; 'to kiss her feet is the utmost man should dream of doing'. Such ideas are remarkably close to Rossetti's vision of love and its eventual fulfilment in eternity. In 'Madonna Mia' (I, 273) Swinburne celebrates the idea in poetry: the lady amid rose bowers, with her heavy golden hair and deep eyes; she is both the incarnation of love—

> Beneath her eyelids deep
> Love lying seems asleep,
> Love, swift to wake, to weep—

and also some emanation of the divinity—

> Only this thing is said;
> That white and gold and red,
> God's three chief words, man's bread
>   And oil and wine,
> Were given her for dowers,
> And kingdom of all hours,
> And grace of goodly flowers
>   And various vine.

'A Ballad of Life' (I, 1) also presents a lady who transfigures all sin, sorrow and death, within whose lips 'my whole soul's life abides' and for whom, should she grace the poet with 'pity', all his days would be as righteous as she. Its companion poem, 'A Ballad of Death' (p. 4), presents another lady, the passage of whose days brought more than peace:

> Ah! in the days when God did good to me,
> Each part about her was a righteous thing;
> Her mouth an almsgiving,
> The glory of her garments charity,
> The beauty of her bosom a good deed,
> In the good days when God kept sight of us;
> Love lay upon her eyes,

And on that hair whereof the world takes heed:
And all her body was more virtuous
Than souls of women fashioned otherwise.

A curious element of Swinburne's work in this vein is that it is somehow not unbalanced by the physical insistence which disturbs the equilibrium of Rossetti's work.[1] The two elements of *The House of Life* which give the ninth sonnet its title, 'Passion and Worship', are occasionally in an uneasy conjunction:

I was a child beneath her touch,—a man
When breast to breast we clung, even I and she,—
A spirit when her spirit looked at me,—
A god when all our life-breath met to fan
Our life-blood, till love's emulous ardours ran,
Fire within fire, desire in deity.

Yet in similar passages Swinburne's insistence on the physical aspects of love seems less disturbing, even when a few lines are removed from their hypnotizing and blurring context:

Behold, my Venus, my soul's body, lies
With my love laid upon her garment-wise,
Feeling my love in all her limbs and hair
And shed between her eyelids through her eyes. (I, 12)

One reason for the difference is that Rossetti's language tries to define real objects and spiritual experience which have some reality for him. But Swinburne rarely pretends to define objects or concepts; although he commands the reader to behold, what follows is less important for its visual or sensual meaning than for its atmospheric harmonies. Rossetti's language being much 'healthier'[2] we *do* react to the objects and concepts presented by it: breast to breast, love's ardour, desire. The poet's feelings for the lady of 'Madonna Mia', however, exist only for the sake of the

[1] See chapter six, p. 236.
[2] See T. S. Eliot, *The Sacred Wood* (1920), p. 149, on Swinburne's poetry: 'The morbidity is not of human feeling but of language. Language in a healthy state presents the object, is so close to the object that the two are identified. They are identified in the verse of Swinburne solely because the object has ceased to exist, because the meaning is merely the hallucination of meaning, because language, uprooted, has adapted itself to an independent life of atmospheric nourishment'.

language's musical movement as it picks up, weaves and plays with sounds:

> She grows with greenest leaves,
> Ripens with reddest sheaves,
> Forgets, remembers, grieves,
> And is not sad.

The personification of Youth in the first sonnet of *The House of Life* suggests both a visual and a conceptual emblem. But in Swinburne's 'Prelude' to *Songs Before Sunrise* the same personification actually matters little in comparison with the musical cadences achieved with it.

This decline in the linguistic health of Swinburne's poetry is directly linked to a decline in its introspection. Only in the very vaguest way do these poems which use certain properties of the *dolce stil nuovo* tell us anything about Swinburne's self-consciousness; what *is* told hardly compels attention and implies a slight degree of self-awareness in the poet.

Many later writers used the same Italian properties and, without Swinburne's mastery over sound and rhythm, produced similarly unrewarding results. But Rossetti's Italian translations and his own work in imitation of them obviously exercised a great attraction for later poets. This mode of introspection, partly because it offered some well defined conventions and vocabulary, served as one vicarious means of identity. The 1890's is a period marked by an extremely eclectic imaginative process and most of its major writers were able to slip into the minds and methods of earlier poets as a means of exploring possibilities for their own consciousness.[1]

Both Wilde and Symons adopt imagery direct from Rossetti; the first in 'La Bella Donna Della Mia Mente' (a Dantesque phrase) where her hair, like the Blessed Damozel's, is like corn; the second in 'Beata Beatrix'. Symons begins this poem on a note of sensual satiety and moves through the 'ecstasy' and 'agony of peace' to the concluding image of Beatrice:

> So I have seen the face of Beatrice,
> In pictures, dead, and in a memory

[1] Yeats makes this point specifically of Arthur Symons, *Autobiographies*, p. 272.

> Seeing the face of Dante out of heaven.
> O, out of heaven, when for my sake you lean,
> Till not a breath of the world may come between
> Our lips that are our souls, and all the seven
> Delighted heavens lean down with you, to bless
> The sacrament of joy, then, with such eyes,
> Closed on so still a new-born Paradise,
> You endure the martyrdom of happiness.[1]

He has drawn upon the Blessed Damozel for Beatrice's leaning out of Heaven and the decorative use of 'mystical' numbers; in another poem, Symons' phrase, 'the fixed paradise of our content'[2] recalls the fixed place or lull of the Blessed Damozel's heaven. The religious evocation of 'martyrdom' and 'sacrament' at the end of 'Beata Beatrix' is a frequent device in other love poems by Symons—the shrine of his lady's eyes (II, 36), the mystical marriage (II, 52), love's mystery (II, 53). The mystical union of body and soul is described with a phrase reminiscent of Rossetti:

> If I think of your soul, I see
> Your body's beauty; and then
> I pray to your body again,
> And your soul answers me. (II, 203)

Wilde lists 'the seven-fold vision of the Florentine' among his poetic treasures and laments that he had not 'trod the road which Dante treading saw the sun of seven circles shine'.[3] In 'A Vision' (p. 762) he asks information of Beatrice, although this use of Dante's guide in Paradise has little purpose beyond a decorative evocation and allusion; she and Dante are again invoked in the final simile of 'Madonna Mia' (p. 716). These eclectic gleanings from other work are borrowed clothes in which to act parts that had, as it were, a guaranteed poetical and introspective quality. Thus Wilde displays a lover's dutiful obeisance ('Even to kiss

[1] *Poems of Arthur Symons* (1919), II, p. 197. All further references will be to these volumes.

[2] II, p. 50. Another poem with distinct echoes of 'The Blessed Damozel' is Neuman's 'The Heavenly Lover', *YB*. XI, 184.

[3] *Works*, pp. 761 and 791. All further references in this section are to this volume.

her feet I am not bold') in his divine vision of the lady; and when he tells the lady in 'Quia Multum Amavi' that 'all night long before thy feet I knelt / Till thou wert wearied of Idolatry' (p. 775) the reader, too, grows weary. Symons protests his utter dependence upon the lady throughout 'Amoris Victima', 'Amoris Exsul', and 'Amor Triumphans'; but the care that held him fettered all his days carries little conviction. Wilde betrays the falsity of the adoption of all these alien conventions when he suggests that 'La Bella Donna Della Mia Mente' is 'fairer than Queen or courtesan' (p. 735). At the point where Salomé intrudes upon the *dolce stil nuovo* its fruitful life is certainly at an end.

Other writers were less perverse, if no less shallow, in their reliance upon the Italian tradition. W. E. Henley's 'Song' in *The Pageant* confidently affirms

> That, winning her, I seem to win
> Out of the drive and dust and din
> A nook of Paradise. (I, 46)

Selwyn Image seems particularly fond of this type of poetry. With frequent echoes of Rossetti's *House of Life* he celebrates the vanity of love:

> Through all the hours of all the days
> I seek for Love through all the ways
> His spirit drives my wandering feet; (*HH*. I, 5)

and asking to worship at love's shrine he also achieves some divine revelation:

> Over his head our lips may meet,
>   Yet soundless is the kiss they frame:
> And, as our souls in union greet
>   His presence, still they breathe no name:
> In the deep heart of heaven, where wells
> God's central spring, 'tis Silence only dwells. (*HH*. V, 111)

The Hobby Horse, which seems hospitable to this type of poetry, printed two cycles of poems by Herbert P. Horne which rather wanly echo Rossetti's sonnet sequence:

> But o'er the scarlet of her mouth,
> Whence those entreated words come forth,

Love hovers all the live-long day
And cannot, through its spell, away.[1]

A writer in *The Dome* lamented the lack in contemporary verse of 'some great compelling thought, some rapturous and passionate purpose'.[2] The need in nineties' poetry for some real and compelling theme was acute indeed and was in no way filled by the *ersatz* troubadour vogue. But those who followed the fashion obviously felt that it did provide some truly 'rapturous and passionate purpose' for their art. It is obviously this purpose which inspires John E. Barlas, for example:

> Yet love, for thee, yet, love, for thy dear grace,
> I walk in dreams as toward the morning star,
>   Through clouds that shine and open out above;
> And all the future flowers about my face,
> And all the past lies looming low afar
>   To me emerging on the heights of love.[3]

And it is presumably the same purpose which informs the publication of Petrarch translations in *The Yellow Book* (IX, 167–8) as well as such limp verses as those where the poet begs to be left to pine a 'little longer at thy feet' (*YB*. III, 19).

It seems certain that Rossetti's work was almost entirely responsible for this vogue; Swinburne and Wilde were deliberate imitators, and there were obviously others. Even Yeats's protestation of his lady's undying beauty has a certain Dantesque tone to it:

> Because of that great nobleness of hers
> The fire that stirs about her, when she stirs,
> Burns but more clearly—[4]

---

[1] From a cycle of six songs, *HH*. III, p. 115. The other group of poems to his mistress are in the first volume, pp. 46–7.

[2] Stephen Phillips, 'A Field for Modern Verse', II, p. 91.

[3] Quoted in an article on his poetry in *The Yellow Book*, XI, p. 89. The echoes of Rossetti seem clear here—the clouds have their parallel in *The House of Life*, LX, the visions of past and future in XLVI and LXII, the hill summit in LXX.

[4] *Collected Poems*, p. 86. Yeats is later able to employ these conventions, as much else of his Pre-Raphaelite inheritance, with a personal and quite individual force (see 'Michael Robartes and the Dancer', for example).

A poem like Frank Freeman's 'Night-piece' not only used Rossetti's favourite image of 'an old moon, drown'd in a pond' but also a Blessed Damozel-like vision of a woman's spirit.[1] More especially the fashion for short sequences of sonnets or songs in the manner of *The House of Life* reveals Rossetti's influence, especially when they concern death and love. Of this sort is William H. Phelps's 'Four Sonnets' in *The Dome*; the poet has built a mystic church in whose courts abound 'Epiphanies of beauty' and 'ethereal crowds of souls', and where he celebrates

> the passion of the worship-hours,
> When love, the purple-bright high priest, precedes
> The chastened priesthood of my inner powers,
> To my heart's heart . . . (VII, 52)

But little of this poetry illuminates the poet's own spirit, the inner landscape of his soul. The very concept of 'soul' has changed. For the Italian poets and in a muddled and insecure way for Rossetti also it had real theological-psychological meaning. Yet although Wilde still praises the mystical union of the soul with the body, the

> sweet unison
> With every pulse of flesh and throb of brain
> The soul in flawless essence high enthroned,
> Against all outer vain attack invincibly bastioned, (p. 789)

the concept has little reality. And generally among Wilde's contemporaries 'soul' signified less the transcendent part of the human complex than the undefined recesses of personality. Occasionally, as if these inadequacies were realized, a poet would exaggerate either of the two elements which originally most characterized the Italian poetry—the mystical or the sensual; but an attempt to imitate merely more slavishly could not save this vogue. It was with some justification that by 1893 John Addington Symonds could note in his essay on 'Ideals of Love' that 'in modern times the purity of chivalrous love has been almost universally suspected'.[2]

[1] *The Dome*, old series III, p. 50.
[2] *In the Key of Blue and other prose essays* (1918), p. 72.

II

All the work that has been discussed so far draws directly upon the conventions of the *dolce stil nuovo*. And simply because they were conventions, long established and with a considerable number of working models, poets could rely upon them without having to do anything original themselves. This can even be seen in some of the less accomplished Italian poems that Rossetti translated; it is abundantly clear in the etiolated verses of Woolner in *The Germ*, or some of Elizabeth Siddal's.[1] Rossetti's 'Blessed Damozel', as has been shown, reveals an uneasy adaptation of the conventions, but its attempt to adapt is a step in the right direction. *The House of Life*, although obviously in some way a product of Rossetti's Italianate enthusiasms, has thrown off much of the dead weight of meaningless conventions by its refusal to rely upon ready-made attitudes and experience.

Rossetti is still interested in love, but his response to it seems much more personal as well as being aware of other aspects of existence that often modify the ideal visions of youth. The prefatory sonnet to *The House of Life* stresses that his main theme is the soul, and a sonnet is a 'memorial from the Soul's eternity / To one dead deathless hour'; but the sestet shows quite clearly that Rossetti's soul is aware of more than just the power of love:

> A Sonnet is a coin: its face reveals
> The soul,—its converse, to what Power 'tis due:—
> Whether for tribute to the august appeals
> Of Life, or dower in Love's high retinue,
> It serve; or, 'mid the dark wharf's cavernous breath,
> In Charon's palm it pay the toll to Death.

The subtitles of the two sections of *The House of Life* reveal that Change and Fate are forces which will ever threaten dreams of

---

[1] See Woolner's 'My Beautiful Lady' and 'Of My Lady In Death'; Siddal's 'The Lust of the Eyes' and 'Gone' in *Ruskin, Rossetti, and Pre-Raphaelitism*, pp. 155 and 153. Woolner's two poems are also available in a useful anthology, *The Pre-Raphaelite Poem*, ed. James D. Merritt (Dutton Paperback Original, New York 1966).

perfectability. It is his awareness of these that gives to Rossetti's work its undoubted originality. As I admitted earlier the poetry which described an ideal love for a beautiful woman was closely connected in Rossetti to an exploration of his own soul; for one thing, he frequently relies upon a beautiful woman as an image of his soul.[1] But the work discussed in the previous section was usually too dependent upon conventions alien to it; whereas the part of Rossetti's work which I shall now discuss has achieved a real independence of those breathless bowers of allegorized love.

When Rossetti wrote of *La Vita Nuova* in his introduction to the translation, he said the work was full of 'undivulged self-communings', a 'poignant sense of abandonment' and of 'refuge in memory' (II, 2). These are precisely the most moving aspects of *The House of Life*, and it seems highly probable that Dante's work suggested to Rossetti an attempt to write an analogous document of the heart. Rossetti's great success lies in the depiction of transient and half-defined states of feeling, the mysteries that lie at the heart of life. His sense of mutability makes him eager to capture often elusive moments of apprehension; it gave them a value that was both precious and powerful. It further placed a burden upon the faculty of memory which had to assist in the recording of these sudden and fugitive insights.

The note which is characteristic of the best in the sequence appears in the fourth sonnet:

> O love, my love! if I no more should see
> Thyself, nor on the earth the shadow of thee,
>   Nor image of thine eyes in any spring,—
> How then should sound upon Life's darkening slope
> The ground-whirl of the perished leaves of Hope,
>   The wind of Death's imperishable wing?[2]

The hopelessness that his sudden apprehension of transience provokes seems a more genuine revelation than the meeting of souls

---

[1] For a discussion of this image of the beautiful woman see chapter five.

[2] This theme he might have found in the Italian poems, but even in his translations he deserts the original text and embroiders upon it in a more individual way, as in the third canzone by Pugliese: 'Nothing of the old years / That comes not back again' (II, p. 303).

described in the octet. So does the opening of 'The Kiss' (VI), the forcefulness of which is not totally dispelled by what follows. Indeed, Rossetti's growing awareness of the power of Change and Fate provides a disquieting note from the very start of *The House of Life*. After the fourth and sixth Change and Fate do not appear explicitly until the twenty-fourth, but the use of seasonal images (XII, XIV, XVII, XVIII and XX) is a subtle reminder of the inevitable fate of youth. With the twenty-fourth, ironically entitled 'Pride of Youth', Rossetti intrudes the note of anguish for the 'change in every hour's recall'. The next sonnet is entitled 'Wingèd Hours', and although the gods of love fling back the 'gathering cloud of Night's ambiguous art' (XXVII) and the following dozen sonnets continue to celebrate various joys of love the note of change makes its inevitable reappearance in 'The Morrow's Message' (XXXVIII). It is then that the 'illusive eyes of Hope' (XLIII) begin to probe first the growing dusk and then the desolate night of 'Without Her' (LIII). As Rossetti feels the increasing pressures of change, he summons memory to help him retain some image of the present and of himself in the present. Memory which was first used to intensify a day of love (XVI) later struggles to preserve its delights:

> When that dead face, bowered in the furthest years,
> Which once was all the life years held for thee,
> Can now scarce bid the tides of memory
> Cast on thy soul a little spray of tears,—(XXXVII)

and finally breaks the heart with its recollections of time past:

> Memory's art
> Parades the Past before thy face, and lures
> Thy spirit to her passionate portraitures:
> Till the tempestuous tide-gates flung apart
> Flood with wild will the hollows of thy heart,
> And thy heart rends thee, and thy body endures. (XLVI)

In Part Two, which is both more subtle and involved as well as less dependent upon the theme of love, Rossetti begins to shore the ruins of change. The very first sonnet of the second part offers the consolation that poetry transfigures the life of the poet, en-

shrines in words his essential soul. The following sonnet stresses
that the poet's own experience is the genesis of his art and as this
emphasis seems to underlie most of Part Two the soul assumes
a dominating importance. Because it is material for the permanence of art, it also seems to acquire stability amid the flux:

> From child to youth; from youth to arduous man;
> From lethargy to fever of the heart;
> From faithful life to dream-dowered days apart;
> From trust to doubt; from doubt to brink of ban;—
> Thus much of change in one swift cycle ran
> Till now. Alas, the soul!—how soon must she
> Accept her primal immortality,—
> The flesh resume its dust whence it began?

And the implication of the sestet of the seventy-third is that the
life of the soul is eternal:

> Miles and miles distant though the last line be,
> And though thy soul sail leagues and leagues beyond,—
> Still, leagues beyond those leagues, there is more sea.

Because the soul has this infinite value, all its images are of equal
permanence and the poet learns to oppose against a sense of
'Lost Days' (LXXXVI) and wasted opportunity the visions which
his soul brings him. But it would simplify *The House of Life*
unduly to imply that Rossetti finds in his soul's experiences the
hope whereby to face transience with calm and optimism. On
the contrary, his sense of 'life's disastrous eld' is too strong to be
overpowered:

> Even so the World's grey Soul to the green World
> Perchance one hour must cry: 'Woe's me, for whom
> Inveteracy of ill portends the doom,—
> Whose heart's old fire in shadow of shame is furl'd:
> While thou even as of yore art journeying,
> All soulless now, yet merry with the Spring!' (XCIII)

In the confused exploration of his own self-awareness in this
sonnet sequence Rossetti does seem to present a contradiction
between accepting the value of the immortal soul as matter for
the permanence of poetry and the soul's despair at the very

transience it opposes. But it is perhaps a paradox in the nature of art to take any vision of the soul's and transfigure it in art:

> So in the Song, the singer's Joy and Pain,
> Its very parents, evermore expand
> To bid the passion's fullgrown birth remain,
> By Art's transfiguring essence subtly spann'd;
> And from that song-cloud shaped as a man's hand
> There comes the sound as of abundant rain. (LX)

The distinctive quality of the introspection appears in Rossetti's sonorous images, the shapes that come eddying forth from his soul. Sometimes they are vague and meaningless, but I think that any attempt to reduce this 'Wild pageant of the accumulated past' (XII) to a prose paraphrase, as W. M. Rossetti has done to assist the readers of *The House of Life*,[1] is not a particularly sensible reaction to it. Rossetti once said to William Sharp:

I do not wrap myself up in my imaginings, it is they that envelop me from the outer world whether I will or no.[2]

This revealing acknowlededgment of his own lack of final control over his imagination (at odds with his other insistence upon the fundamental brainwork of poetry) does at least suggest that logical analysis would not be a profitable approach to this sonnet sequence or to such poems as 'The Stream's Secret' where the introspection is the same. What Rossetti's imagination offers is various states of feeling, at times intense and immensely poignant, but usually unrelated to explicit experience and often articulated with little precise imagery. Rossetti presumably had focused his mind upon certain experiences and made his comment on them through the sonnet; but the actual event is not presented or, at best, only hinted.[3] This vagueness is essential to his method,

---

[1] In *Dante Gabriel Rossetti as Designer and Writer* (1889), pp. 179–262. See also a similar attempt by John Masefield, *Thanks Before Going: Notes on some of the original poems of Dante Gabriel Rossetti* (1946).

[2] 'The Rossettis', *The Fortnightly* (1886), pp. 414 ff.

[3] See R. C. Wallerstein, 'Personal Experience in Rossetti's *House of Life*', *PMLA* (1923), XLII, pp. 492–504. But there is also the fact that in trying to emulate *La Vita Nuova* Rossetti relied only on his sonnets, while Dante set his poetry among prose passages which both help to explain the poetry and act as a background to it.

because he is concerned less with the conscious efforts of his love
than with the half-divined, half-articulated state of his mind; as a
contemporary American poet says—

> Some shapes cannot be seen in a glass,
> those are the ones the heart breaks at.[1]

Hence Rossetti's use of strongly emotive images, like the one

> where wan water trembles in the grove
> And the wan moon is all the light thereof, (IX)

or the other where

> through dark forest boughs in flight
> The wind swoops onward brandishing the light. (LXIV)

These have no precise meaning, except perhaps as natural phenomena, though even then it is difficult to visualize wind brandish-
ing the light; but their function is much more than that of natural
description. They serve to suggest and even stand for various of
'the soul's sphere of infinite images' (LXII).

The sonnet in which that phrase occurs offers a characteristic
example of Rossetti's introspection and is worth considering, for,
although the impact of *The House of Life* is an accumulative one,
not to be judged from single images or even single sonnets, it is
still possible to pin down the essential nature of Rossetti's imagination. The sonnet, entitled 'The Soul's Sphere', begins by
offering various images, two of them visual:

> Some prisoned moon in steep cloud-fastnesses,—
> Throned queen and thralled; some dying sun whose pyre
> Blazed with momentous memorable fire;—
> Who hath not yearned and fed his heart with these?
> Who, sleepless, hath not anguished to appease
> Tragical shadow's realm of sound and sight
> Conjectured in the lamentable night? . . .
> Lo! the soul's sphere of infinite images!

[1] Howard Nemerov, 'Holding the Mirror Up to Nature', *Five American Poets*,
ed. T. Gunn and T. Hughes (1963), p. 40.

What sense shall count them? Whether it forecast
　　The rose-winged hours that flutter in the van
　　Of Love's unquestioning unrevealèd span,—
　　Visions of golden futures: or that last
　　Wild pageant of the accumulated past
　　That clangs and flashes for a drowning man.

The sum of the sonnet's meaning is virtually contained in the
eighth and ninth lines, where Rossetti marvels at the difficulty of
assessing the infinite images of the soul. The remaining lines offer
examples of these images, suggested impressionistically and fleet-
ingly, which is assisted by the absence of main verbs. The first
two are precise enough descriptions, but their final effect is made
somewhat vaguer by the emotive associations—'prisoned' and
'thralled', with their impression of some beauty locked in a
tyrant's castle, and 'momentous memorable' and the implications
of death. This seems Rossetti's special device—a blurring of
initial precisions by the addition of some emotional colouring;
or, alternatively in the last lines, a sudden, and in this case, brilliant definition of a grand but potentially vague image with a
verb like 'clangs', which suggests the terrifying reality of a death
by drowning. But in either case the image is neither totally precise nor utterly vague; probably a more casual reading would not
be upset by any imprecision at all, yet would accept the poet's
sense of the impossibility of 'counting' them.

The vagueness has further implications. The phrase, 'fed his
heart', implies Rossetti's uncritical absorption in a retreat from a
reality which is inhospitable to his imagination. While the first
four lines reveal an impressionable response to natural scenery
which serves perhaps as a tangible equivalent for the poet's emotions, the next four ambiguously suggest his wish to contrive
these infinite images within the narrow chamber of his own mind.
He seeks, that is to say, an escape from a world which always
harasses the sensual apprehension of fugitive images. In his mind
he can perhaps create them again or afresh, 'a solitary prisoner'—
as Pater says in the 'Conclusion'—in his 'own dream of a world'.
And the external world as an objective reality becomes a meaning-

less concept. What T. S. Eliot writes in explanation of Bradley is true also of Rossetti and the Pre-Raphaelite introspection:

everything, the whole world, is private to myself. Internal and external are thus not adjectives applied to different contents with the same world; they are different points of view.[1]

III

These shifting perspectives, the increasing isolation and authority of the individual mind and the consequent difficulties of reading and judging it are confirmed in other Pre-Raphaelite writers.

Rossetti at his best reveals intricate attitudes of his mind in images that might not expose a particular experience but yet would focus his feeling and our response to it; but these are not found in Swinburne. I should make clear that this in itself is no fault, though I prefer Rossetti simply because he can offer them, while Swinburne's verbal harmonies do not satisfy for as long. But the effect of Swinburne's type of poetry upon later writers could have been very unfortunate. His is sufficiently close to Rossetti's poetry to be associated with the introspection for which Rossetti obviously was known:

> If yet these twain survive your worldly breath,
> Joy trampling sorrow, life devouring death,
> If perfect life possess your life all through
> And like your words your souls be deathless too,
> To-night, of all whom night encompasseth,
> My soul would commune with one soul of you. (III, 12)

> The scent and shadow shed about me make
> The very soul in all my senses ache; (I, 14)

Yet the net self-revelation of two such passages is diffuse and, in the final resort, they are as impersonal as masks. They were nevertheless valued for their introspective qualities; Wratislaw could write of *Poems and Ballads* that 'The most violent of its poems are, as it were, the visions of an opium eater, the dreams

---

[1] Quoted Hugh Kenner, *The Invisible Poet*, pp. 53–4.

of an exasperated imagination', and Swinburne himself called them 'studies of passion and sensation'.[1]

As we have seen in the discussion of the amatory conventions, Swinburne's introspection is blurred and hazy. This danger increases whenever he cannot draw upon conventions to shape and define experience. While his poetry gives the impression of a mind revealed it is virtually impossible to say what the nature of that mind is. His very words obscure the spirit they should express. His remark in 'The Triumph of Time' seems, then, curiously apt:

> I will keep my soul in a place out of sight
> Far off, where the pulse of it is not heard. (I. 40)

But this does not prevent, even in that poem, the frequent use of the word 'soul', which features in the verbal kaleidoscope as evidently important and sonorous:

> I saw my soul at rest upon a day
> As a bird sleeping in the nest of night,
> Among soft leaves that give the starlight way
> To touch its wings but not its eyes with light;
> So that it knew as one in visions may,
> And knew not as men waking, of delight. (III, 34)

> In the sweet low light of thy face, under heavens
> untrod by the sun,
> Let my soul with their souls find place, and forget
> what is done and undone. (I, 73)

> So to my soul in sure fashion
> Your savage stamp and savour hangs;
> The print and perfume of old passion,
> The wild-beast mark of panther's fangs. (III, 33)

But at almost every occurrence it becomes fuzzy, letting meaning surrender to alliteration or rhythm, as in the first and second

---

[1] Theodore Wratislaw, *Algernon Charles Swinburne, A Study* (1900), pp. 38–9; Swinburne, 'Dedicatory Epistle', I, vi.

examples, or to a world where human feelings have no existence, as in the third.[1]

This tendency is particularly striking in those poems where a *persona* could focus his introspection. The use of Tannhäuser in 'Laus Veneris' and of Sappho in 'Anactoria' could offer a narrative or psychological framework, but the tensions and anguished perplexities which Swinburne attributes to the speakers are not given any such frame of reference. These poems suffer as much as those in which he speaks in his proper person from the often hysterical *montage* of his ideas and emotions.

Pater, who confessed a debt to Swinburne,[2] managed to focus his introspection with greater success and assurance. This was because he frequently chooses to identify his own self-consciousness with the work of other artists about whom he writes. *The Renaissance* may be read as a series of *personae* through whom Pater communicates his own insights.[3] It is presumably the example of such a book as this that leads George Moore to emphasize that criticism is rather 'the story of the critic's soul than . . . an exact science'.[4] The 'Conclusion', despite the studied impartiality of the donnish 'we', contains the most moving account of the introspective imagination at a crucial stage in its history:

Experience, already reduced to a group of impressions, is ringed around for each one of us by that thick wall of personality through which no real voice has ever pierced on its way to us, or from us to that which we can only conjecture to be without. Every one of those impressions is the impression of the individual in his isolation. . . . (p. 248)

---

[1] Equally the frequent use of the first person pronoun in 'The Triumph of Time' blurs the effect; especially in the two stanzas beginning, 'Where the dead red leaves of the year lie rotten . . .' (I, pp. 41–2).

[2] See *Swinburne Letters*, II, 241.

[3] G. Tillotson has called Pater's criticism 'autobiographical poetry', *Criticism and the Nineteenth Century* (1950), p. 30. R. Wellek also suggests that Pater's frequent use of 'sincere' in his criticism eventually becomes a term defining faithfulness to inner vision, 'Walter Pater's Literary Theory and Criticism', *Victorian Studies* (1957), I, 38–9.

[4] Quoted Tindall, *Forces in Modern British Literature* (Vintage Books, New York 1956), p. 13. Cf. *The Savoy* (I, 144) which champions the highly subjective school of criticism, and Symons who called *Imaginary Portraits* 'The study of a soul, or rather of a consciousness' (*A Study of Walter Pater* (1932), p. 47).

Where Pater does not image his own mind through his readings of other arts, his characteristic proceeding is to use as *personae* some solitary reflective consciousness like Marius or Florian Deleal. And here he is saved from Swinburne's haziness by his sustained insight into the sensations of the mind as well as by his addiction to finite objects.

Pater's own writing crystallized certain ideas and methods which had already been present, as he realized, in Rossetti. Pater's essay on Rossetti's poetry begins by noting its 'perfect sincerity' and continues:

His own meaning was always personal and even recondite, in a certain sense learned and casuistical, sometimes complex or obscure; but the term was always, one could see, deliberately chosen from many competitors, as *the just transcript of that peculiar phase of soul which he alone knew*, precisely as he knew it.[1]

The peculiar phases of the soul well describe those shifting images of *The House of Life*, some of which were discussed in the sixty-second sonnet. The phrase also sums up an aspect of Pater's own art, 'the gradual expansion of the soul', for instance, that he traces in 'The Child in the House', or 'the inward world of thought and feeling' he celebrates in the 'Conclusion'.[2] When he says that for Rossetti common things were full of human or 'personal' expression (p. 219), he is again describing a special aspect of his own sensibility whose 'sharp and eager observation' scanned hand or face, hills or sea for moods of passion or intellectual excitement. His sensibility even displays in his famous Giaconda passage that 'certain feverishness of soul' that he rightly notes in Rossetti (p. 218). And in a passage, to which Symons referred in his later essay on Rossetti, he is described in terms close to those of the 'Conclusion':

To Rossetti it is so always, because to him life is a crisis at every moment. A sustained impressibility towards the mysterious conditions of man's everyday life, towards the very mystery itself in it, gives a singular gravity to all his work . . . (p. 220)

[1] *Appreciations*, p. 207, my italics. The essay was published first in 1883.
[2] 'The Child in the House', *Miscellaneous Studies* (1910), p. 73, and *The Renaissance* (1888), p. 247.

The arresting images which illuminate the best sections of *The House of Life* are surely Rossetti's equivalent of seizing upon perfect moments in the perpetual flight of daily impressions, which Pater counsels; for both authors the self comprises a series of momentary impressions. Rossetti even defines a sonnet as 'a moment's monument'; if Pater found 'monument' too concrete and definitive a term for the impressionistic sensitivity he advocated, Rossetti's idea of a sonnet is very close to the technique of Giorgione's school which Pater praises:

Such ideal instants the school of Giorgione selects, with its admirable tact, from that feverish, tumultuously coloured life of the old citizens of Venice—exquisite pauses in time, in which, arrested thus, we seem to be spectators of all the fulness of existence, and which are like some consummate extract or quintessence of life.[1]

The nineties would have noted this introspective similarity all the more because Rossetti and Pater also shared a strong apprehension of life's transience. A sense of perpetual flux is the premise upon which Pater builds his 'Conclusion', as it is the note which sounds throughout *The House of Life*. Both writers oppose this rapid passage of time with moments of greater spiritual intensity—Rossetti's infinite images of the immortal soul, Pater's 'any exquisite passion, or any contribution to knowledge that seems . . . to set the spirit free for a moment'.[2] Both writers invoke memory to preserve their sensations from oblivion.[3]

A third Pre-Raphaelite writer besides Swinburne and Pater whose unique temperament offered similar examples of introspection was Christina Rossetti. Her work was much admired by Arthur Symons[4] and even attracted the attention of a latter-day symbolist, Teodor de Wyzewa. He found her 'un symbol sans pareil de la poésie', her verses 'limpides et chantants, ces

---

[1] *The Renaissance*, pp. 156–7.
[2] Ibid., p. 250.
[3] For Rossetti see supra p. 94, and for Pater see 'The Child in the House', *Miscellaneous Studies*, p. 186.
[4] He singles her out as the pre-eminent poet of 1893 in 'La Littérature anglaise en 1893', *Mercure de France* (January–April 1894).

adorables soupirs'.[1] From this it is obvious that her piety and moral fervour were no obstacle to an appreciation of the nostalgia and pessimism which were otherwise the most characteristic aspects of her poetry.

Christina's large output of poetry is generally distinguished by its expression of private emotions; in this she much resembles the heroine of her own children's tale, *Maud*, whose insistent self-examination becomes a puritanical introspection of soul. 'Soul', for Christina Rossetti, inevitably has strong religious overtones and provides a large proportion of her poetry with its subject; but often the context does not make the religious emphasis particularly clear:

> Dumb I was when the ruin fell,
> Dumb I remain and will never tell;
> O my soul, I talk with thee,
> But not another the sight must see.

> And, though young spring and summer pass away,
> The autumn and cold winter come again,
> And though my soul, being tired of its pain,
> Pass from the ancient earth, and though my clay
> Return to dust, my tongue shall not complain:—
> No man shall mock me after this my day.[2]

It is this type of introspection that inevitably identified her with Dante Gabriel.[3] Even in a poem such as 'A Soul', which obviously refers to spiritual faith, the final effect is similar, in its imagery especially, to some of her brother's sonnets:

> Her face is steadfast toward the shadowy land,
> For dim beyond it looms the land of day:
> Her feet are steadfast, all the arduous way

---

[1] 'Une Femme-Poète Anglaise: Christina Rossetti', *Revue des Deux Mondes*, XII, no. 15 (1908), pp. 923 and 927.

[2] *The Poetical Works*, pp. 331 and 290. All further references are to this volume.

[3] He expressed approval of 'Amor Mundi', where earthly love is suddenly made aware of its insubstantiality, and of 'Love Lies Bleeding', with its resonant image of memory: 'Caught after glow thrown back from long-set days / Caught echoes of all music past away.'

> That foot-track doth not waver on the sand.
> She stands there like a beacon through the night,
>   A pale clear beacon where the storm-drift is—
> She stands alone, a wonder deathly-white:
> She stands there patient nerved with inner might,
>   Indomitable in her feebleness,
> Her face and will athirst against the light. (p. 311)

The two sequences of her sonnets, 'Monna Innominata' and 'Later Life',[1] would also have suggested a real connection between her own introspection and her brother's. The latter deals with her expectancies in the world to come, but the reflective tone of the whole continuously emphasizes her spirit's responses to its present, earthly predicament:

> I am sick of where I am and where I am not,
>   I am sick of foresight and of memory,
>   I am sick of all I have and all I see,
> I am sick of self . . . (p. 78)

But despite this revulsion from herself, her soul is nevertheless the object of a good deal of this sequence:

> So tired am I, so weary of today,
>   So unrefreshed from fore-gone weariness,
>   So overburdened by foreseen distress . . .
> Half-starved of soul and heartsick utterly. (p. 74)

This soulful quality has no religious justification in 'Monna Innominata'. The sequence purports to be the work of an anonymous lady loved by some unknown predecessor of Dante and Petrarch, quotations from whose work preface each sonnet. Christina manages very few arresting images like her brother's, but the vaguer outpourings are attempts to define a response to love that recall his own sonnet sequence:

> The longing of a heart pent up forlorn,
>   A silent heart whose silence loves and longs;
>   The silence of a heart which sang its songs
> While youth and beauty made a summer morn,
> Silence of love that cannot sing again. (p. 64)

---

[1] Also perhaps the Italian sequence, *Il Rosseggiar dell'Oriente*, not published until after her death, but more deeply introspective than the other two.

Also similar to Dante Gabriel is such a remark as 'My hope hangs waning, waxing . . .' (p. 59), or such an image as that produced by the sight of mountains which 'Struck harmonies from silent chords which burst / Out into song, a song by memory nursed' (p. 80).

But the aspect of her poetry which seems to have had the most influence upon the nineties was that to which Dante Gabriel referred when he described his sister as 'seated by the grave of buried hope'.[1] Like her brother and like Pater, though for explicitly devotional reasons, she saw the transience and the vanity of all earthly things. Part of her poetry surmounts this and celebrates the divine security of immortal life: as she wrote at the age of fourteen:

> Yes, for aye in heaven doth dwell
> Glory indestructible,
> What here below finds tainted birth
> In the corrupted sons of earth.[2]

But another part of her poetry seems too fascinated with that earthly corruption to be able to seek the consolations of immortality. The theme of 'tainted birth' harrows her soul and engenders a morbid preoccupation and pessimism:

> But all too sure of what life is, to dread,
> Learned I that love and hope are fallacies. (p. 113)

> . . . this world of hope deferred,
> This world of perishable stuff:— (p. 192)

> Ê vanità il fiorir
> Di questa vita che menian costì.
> Odi che dice e piange: È vanità
> Questo che nasce e muore amor mondan; (p. 453)

Not only do many of her wounds seem self-inflicted but there is a real suspicion that she enjoys this pessimism: in *Seek and Find* (1879) she writes that

---

[1] *Family Letters of Christina Rossetti*, p. 75.
[2] From a small volume of her poems privately printed by her grandfather Polidori in 1847.

Vanity of vanities . . . amounts to so exquisite a dirge over dead hope and paralyzed effort that we are almost ready to fall in love with our own desolation. (p. 272)

But whether or not Christina *did* relish her desolation, it was an attitude which appealed to the nineties;[1] as minor writers, they seemed to seize those aspects of the Pre-Raphaelite legacy which were most easily recreated in their own work. Notes of pessimism and frustrated love are somehow reproducible at second-hand without direct experience; perhaps negative states of mind were attractive because they gave an immediate impression of intensity and personal feeling.

IV

The Pre-Raphaelite introspection, then, from which the nineties took much of their inspiration was a composite affair. Rossetti's *House of Life* provided the dominant style and ideas, with its impressionistic exploration of the soul's *selva oscura*. His sister, often reminiscent of him, contributed the '*chiaroscuro* of deferred hope'[2] which matched his own despair at the transience of life. But while Christina Rossetti countered this by concentrating upon the permanence of the next life, her brother's work and Pater's reflect the artist's response in their concern for the notation and preservation of intense moments of spiritual existence. Pater generally confirmed the Pre-Raphaelite stress upon introspective vision as well as gave it more technical confidence by his own practice. Swinburne's main contribution, on the other hand, to the articulation of his psyche was an intoxicating diffuseness.

Neither the Rossettis nor Pater are, of course, devoid of faults. They all, like Swinburne, tend to blur their emotions and to substitute 'atmosphere', and the Rossettis incline towards romantic generalizations: 'Il Rosseggiar', for example, shows Christina

[1] See Symons who typically confesses to being 'half in love with sadness' (II, p. 122). Even Morris seems prone to this love of his own desolation and in 'Hapless Love' he writes that 'To my heart / My love and sorrow must I press; / It knoweth its own bitterness'.

[2] Robin Ironside, in the introduction to *Poems by Christina Rossetti, selected and with an introduction* (1957), p. 17.

more obviously in love with love than with her lover. But the virtue of each is a real concern with nuances of mental and spiritual life. Furthermore, they all seem aware of the constrictions imposed by their own mode of imagination. Christina Rossetti is alert to the isolation and frustration of a 'heart pent up forlorn' (p. 64), just as Pater realized the unrelated and disillusioning privacy of this subjectivity:

> Deprived of that exhilarating yet pacific outlook, imprisoned now in the narrow cell of his own subjective experience, the action of a powerful nature will be intense, yet exclusive and peculiar.[1]

But too many later writers in the 1890's are unaware of these limitations. If Christina Rossetti could talk of one of her poems as 'something of a genuine lyric cry',[2] subsequent *cris de coeur* seem less genuine and reveal less precisely the intricacies of the soul's existence. Above all they seem too easy, unperturbed by the resistance which the Rossettis or Pater encountered in expressing their introspection, with the result that the creation of moments of heightened insight is not sharpened by constant anxiety about either the artistic or psychological reality.

The House of Life clearly served as a point of reference for writers of the 1890's. When *The Hobby Horse* reviewed the sonnets of John Gambril Nicholson it commented upon their obvious debt to Rossetti's sequence (VII, 132). Elsewhere in the magazine its editor affirmed the 'growing tendency amongst our young writers not only to imitate him, but to imitate him in his least sound work, his sonnets'.[3] Twenty pages later are verses by J. Addington Symonds which support Horne's assertion: the figure in his 'Narcissus Flower', with 'dreaming poet's eyes', leans

> Face-forward o'er the hurrying streamlet's gloom,
> Bending dark brows of yearning, dim surmise,
> To search time's turbid flood with prescient mind.

---

[1] 'Prosper Mérimée', *Miscellaneous Studies*, p. 12.
[2] *Family Letters of Christina Rossetti*, p. 65.
[3] *HH.* II, p. 101. It is presumably not the sonnet form which is unsound, but the dangers inherent in Rossetti's use of it in *The House of Life*.

The last line might be quite a good definition of Rossetti's poetic task in *The House of Life*; but Symonds *tells* what his figure is doing rather than *shows* us the results of its search; 'dim surmise' also blurs the picture and is, furthermore, at odds with the implications of 'prescient'. It seems rather as if Symonds only has to stress the 'dreaming poet' and add words of resonant vagueness like 'surmise' and 'prescient' to suggest a spirit's *selva oscura*. In another of his sonnets Symonds achieves the same effect with such phrases as 'lady of dreams and death', 'slumberous eyes of fate' and (a very Rossetti-like phrase) 'the whirlpool of life's troubled sea'. The sub-conscious depths of a mind are suggested by obscure words—'gloom', 'dark', 'dim'—for which a minimum of effort is required by the poet.

Lionel Johnson warned his contemporaries against the obscurity or luxuriance of Rossetti's 'less happy manner' (*HH.* VI, 157); but to little effect. In the second book of the Rhymers' Club Todhunter longs for some escape from life's pressures:

> Yes, this rich death were best:
> Lay poison on thy lips, kiss me to sleep,
> Or on the siren billow of thy breast
> Bring some voluptuous Lethe for life's pain,
> Some languorous nepenthe that will creep
> Drowsily from vein to vein. (p. 62)

The sonnet, 'Passion', contributed to *The Yellow Book* by 'Richard Garnett, LL.D., C.B.' tells of

> This flame of Passion that so high in air,
> By spice and balsam of the spirit fed,
> With fire and fume vast Heaven hath overspread,
> And blots the stars with smoke, or dims with glare. (VII, 149)

Again, the discussion is in sonorous, dim generalities. The frequent attempt to find correlatives of passion and pain in natural features is Rossetti's own method, but in other hands the effect is stale and just as general:

> When all the passion and the pain
> That forged our flesh and spirit one
> Are past, and sweet desire is vain,
> And youth and hope and life are gone,

> Will then our end be like the west,
>> Where sunset fires have paled to gloom,
> But give their gorgeous crimson's best
>> To light with splendour day's long doom?[1]

Much of the feebleness arises from the very fact that writers seem to delight in generalities, as in Olive Custance's poem—

> The pent-up passion of her soul
>> Deepens the pallor of her face,
> Against her throbbing heart the whole
>> Wide sorrow of the world finds place,
> And deep compassion and love's grace. (*YB.* VII, 203)

That also recalls Pater's Gioconda whose face all the experience of the world had etched and moulded.

The obscurity and luxuriance of Rossetti's 'less happy manner' is apparent in writers who ostensibly draw their main inspiration from France. Gray confesses in *Silverpoints* that 'in my soul the mists upcurl / of infinite love'.[2] Through the pages of Moore's *Flowers of Passion* wanders the ghost of Rossetti's soul-mate, which Moore uses in an attempt to illuminate moments of his own spiritual life:

> Dreaming she lies with fast closed eyes
>> Within the dim alcove,
> As I bend over her she seems to stir
>> With the instinct of my love,
> For down the streams of her drifting dreams
>> I may be the spirit above.[3]

Symons follows more the tradition of *The House of Life* and his poetry displays many characteristics found in Rossetti's sonnet sequence. In *Figures of Several Centuries* he quotes Pater's remark that life for Rossetti is 'a crisis at every moment' and added that he meant the 'inner life'. His own verse, full of the

[1] *YB.* VII, p. 261. Or in the Swinburnean vein there is the 'Hymn to the Sea' (*YB.* V, pp. 11–18) where the sea is used as a vague analogue to the soul's ebb and flow.
[2] *Silverpoints* (1893), p. xxxii.
[3] *Flowers of Passion* (1878), p. 79. Also see chapter five, p. 197.

'poisonous mist of memories' (II, 13), is the record of an intense contemplation of these inner crises:

> Love, once a simple madness, now observes
> The stages of his passionate disease. (I, 132)

But more than in other poets of the period Symons gives the impression of cultivating, even fabricating, these moments of crisis: 'Passionately we play the self-same parts / Our fathers have played passionately yesterday' (I, 79). Symons's long poem published in *The Savoy* (VIII), entitled 'Mundi Victima', is a chronicle of passionate crises:

> Your soul I never knew, I guessed at it,
> A dim abode of what indefinite
> And of what poisonous possibilities! (II, 53)

the 'poison' is perhaps Baudelaire's, but the idea of the soul is surely Rossetti's. Symons had rather glibly defended Rossetti's dreams as being precise provided we do not come outside them[1] and his 'Mundi Victima', like his other poetry, aims at this same ambiguous precision:

> To have won, amid the tumults round about,
> The shade of a great silence from the shout
> Of the world's battles and the idle cry
> Of those vain faiths for which men live and die!
> And have we not tasted the very peace
> So passionate an escape must needs release,
> Being from the world so strangely set apart,
> The inmost peace that is the whirlpool's heart? (II, 54)

> break
> The mould of this void spirit, scatter it
> Into the vague and shoreless infinite,
> Pour it upon the restless arrogant
> Winds of tumultuous spaces; grant, O grant
> That the loosed sails of this determinate soul
> Hurry it to disaster, and the goal
> Of swiftest shipwreck; that this soul descend
> The unending depths until oblivion end

[1] *Figures of Several Centuries*, p. 203.

III

> In self-oblivion, and at last be lost
> Where never any other wandering ghost,
> Voyaging from other worlds remembered not,
> May find it and remind of things forgot. (II, 6–7)

Symons had also said rather unfairly of Rossetti's poetry that it is 'the sound of a voice, rather than anything said';[1] but that is much more adequate a judgment of his own poetry.

The real fascination of Rossetti's sonnets for the nineties was their revelation of intense moments of emotion. Yeats remembers how in the years around 1890 he wanted 'the strongest passions', 'some moment of passionate experience'.[2] In 'The Tables of the Law' he describes his friend's pictures as a product of 'temperaments which seek always an absolute of emotion', and sees the symbolists and the Pre-Raphaelites as examples of such temperaments (S. VII, 80). But absolute emotions are easy perhaps only for those whose introspective privacy secludes them from any comparisons with emotional realities. High ideals of the kind Yeats's friend cherished are liable to produce overwrought poets, all eager for absolute emotions, yet all liable to disillusionment. It is not surprising that many ended up at 'The House Desolate' which Rosamund Marriott Watson described:

> Pale as the dead are they that dwell herein,
> Worn with vain strife and wrung with vain regret.
> (YB. VII, 23)

They lose control of thoughts and language in their desperate attempts

> To drift with every passion till my soul
> Is a stringed lute on which all winds can play.[3]

They surrender themselves to the 'delicious luxuries of introspection' (P. I, 133), and to the soulfulness which Gleeson White had praised in Rossetti's art.[4] In their poetry souls are seen on Lethe Bank, singing in the twilight, lost in mist, or forever greeting a new day;[5] in all these are echoes, faint or strong, of Rossetti's voice. Special interest is shown in any moment or experience

---

[1] *Figures of Several Centuries*, p. 202.   [2] *Autobiographies*, pp. 125 and 269.
[3] *The Works of Oscar Wilde*, p. 693.   [4] *The Dome*, old series II, p. 93.
[5] Respectively *S*. VI, p. 55, *YB*. III, p. 134, *YB*. XII, p. 281, and *HH*. I, p. 9.

which would make 'the soul's garden' bloom (*YB*. III, 153); so Symons anxiously looks forward, in Rossetti-like tones, to the possibility of momentous hours to come—

> Out of the multitudinous hours
> Of life sealed fast for us by fate,
> Are any hours that yet await
> Our coming, worthy to be ours? (*S*. III, 58)

Yeats, on the other hand, celebrates an hour that is almost over—

> The hour of the waning of love has beset us,
> And weary and worn are our sad souls now;
> Let us part, ere the season of passion forget us,
> With a kiss and a tear on thy drooping brow.[1]

Examples could be offered indefinitely; but however far one searched, the verdict of the poet in Johnson's ironic tale, 'Incurable', on his own introspection would still hold: 'though he should vivisect his soul *in public* for evermore, he would find there nothing worth revealing'.[2]

Much of the Pre-Raphaelite-inspired work of the nineties is concerned with reproducing the personal insights and individual manner of other writers, like Rossetti. This is confirmed by Horne's remark about the fascination with which Rossetti's personality was regarded: 'For us who only knew him through his works, this personality has a magic greater than that of any other man of his time' (*HH*. II, 98). This led writers to imitate those aspects of Rossetti's poetry which were seen as the central elements of his personality: the yearning, for example, the sonority and dim vagueness, the soulfulness, the eagerness for each moment's monument, and generally the 'sound of a voice' to which Symons drew attention.

But the sound of the voice rarely carries conviction by itself. Occasionally, as in Eva Gore-Booth's sequence of sonnets, 'Finger-Posts', there are moments when Rossetti's voice is less insistent and more genuine tones are heard:

> Swift windy beams split through the leafy screen,
> And pierce the heavy shroud of waving green,

---

[1] *Collected Poems*, p. 16.   [2] *P*. I, p. 131—my italics!

Until the narrow pathway feels at length
The strength of sunshine and the light of rain,
And broadens out into the open plain.

But, at a moment's notice, the speaker succumbs to language which is not hers, and Rossetti-like phrases, huge cloudy symbols of the soul's romance, obtrude again—

This is the road of Hope, that some men call
The way of Love, far out of human sight,
Amid strange mansions of austere delight;
A way of shadows, pale, aethereal,
High among stars and storm, outsoaring all
The silent glories of each lonely height,
Above the tumult of the windy night.[1]

Rossetti's voice had been perhaps most impressive when he could identify the images of his soul with some momentous hour of the day, as in 'Silent Noon' (XIX) or 'The Heart of the Night' (LXVI); poets in the nineties followed this device. Twilight was especially popular as the appropriate landscape for an uneasy soul: in 'A Mood' Olive Custance writes:

Between the dark lands and the sunset lands
My soul walks wearily with aching eyes: (*YB*. VIII, 341)

and William Watson uses the visionary glow 'At the hushed brink of twilight' which is eloquent of 'memory, foresight, and life's ebb and flow' as an analogy for the first recognition in a woman's fair face of the 'invasion of the vandal years' (*YB*. I, 113). But for the more perfect moments of the soul, noon was more suitable:

My soul is still as summer noon—
    Its inmost shrines are full of sleep;
But when the stars of dreamland swoon
    'Twill wake and weep. (*YB*. VI, 215)

It is all very much as a character of Henry Harland's remarked: 'the idea is stolen. It's almost a literal translation from Rossetti.

[1] *YB*. X, p. 214. Cf. 'Love's throne was not with these; but far above / All passionate winds . . .' (*The House of Life*, I).

What with a little imagination and a little ingenuity, one can do wonderfully well on other people's experience.'[1]

Christina Rossetti's experience also provided material for others' introspection. If one could feel safe in attributing a sense of humour to certain of the nineties writers, one could argue that they were merely parodying Christina's more solemn moments of abnegation and pessimism. L. Housman, for example,

> For I am like a withered brook
>   Which water flows not through,
> Since Death hath laid a dear rebuke
>   On all my thoughts of you: (*D*. IV, 171)

or Charles Catty's 'Song of Sorrow' (*YB*. IX, 157); or Rosamund Marriott-Watson's

> Bury me deep when I am dead
>   Far from the woods where sweet birds sing;
> Lap me in sullen stone and lead,
>   Lest my poor spirit should feel the spring. (*YB*. V, 71)

Ernest Dowson and Selwyn Image were the two most ardent followers of her theme of 'vanity of vanities'. Dowson, especially, contrives to exercise his own delicate metrical talent and at the same time allude to her mild rhythms and resigned tone:

> The long, long winter weather,
>   These many years and days,
> Since she, and Death, together,
>   Left me the wearier ways:
>   And now, these tardy bays!
>
> Outside, the world is wild and passionate;
>   Man's weary laughter and his sick despair
> Entreat at their impenetrable gate:
>   They heed no voices in their dream of prayer.[2]

Image printed two poems on 'Vanitas' or 'Vanity of vanity' in *The Hobby Horse* (I and III), and in both Christina's theme is

---

[1] 'Castles near Spain', *The Eighteen-Nineties, a Period Anthology*, etc., chosen by Martin Secker (1948), p. 173.

[2] Respectively *R*. I, pp. 69–70, and *HH*. VI, p. 137. 'They' in the second extract are nuns.

combined with Swinburnean cruelness and Rossetti's allegory of love. The note of pessimism was in no way a specifically Pre-Raphaelite or even English characteristic; but when it sounds in the nineties (and it is evidently a fashionable note) Christina Rossetti's influence can be heard, sometimes in a rhythm, sometimes in the actual tone of the self-abnegation:

> I watch you pass and pass,
>   Serene and cold: I lay
> My lips upon your trodden, daisied grass,
>   And turn my life away. (*HH*. VI, 138)

Pater's influence, like Christina's, mingles with others; but his dominant notes can also be distinguished among the other borrowed voices. Arthur Symon's 'Credo' is a versification of part of the 'Conclusion' to *The Renaissance*—

> For of our time we lose so large a part
>   In serious trifles, and so oft let slip
>   The wine of every moment at the lip
> Its moment, and the moment of the heart.[1]

The infinite images of Rossetti's soul, his heart's moments, are recorded in sonnets which he describes in the introductory verses to *The House of Life* as 'monuments', achieved and permanent records of transient experience. Pater makes this point more directly in the 'Conclusion' when he emphasized how experience must be captured and recorded. Johnson echoes the same concern when he talked of literature as 'the evocation of truth from the passing show of things' (*HH*. VI, 64). And when Yeats came to construct his theories of art from the sacred books of the past he found that Pater's philosophy was confirmed by Blake, whom he quotes in *The Savoy* (IV, 33):

Every time less than a pulsation of the artery is equal in its tenor and value to six thousand years, for in this period the poet's work is done, and all the great events of time start forth, and are conceived: in such a period, within a moment, a pulsation of the artery.

[1] Originally *YB*. III, 49. Also *Poems*, I, 174.

But the danger of making evocation the essence of literature or of comparing poetry to a pulsation of an artery was the encouragement it gave to vague intensity or the cultivation of mere mood.

V

What Pater calls 'the narrow chamber of the individual mind'[1] gets claustrophobic by the century's end and rarely individual. Too much imitation of a few writers produced a uniformity of introspection where genuine voices are often silenced by borrowed accents and where Coleridge's great principle of the all-importance of the self offers few poetic possibilities.

When the Pre-Raphaelite movement began it seemed as if the Romantic confidence in the unique sensibility of the individual could be reaffirmed. Rossetti, especially, showed himself capable of poetry which defined inner experience with strong feeling and precision of a sort. He seemed the answer to Coventry Patmore's complaint that a highly self-conscious century had not produced poets self-conscious enough, for the 'only system now possible [is] the psychological'.[2] Rossetti seemed at times to possess enough imaginative insight into his own psyche to reaffirm the reality of the inner vision in a way that might have satisfied Patmore. But when it becomes the only reality its literary, let alone its psychological, health is endangered. This happened with Rossetti and increasingly with those who followed him.

A writer in *The Hobby Horse* deplored this 'age of ours [which] has been all for the assertion of personal feeling, for the unrestrained expression of individual sentiment';[3] but what had become deplorable was not the assertion, but the poetry it produced. The faults were several. Often instead of the poetry *being* introspection, it spent too much time talking about it. Both

---

[1] *The Renaissance*, p. 248.

[2] *Pre-Raphaelite Diaries and Letters*, p. 233. Patmore's hope was to be fulfilled most successfully in the prose fiction of the movement: see chapter six, *passim*.

[3] *HH*. IV, 107. The author goes on to suggest a return to the methods of Pope and Addison.

Rossetti and Pater invoked memory as an aid to imagination, but it was to become sufficient in itself:

> Ambition, love and all the thoughts that burn
> We lose too soon, and only find delight
> In withered husks of some dead memory.[1]

And the memory frequently seems to be of other literature not of first-hand experience. Nor was it always clear how many poets were aware of their borrowed clothes. If one were to divide them, after Auden's fashion, into 'the sane who know they are acting and the mad who do not', the insanity rate might be extremely high. For few can we claim, as Wilde was to do for himself, that the imitation of other people's art was not insincerity, but 'a method by which we can multiply our personalities'.[2] Maybe for some poets like Wilde or Symons it was a genuine intellectual attempt to find themselves vicariously. But such is not the impression their poetry finally gives; while for lesser talents imitation of an introspection established by earlier Pre-Raphaelites was only a convenient means of pretending to be poets.

After the 1890's the reaction against unrestrained self-expression was inevitable. Yeats, who had learnt its limitations the hard way, seems to have made the elimination or restriction of self an important part of his creative procedure.[3] Later still both Pound and Eliot—Hugh Kenner's 'invisible Poet'—hide themselves behind the masks of their various *personae*.

[1] *The Works of Oscar Wilde*, p. 801.
[2] Ibid., p. 171.
[3] See the interesting discussion of Yeats's composition in Jon Stallworthy, *Between the Lines: Yeats's Poetry in the Making* (1963).

CHAPTER FOUR

Symbolism:
'The Dialect of a Far Country'

A symbol is indeed the only possible expression of some invisible essence

—W. B. Yeats

A faculty for truth is a power of distinguishing and fixing delicate and fugitive details

—Walter Pater

I

PRE-RAPHAELITE INTROSPECTION presents an interesting and authentic parallel to one aspect of French symbolism, normally acknowledged,[1] which is an obsession with self. What the *Oxford and Cambridge Magazine* identified as the 'general subjective tendency of modern imagination; i.e. that which directs itself to express the opinions, passions and perplexities of the writer' (p. 717) was a feature of later romanticism in France and England. So much of what Yeats admired in French symbolism had its counterpart also in earlier nineteenth-century English literature, especially the Pre-Raphaelite movement and the imagination of William Blake, whom it was the special enthusiasm of the Pre-Raphaelites to promote in the later part of the century. Similarly what Symons admired in French symbolism was present just as much in those aspects of introspection discussed in the previous

[1] See Edmund Wilson, *Axel's Castle* (New York 1959), p. 22, and A. G. Lehmann, *The Symbolist Aesthetic in France* (Oxford 1950), *passim*.

chapter. The spiritual world was the reality for Rossetti as for de l'Isle-Adam; dream, atmosphere and evocation were his element as well as Nerval's; the weariness and sadness of de l'Isle-Adam or Verlaine were present in both the Rossettis, as was Laforgue's self-pity. Introspection is clearly a distinct element in the symbolist aesthetic.

But it is only one element of a movement of the imagination in which the central, controlling doctrine was a rejection of all logical, material and external phenomena in favour of the unseen mysteries which lie in the more satisfyingly authentic world behind. Obviously introspection like Rossetti's has its place in this larger definition of symbolism, for he explores the mysteries of the soul which its infinite images reveal to him. But a wider range of the Pre-Raphaelite imagination than its introspection has to be invoked to sustain the claim, often advanced but infrequently illustrated, that 'the Pre-Raphaelites . . . were launched by an impulse similar to that of the symbolists'.[1]

The paths of English and French symbolism converge most prominently in the work of such 1890's critics as W. B. Yeats and Arthur Symons. In their work the Pre-Raphaelite and French imaginations find mutually hospitable ground. In *The Symbolist Movement in Literature*, for instance, though Symons's concern is specifically with French writers, his allusion to Carlyle in the introduction invokes a theorist to whom Pre-Raphaelite symbolism had also looked. Both Symons in his brief quotations from Carlyle and the author of the five articles in the *Oxford and Cambridge Magazine*[2] show that Carlyle's discussion of symbols is important for its emphasis on penetrating the external forms of things to discern their essence. In the silent heart of things are the eternal secrets which a symbol both conceals and reveals; Symons quotes—'In the Symbol proper . . . there is ever, more or less distinctly and directly, some embodiment and revelation of the Infinite'.[3]

[1] Edmund Wilson, op. cit., p. 23.

[2] The author was Vernon Lushington, and the articles appear on pp. 193–211, 292–310, 336–52, 697–712 and 743–71.

[3] *The Symbolist Movement in Literature* (Dutton Everyman Paperbacks, New York 1958), p. 2. All further references are to this volume.

Nor can we ignore, however difficult it may be to determine at all precisely, the effect on Symons of his contact and discussions with W. B. Yeats,[1] who had a more intimate knowledge of Pre-Raphaelite predecessors and their place in symbolism. Symons and Yeats were together in Ireland in 1896; it was the year both of Yeats's essays on Blake in *The Savoy*, which Symons edited, and of Symons's first essays to recognize symbolism. Symons may have been uneasy about Yeats's involvement with the occult, but this need not have precluded his being educated in other matters of symbolism. Some of the essays collected by Yeats in *Ideas of Good and Evil* (1903) were written before Symons gathered his articles together into *The Symbolist Movement in Literature* (1899). This book was dedicated to Yeats as 'the chief representative of that movement in our country'. Much of Symons's discussion of French literature is couched in terms close to those Yeats uses in his wider range of reference. It is perfectly obvious that, temperamental inclinations apart, both men sought similar discoveries in later romanticism. What Yeats emphasizes in Pre-Raphaelite and English symbolism Symons also stresses in his readings of French literature. Symons's later essays on Pre-Raphaelites[2] invoke much of Yeats's dialect and preoccupations; Symons seems to consolidate what he had said of late French romanticism by identifying similar spiritual and artistic manifestations in an English movement which Yeats had the advantage of knowing at first hand. It seems inevitable then that Yeats's first-hand knowledge of Pre-Raphaelite arts conditioned his explorations of symbolism and perhaps even coloured or directed those of Symons. So it will be useful to determine in some detail the nature of their ideas on symbolism, expounded right at the close of the century, before isolating the specific Pre-Raphaelite contribution from 1848.

Both Symons and Yeats saw that the symbolist movement was based upon a reaction against the rationalism of the eighteenth

---

[1] See, for example, 'The Isles of Arran' (*S.* VIII), in which Symons discusses his talks with Yeats during their Irish trip.

[2] On G. F. Watts in *Studies in Seven Arts* (1906) and on Rossetti in *Studies in Strange Souls* (1929).

century and a further revulsion from nineteenth-century material-ism.[1] They welcomed it because it required the artist to see past the mere phenomena of life to a world of the subconscious, of magic, of suggestion, and of invisible essences. For Yeats, sym-bolism entailed a rejection of descriptions for their own sakes and of mere anecdotage, and a refusal to brood over 'scientific opinion' (p. 163). As he said to Sturge Moore, the creation or enjoyment of a work of art is an 'escape from the constraint of our nature and from that of external things'.[2]

Similarly Symons saw symbolism as an 'attempt to spiritualize literature, to evade . . . the old bondage of exteriority' (p. 5). In the writers he discussed he championed their escape from rational-ism, from a devotion to mere exteriority and from the rule of will. In Laforgue's *Moralités Légendaires* Symons stresses both the 'haste to escape from whatever weighs too heavily on the liberty of the moment' (p. 60) and the poetry's 'instantaneous notation' of its subject (p. 57), which deliberately evades the pressures of laborious description. Nerval's sonnets were also composed in a state of 'supernaturalistic' meditation (p. 18). De l'Isle-Adam revolted against the limitations of a scientific explana-tion of existence. Symons quotes him on 'Toute cette vieille Extériorité, maligne, compliquée, inflexible' and comments

that illusion . . . Science accepts for the one reality; it must be the whole effort of one's consciousness to escape from its entanglements, to dominate it, or to ignore it, and one's art must be the building of an ideal world beyond its access (p. 24).

Verlaine's reflections are never the speech of reason (p. 46), and in Rimbaud's sacred disorder of the mind the rule of will has surrendered to hallucination (p. 39).

Yeats, too, required the works of symbolism to be released from 'the pressure of the will'. When the will no longer controls our thoughts, we may relapse into a state of 'real trance' where

---

[1] Yeats, *Essays and Introductions*, p. 187. All further references are to this volume. For Symons see the following discussion.

[2] Quoted R. Skelton and A. Saddlemayer (eds.), *The World of W. B. Yeats* (Victoria, B. C. 1964), p. 54.

the mind is 'unfolded in symbols' (p. 159). This release into the subconscious, into a dream world, into trance, is of great importance to Yeats. It was linked inextricably with magic which, as he began to study it, convinced him 'that images well up before the mind's eye from a deeper source than conscious or subconscious memory'.[1] In one of his *Last Poems*, 'Under Ben Bulben', he explains the same idea—

> forms that are or seem
> When sleepers wake and yet still dream,
> And when it's vanished still declare,
> With only bed and bedstead there,
> That heavens had opened.

One state of being where the will and exterior reality are not in control is madness and, with his interest in contemporary French writing, it was perhaps inevitable that Yeats should quote Gérard de Nerval on his insanity:

I then saw, vaguely drifting into form, plastic images of antiquity, which outlined themselves, became definite, and seemed to represent symbols of which I only seized the idea with difficulty (p. 162).

Symons also notes that Nerval was at his best as a writer, 'really wise [and] passionate', when insane (p. 10).

Symbolic vision required new techniques, as both writers realized. Yeats's admiration for Blake was founded on his pioneer work of creating a language capable of conveying a world that was not of everyday actuality. He excuses confusions and obscurities in Blake by saying that it was 'because he spoke of things for whose speaking he could find no models in the world he knew' (p. 111); and later that 'he was a symbolist who had to invent his symbols'. To convey illusive essences, to capture whatever it is that exists beyond the phenomenal world required, as Yeats realized, an exceptional technique: 'you cannot give a body to something that moves beyond the senses, unless your words are as subtle, as complex, as full of mysterious life, as a body of a flower or of a woman' (p. 164). Yeats perpetually insisted upon the importance of technical resources—'perfection of thought and

---

[1] *Autobiographies*, p. 183.

feeling, and . . . of form',[1] rhythms that are not the invention of
the will but wavering and meditative (p. 163); he even goes so
far as to acknowledge that more effective than symbol is 'pure
sound' (p. 156).

Symons was similarly impressed by the technical advances of
French writers: by Rimbaud's new way of writing prose (p. 40),
by the Goncourts' 'desperate endeavour to give sensation, to
flash the impression of a moment, to preserve the very heat and
motion of life'.[2] To build the ideal world of the symbolist's
vision requires of the poet a rejection of the old 'bondage of
rhetoric' (p. 5); Symons continues by stressing that descriptions
should be replaced by evocation and regular verse beats by more
subtle rhythms, and that mystery should be feared no longer. Like
Yeats, he praises pure sound—'words which create an atmosphere
by the actual suggestive quality of their syllables' (p. 19). These
technical needs of symbolism, as Symons saw them, were all
fulfilled in the rhythms of dance. Ballet 'dissolves the will into
slumber' and is disturbed by no intrusion of words: 'the dancer,
with her gesture, all pure symbol, evokes, from her mere beautiful
motion, idea, sensation, all that one need ever know of event'.[3]

For these two writers symbolism meant an art which penetrates beyond ordinary circumstance. The wisdom which rewards
this penetration is defined in different ways for different writers:
for de l'Isle-Adam it is a vision of 'an ideal world'; for Verlaine,
of 'the essential parts of things, or precisely those aspects which
most other people would pass by'; for Nerval, 'unknown harmonies'; and for Mallarmé, 'all the correspondence of the universe, the supreme Music'.[4] For Yeats, the vision is of 'truth in
the depths of the mind when the eyes are closed' (p. 28). One
assumes that the truth found there will be 'some invisible essence'

---

[1] Arnold, quoted ibid., p. 313.

[2] 'The Decadent Movement in Literature', *Harper's New Monthly Magazine*
(November 1893), p. 860. It is because of similar interests that on the previous
page Symons indentifies symbolism with impressionism.

[3] 'The World as Ballet', *Studies in Seven Arts*, pp. 389–91. For a detailed
discussion of the symbolist image of the dance see Frank Kermode, *The Romantic
Image* (1957).

[4] Op. cit., pp. 24, 42, 17 and 73 respectively.

(p. 116), 'the Divine Essence' (p. 148), or 'the essences of things ... not things' (p. 193). The key to these noumena are symbols, which are the only means of conveying the divine truths, of making visible the 'soul of things'.[1]

Yeats was perfectly aware of the Pre-Raphaelite contribution to this symbolist imagination. Reactions against materialism and rationalism came to perfection, he says, with the Pre-Raphaelites in England (p. 187). In his essay on 'Symbolism in Painting' Rossetti is cited enthusiastically. He felt strongly that Rossetti 'desired a world of essences, of unmixed powers, of impossible purities' (p. 53) and that he demonstrated his concern for the perfection of thought, feeling and form which could express that world.[2] Rossetti also saw the 'supernatural beauty, the impossible beauty' (p. 64).

It is also, I believe, no accident that Yeats should choose the beryl stone to image poetry's return to symbolism. For the beryl stone of Rossetti's 'Rose Mary' is the same as Yeats's, 'enchanted by our fathers that it might unfold the pictures in its heart, and not to mirror our own excited faces, or the boughs waving outside the window' (p. 163). At the first occasion on which Rossetti describes the stone, he might well be articulating Yeats's own interests in symbolic vision:

> Shaped it was to a shadowy sphere,—
> World of our world, the sun's compeer,
> That bears and buries the toiling year.
>
> With shuddering light 'twas stirred and strewn
> Like the cloud-nest of the wading moon:
> Freaked it was as the bubble's ball,
> Rainbow-hued through a misty pall
> Like the middle light of the waterfall.
>
> Shadows dwelt in its teeming girth
> Of the known and unknown things of earth;
> The cloud above and the wave around,—
> The central fire at the sphere's heart bound,
> Like doomsday prisoned underground. (I, 104)

[1] The phrase is Symons's, p. 5. Cf. Yeats, p. 28.
[2] P. 53. Cf. *Autobiographies*, p. 313.

The shadows, the hazy mists, the unknown things and the central fire seem to be the same characteristics as Yeats admired in symbolism.[1]

Further, Yeats links Blake's invention of symbols with Blake's search for a mythology.[2] A similar connection between symbolism and mythology he saw had marked much of the Pre-Raphaelite movement from 1848 until the time of his own earliest work. It had searched for a variety of mythologies—Scandinavian, Celtic, that of *il dolce stil nuovo*, mediaeval French—which were popular mainly because they were modes of apprehending a reality which the nineteenth century saw as most productive of great and satisfying works of art.[3] The Pre-Raphaelite return to earlier ages was an attempt to find a means of exploring depths of feeling which Victorian life seemed to deny them. The daily existence of their age seemed to have little of that spiritual and human significance which life had apparently held for such artists as Dante or Giotto. These 'mythologies' attracted the Pre-Raphaelites because they did not betray a cleavage between daily visible facts and accepted truths and values; because, in short, they offered symbols which could reveal 'divine essences'. Yeats praised the Scandinavian tradition in Wagner and Morris because it introduced the 'most passionate element in the arts of the modern world' (p. 186); Scandinavian mythology was fraught with strong passions, and strong passions stirred life at the very roots of being, penetrating to those invisible essences which were the concern of symbolism. Rossetti had thought the same way about the idealization of woman in *il dolce stil nuovo*.

Both Yeats and Symons invoke Blake in their fabric of symbolist history and here, specifically, the Pre-Raphaelite inspira-

[1] Like Yeats, Rossetti was intrigued by the occult: see C. K. Hyder, 'Rossetti's *Rose Mary*: A Study in the Occult', Victorian Poetry, I (1963), pp. 197 ff.

[2] P. 114. Cf. Symons in *The Dome*, new series I, p. 71, on a similar connection between legend and symbolism in Wagner.

[3] See Yeats's essay on 'The Celtic Element in Literature' (pp. 173 ff.). Also see H. House, *All in Due Time* (1955), pp. 151–8, and J. Chiari, *Symbolisme from Poe to Mallarmé*, p. 33: the latter notes that the Pre-Raphaelite interest in the Middle Ages 'was part of a conscious search for roots in a world stultified and desecrated by abstractions and materialism'.

tion and example were strong.[1] Blake is an artist whom Matthew Arnold strangely omits from his pantheon of great romantics. It was left to the central members of the Pre-Raphaelite movement to energize a revival of interest and enthusiasm. Both Rossettis contribued to the first major homage paid to Blake in the nineteenth century—Alexander Gilchrist's *Life of William Blake with Selections from his Poems and other writings*. It was issued in 1863, two years after Gilchrist's death, having been completed and seen through the press by D. G. Rossetti; a revised and enlarged edition appeared in 1880. Meanwhile Swinburne had published his 'critical essay' on Blake in 1868, an enterprise that grew from a review of the Gilchrist volume. W. M. Rossetti edited and introduced the Aldine edition of Blake's poetry of 1874.

It was the Gilchrist edition which Yeats's father put into his hands about 1881 and which he found 'decorated with wonderful and mysterious pictures that no-one understood, and containing writings that many thought had no meaning at all'.[2] And among the 'brotherhood' of Pre-Raphaelite-inspired artists with whom his father was intimate Blake was admired and cultivated. So it is not perhaps surprising in view of this background of interest in Blake that Yeats should himself be in part responsible for the major work of rehabilitation: jointly with Edwin Ellis he produced a three-volume edition in 1893 of which two volumes were introduction and commentary. Symons also contributed to this enthusiasm, but his book on Blake is much later—1907—and it mainly recapitulates most of the Pre-Raphaelite tradition of admiration. Nor were these the only enthusiasts in the 1890's[3] for a writer and artist who offered later Victorians an example of the 'exalted visionary'. And, as both Yeats and Symons announced, Blake further offered the example of a man who had fashioned a new 'language of spiritual utterance' (Yeats), a 'dialect of a far country' (Swinburne) in which to speak of his visions.[4]

---

[1] See a fuller discussion, infra p. 167 ff.

[2] Quoted D. Gordon and Ian Fletcher, *W. B. Yeats: Images of a Poet* (1961), p. 92. I am indebted to their section on symbolic art for my own discussion.

[3] See both *The Hobby Horse* and *The Dial, passim*.

[4] E. J. Ellis and W. B. Yeats, *The Works of William Blake* (1893), I, xi, and A. C. Swinburne, *William Blake. A Critical Essay* (2nd ed., 1868), p. 47.

II

Yeats was the first to appreciate how much the actual practice of the Pre-Raphaelite arts endorsed the more vocal and formulated programme of French symbolism. The English movement concerned itself little with theories—except perhaps in their attempts to explain Blake[1]—but in their original work can be found examples of symbolist art which, sometimes tentatively, sometimes with real confidence, explore areas of experience that we have seen Yeats and Symons celebrate. A great deal of Pre-Raphaelite interest is devoted to aspects of life for which a symbol is the best possible expression—the inward dramas of the soul, a divine world of ideal beauty or of invisible essences. Words or pigment 'are used not to describe the phenomena, but to suggest the noumena, the very idea of the thing'.[2] Even Holman Hunt's detailed verisimilitude, as in *The Awakened Conscience*, is used to convey a profound state of being; Hunt himself wrote that the man in the picture might be seen as 'the unconscious utterer of a divine message'.[3]

But while Yeats acknowledged this general precedence he went into few details; Symons was to offer more. This chapter seeks to expand their suggestions and provide a fuller account of the Pre-Raphaelite contribution to what may, restrospectively, be seen as a movement of European dimensions. It seems best to focus the discussion on three areas of symbolism. Firstly, Pre-Raphaelite art displays an interest in an existence beyond mere exterior description, anecdotage, or the perceptions and clarity of the waking mind; an interest in trance and dreams, in what Rilke called the 'flowering of our inwardness', in mythological worlds whose significance does not lie upon the surface; they were obsessed with transience and the complementary search for a more stable and authentic world of noumenous existence. Secondly, the Pre-Raphaelite apprehension of the unheard music,

---

[1] See D. G. Rossetti on Blake's writings on art in the *Descriptive Catalogue* and the *Public Address*, which he considers (Gilchrist edition, II, 137) the best things ever said about art.

[2] Chiari, op. cit., p. 116.

[3] Quoted Ironside, *Pre-Raphaelite Painters*, p. 31.

the invisible essences and divine mysteries of existence forced them to evoke them by the musical and atmospheric use of language. Their arts aspired to the condition of music in order to articulate a 'musicalité intérieure', and in this they offer a distinct parallel to the French interest in music as a possible dialect for symbolism. Thirdly, the revival of interest in Blake, already alluded to briefly; in discussing this our interest will be chiefly how the Pre-Raphaelite discovery of Blake confirmed much of their own artistic endeavours and how their explanations of his idealism promoted their most sustained *theoretical* formulations of symbolism.

III

From its earliest stages the Pre-Raphaelite Brotherhood used exact and detailed representation of objects less as an end in itself than as a vision or suggestion of greater things, like Father Hilary in Rossetti's 'World's Worth' who finds in the wind-stirred pools of water on the church roof an analogy of his own despair. John Ruskin pointed out in his letters to *The Times* that the details in Holman Hunt's pictures are revelations of much more, like the ivy-choked door at which Christ knocks in *The Light of the World*, or the new books in *The Awakened Conscience* 'marked with no happy wearing of beloved pages'.[1]

Contributors to both magazines of the movement reveal an interest in external phenomena which have symbolic implications. W. M. Rossetti wrote of his brother's poem, 'My Sister's Sleep', which appeared in *The Germ*, that the poem 'shows in an eminent degree one of the influences which guided the movement: the intimate intertexture of a spiritual sense with a material form; *small actualities made vocal of lofty meanings*'.[2] The remark is more significant than the poem upon which it comments, and it may be hindsight on W. M. Rossetti's part, an attempt to adjust the history of the Pre-Raphaelite movement to later symbolist enthusiasms. But it is supported in practice by several items in *The Germ*.

[1] *Works*, XII, p. 335.
[2] Introduction to facsimile of *The Germ*, p. 19, my italics.

In Bell Scott's 'Morning Sleep' the poet's eyes are 'in a continual dreaming, mingling earth / And heaven with vagrant fantasies' and he is granted, through this 'golden atmosphere', a vision of the 'forms of immortalities'. William Michael Rossetti speculates on 'the reconciling vision' beyond 'mortality's stern screen', and the use of screen is similar to later symbolists' references to the intractible barrier of the external world. He also offers a poem describing a series of minutely observed natural objects beside some summer water: in case we ignore the ulterior purpose the last stanza asks, 'Is not this something more than idle play?' Similarly, Thomas Woolner's 'Emblems' presents two stanzas of natural, yet symbolic description, to which he then fits a further six of interpretation.

The Germ also displays a corresponding interest in visions which rely only slightly upon details of the real world and which by-pass them to focus upon intense experiences and noumenous insights. Christina Rossetti's 'Dream Land' is a vision of death's shadowy land, where the purple twilight and the sunless rivers are the essence of a release from life. Her brother's Blessed Damozel dreams of the ideal, spiritual fulfilment of her love, and in 'Hand and Soul' the artist's realization of the importance of his integrity is given him in a vision by a lady in grey and green raiment, who is the image of his soul.

These interests continue in the *Magazine* for 1856, which as well as being more coherent and less diversified than *The Germ* shows an interest in the theories of symbol. In addition to the discussions of Carlyle's ideas on symbolism there is a consideration of Tennyson in the rôle of 'Interpreter', which anticipates the symbolist idea of the poet as the *déchiffreur de l'univers*.[1] Burne-Jones recalled Rossetti to the readers of the *Magazine* as the author of 'The Blessed Damozel', which was reprinted, and of the symbolic story, 'Hand and Soul'; Lushington explains the symbolism of Rossetti's *Dante's Vision of Beatrice* at great length.

The use of dreams and vision, as methods for communicating further truths, increases in the *Magazine*. Seven stories out of

[1] The phrase is Mallarmé's: cf. 'Art is mediation by genius which reveals what truly is' (Chiari, op. cit., p. 45).

seventeen use a dream or imaginative reverie to introduce their visions, while others indulge in passages of impressionistic description which create much the same effect.[1] In Dixon's 'The Rivals' there is the 'beautiful vision' of the girl in the suburban garden, caught in purple sunlight, with a 'mist of light about the clouds' (p. 36). Burne-Jones's 'The Cousins' shows the distracted narrator's mind in 'some weird trance' where 'human faces grew ever vague and indistinct and shadowy' (p. 26).

Morris, together with an obvious imitation of Morris by Fulford,[2] provides the most interesting example of dream-worlds whose significance is more than what is merely stated. In 'The Story of the Unknown Church' (pp. 28-33) a mediaeval mason dreams on the scaffold where he is carving. In his dream he is able to see 'even very far off things much clearer than we see real material things on the earth'. This heightened awareness produces a sequence of visions linked in a strange *montage*:

. . . and there was something in the moving of the water-lilies as the breast of the horse swept them aside, that suddenly took away the thought of Abraham and brought a strange dream of lands I had never seen; and the first was of a place where I was quite alone, standing by the side of a river and there was the sound of singing a very long way off, but no living thing of any kind could be seen, and the land was quite flat, quite without hills, and quite without trees too, and the river wound very much, making all kinds of quaint curves, and on the other side where I stood there grew nothing but long grass, but on the other side grew, quite on the horizon, a great sea of red corn-poppies, only paths of white lilies wound all among them, with here and there a great golden sun-flower . . . and I stooped to drink of the water of the river, and as soon as the water touched my lips, lo! the river vanished, and the flat country with its poppies and lilies, and I dreamed that I was in a boat by myself again, floating in an almost land-locked bay of the northern sea, under a cliff of dark basalt. . . . So I reached out my arms to him, and suddenly I was walking with him in a lovely garden, and we said nothing, for the music which I had

[1] Rossetti in a letter to Allingham referred to the authors of tales in the *Magazine* as coming from 'dreamland' (*Letters*, I, 293).

[2] 'A Night in a Cathedral' (pp. 310-16), also a form of reverie, where the darkened building stimulates the modern visitor's perception until he envisions the original construction of the cathedral.

heard at first was sounding close to me now, and there were many birds in the boughs of the trees: oh, such birds! gold and ruby, and emerald, but they sung not at all, but were quite silent, as though they too were listening to the music. Now all this time Amyot and I had been looking at each other, but just then I turned my head away from him, and as soon as I did so, the music ended with a long wail, and when I turned again Amyot was gone; then I felt even more sad and sick at heart than I had before when I was by the river, and I leaned against a tree, and put my hands before my eyes. When I looked again the garden was gone, and I knew not where I was, and presently all my dreams were gone.

These mysterious dreams are told with a brilliant perception ('perfect in colour and form, sweet sounds and shapes') and a carefully controlled imprecision, as if the exactitude of the suggestion would conjure up images of another reality. For, as the mason remarks later in the tale, 'I . . . seemed quite away out of the world.' The passage recalls Mallarmé's remark in *Sur l'Évolution littéraire* that 'La contemplation des objets, l'image s'envolant des rêveries suscitées par eux, sont la chant'.[1]

Morris also contributed an article on Amiens. His rhetorical farewell to the cathedral[2] presents a vision of the building which is infinitely more than the sum of all the parts described. From the 'twined mystery of the great flamboyant rose window' to the 'spire that seems to rock, when across it, in the wild February nights, the clouds go westward', Morris clothes the building in such a devotional intensity and more than natural radiance that it seems to become a symbol of all the history and mysteries of the catholic church.

Ruskin had used a similar technique with great success. But Morris achieves greater compression by using suggestion and rejecting Ruskin's more laboured exposition. The chapter on Torcello in the second volume of *The Stones of Venice* is an excellent example of the method which might have impressed the young Morris. From the opening description of the 'waste of wild sea moor' to the final vision of the Duomo as the goodly

---

[1] *Oeuvres Complètes* (Bibliothèque de la Pléiade, Paris 1945), p. 869.
[2] *Oxford and Cambridge Magazine*, pp. 99–110. Part of the passage is quoted infra p. 160.

temple-ship of the church, Ruskin sees the architectural and topographical accidents as symbolic representations of greater, invisible
things. The cathedral of Torcello, Ruskin insists, is 'exactly typical of the spiritual condition which every Christian ought to
recognize in himself, a state of homelessness on earth, except so
far as he can make the Most High his habitation'. The lightness
and brightness of the building reveal to Ruskin, in conjunction
with the two famous mosaics, that the spirit of that early church
was of tangible hope and comfort rather than threatenings and
mysteries, of humbleness before Christ, and of deep sorrow and
sacred courage.

Morris refined considerably upon such a method, eliminating
especially the explicit morality and the lengthy interpretations of
phenomena, allowing the special mysteries of the noumena to
suggest themselves. Morris's influence in this method of description seems to have reached Arthur Symons, whose essay on
'Cathedrals' of 1903 evinces a curiously Morris-like absorption.
His evocations of the 'genius' or 'temper' of the buildings are
statements of the symbolic 'soul in stone' of each: Cologne is
'one of the unconsoling images of eternity. . . . It shelters no
dreams, only a calm certainty, as of a mind which has reasoned
itself sure.' At Bourges the double aisles around the church offer
a pattern of mysterious lines whose 'evasiveness is like a last,
less definite suggestion completing what is frank and precise in
the bare elegance of the structure'.[1]

Morris's tale of 'The Hollow Land' (pp. 565–77 and 632–41)
presents the most important use of his symbolist method in the
Oxford and Cambridge Magazine. The narrator begins by admit-
ting that the Hollow Land is always dreamed of and is indeed
only a dream. It seems the first of Morris's quasi-paradises, a
first wood beyond the world, a first well at the world's end. Like
those later evocations of such ideals it seems exactly and precisely
recorded:

a great *hollow* land, the rocks going down on this side in precipices,
then reaches and reaches of loveliest country, trees and flowers, and

---

[1] *Studies in Seven Arts*, pp. 151 ff.

corn, then the hills, green and blue, and purple, till their ledges reached the white snowy mountains at last (p. 576).

In that passage it is probably the superlatives and the insistence upon colours that evoke a picture of a more than natural landscape. Paradoxically, for all this careful description, quite what significance to give this hollow land is left vague. It is certainly an ideal domain, like the one for which *le grand Meaulnes* spent his life searching. (Alain Fournier, an admirer of the Pre-Raphaelites, must assuredly have Morris's tales most in mind in his great novel.) But whether the Hollow Land represents a perfect life, or whether its blue shadowings hint at an *after*-life, remains unclear; even the ending—golden deserted streets, the fair palace, the great space of flowers—offers no surer clue to interpretation. Yet there is an emphatic and quite assured handling of a symbolic landscape, suggesting if only vaguely some 'lofty meaning'.

Morris's talents lie most obviously in decoration. It is fascinating to note how in the passage, quoted above, of the mason on his scaffold the natural details focus into the patterns of a Morris design. But in his literary art the most characteristic tendency of his imagination, apart from decoration,[1] is towards the magical and suggestive symbolism we have seen in his stories. If he became more diffuse and quaint after *The Hollow Land*, he also gained assurance by the time of, say, *The Wood Beyond the World*, published nearly forty years after the *Oxford and Cambridge Magazine*. These later romances continue to evoke some landscape of the spirit, to suggest something beyond the mere telling of a tale.

In a review of *The Well at the World's End* Swinburne raised the central difficulty about Morris's symbolism. He recalls the author's disclaiming any allegorical intention in *The Wood Beyond the World* and continues:

No commentator, I should hope, will ever waste his time on the childish task of inventing an occult significance for the incidents and adventures, the lurid and the lovely landscape . . . in this later and yet more magically beautiful tale.[2]

[1] See, for example, 'The Sailing of the Sword' or 'The Red Roses Across the Moon' which anticipate the colour symphonies of later symbolists.
[2] Pierpont Morgan Library MS., no. MA 1731.

He is right to insist that for neither is it easy to invent an occult significance. Yet one seizes upon Swinburne's use of 'magically', as perhaps he was himself doing, to explain that these two works do in fact imply more than the total effect of the incidents narrated. Just as for Pater the smile of Leonardo's *John the Baptist* suggested something far beyond 'outward gesture or circumstance',[1] so I believe do Morris's romances. It is perhaps left deliberately vague what that something is, so that each reader might improvise for himself.

Morris himself offers certain signposts, not least by inferences in his titles, which suggest more than description or narrative. In *The Story of the Glittering Plain or the Land of Living Men* the alternative title explains the magical significance of the Plain. Then, on the second page, one idea or abstraction which the Plain may be said to symbolize is brought explicitly to our attention by the three horsemen who seek the land where they may 'forget the days of Sorrow'. When Hallblithe discovers that the land is also free from foes and fear, its symbolic significance is even clearer; equally when Hallblithe and Puny Fox return to Cleveland and to a more normal life (no wizardry, for instance!), the moral significance again obtrudes somewhat abstractly. Yet Morris's hints and indications offer only the general outline, and the reader's fancy is still allowed to exercise itself. But what remains clear is that just as in his decorative designs he moved away from the representational towards suggestive, symbolic shapes, so in his narratives. Walter Pater might well have been referring to Morris's romances when in his essay on Rossetti he said that 'Dream-land . . . is to him . . . a real country, a veritable expansion of, or addition to, our waking life'.[2]

For Morris one means by which he extended his waking life was by a celebration of Utopias. He once warned his readers that the only way to read a Utopia was as an expression of the author's temperament.[3] These symbolic romances, less explicit

---

[1] *The Renaissance*, p. 122.

[2] *Appreciations*, p. 214. These were the very terms in which Yeats and Symons saw symbolism's superiority over realism.

[3] See Margaret R. Greenan, *William Morris, Mediaevalist and Revolutionary*, p. 134.

Utopias than *News From Nowhere*, present stories charged with some ideal significance, pointed perhaps for Morris himself but not successfully communicated to others. Yeats admitted the necessary 'monotony in the work of the symbolist who can only make symbols out of the things that *he* loves'.[1] Perhaps a similar cause limits also the success of articulation in Morris. Some compelling personal significance, some intense private dream stamps many scenes in these romances—the loss of the Hollow Land or the scene where Ursula and Ralph drink at the Well or the scene where the girl appears as the Queen of Summer in *The Wood*. And the journeys upon which his characters embark seem also some personal extension (again Alain Fournier's novel springs to mind) of the Grail quest, which represented for the Pre-Raphaelites the ideals for which there was no utilitarian justification, which were even beyond precise definition.[2]

Much Pre-Raphaelite symbolism, like Morris's prose romances, is undeniably extremely private. Indeed, it has been plausibly suggested that their inaccessible symbolism attracted the later aesthetic movement just as it lost them popular appeal.[3] Their most public symbolism probably occurs in their painting, where it needed to fix upon visible items and could not indulge in the impressionistic suggestion we have seen in Morris's romances. Partly because they were committed to detailed reproduction of the minute actualities of what they saw, their paintings stress the phenomenal world more precisely than their writings usually do. They wished to avoid the stereotyped mannerisms fostered at the Academy schools and to devote themselves to faithful renderings of the external world. They invoked their own first-hand vision and rejected the borrowed style (that necessarily involved borrowed visions) of Reynolds's imitators. But although this programme produced detailed accounts of the phenomenal world the emphasis upon their own vision and imagination tended to elicit unique and absorbed private accounts. These often have

[1] *A Book of Images* by W. T. Horton and introduced by W. B. Yeats (1898), p. 15.
[2] See Beerbohm's cartoon of Jowett enquiring of Rossetti what would be done with the Grail when it was found, *Rossetti and his Circle* (1922), no. 4.
[3] J. H. Buckley, *The Victorian Temper*, p. 165.

an intensity of insight into the scene depicted which illuminates more than its physical accidents.

The most obvious example of this is what might be called the 'moral symbolism' of Holman Hunt. *The Hireling Shepherd* (1851) was intended as 'a rebuke to the sectarian vanities and vital negligences of the day';[1] the shepherd is a symbol of the muddle-headed pastor who neglects his duties, and almost each detail of the picture has a similar symbolic relevance. But this symbolic reference is hampered by the precise description; frequently we have to rely on catalogue notes to identify all the implications. Hunt's dedication to the early Pre-Raphaelite doctrine of fidelity of natural description and his impulse to make each painting a moral symbol are often at odds with each other. He would rise at four every morning and climb Magdalen Tower to catch the sunrise, painting each detail of *May Morning on Magdalen Tower* with infinite care. But he then added flowers at the choristers' feet to symbolize Spring and, because to greet the dawn is an ancient rite, he also introduces a venerable Parsee among the college fellows.[2] The realism of *The Scapegoat*, over which he had so much difficulty rendering the exact details of the scene, hardly allows any symbolism to become apparent. As the art critic in *The Athenaeum* suggested rather scornfully, it is 'impossible to paint a goat, though its eyes were upturned with human passions, that could explain any allegory or hidden type'.[3] But a further reason for the obscurity of Hunt's symbolism is the highly personal notions he brought to his painting. His remarks about *The Light of the World* disclaim any traditional, iconographical symbolism:

I may say that any occult meaning in the details of my design was not based upon ecclesiastical or archaic symbolism, but derived from obvious reflectiveness. My types were of natural figures such as language had originally employed to express transcendental ideas,

[1] Quoted Ironside, op. cit., p. 28.

[2] See T. S. R. Boase, *English Art 1800–1870* (Oxford 1959), p. 298.

[3] Quoted Hunt, *Pre-Raphaelitism and the Pre-Raphaelite Brotherhood*, II, 111. Interestingly Launcelot Andrewes in one of his sermons offers the example of the scapegoat as a type or figure which is 'shadowed out darkly, rather than clearly expressed'.

and they were used by me with no confidence that they would interest any other mind than my own.[1]

The picture relies, in fact, upon literary and biblical allusions, interpreted in a highly personal fashion.

Some Pre-Raphaelite painting did use, as Yeats notices, 'traditional symbolism' (p. 150). This meant either orthodox iconography or allegorical devices. In the first category come the lilies and doves of Rossetti's *Annunciation* and *Girlhood of Mary Virgin*, the passion flowers in the background of *Mary Magdalene*, the well of life in *Mary Magdalene leaving the House of Feasting*, or the dove in *Beata Beatrix*, crowned with a halo like the bird of the annunciation and in its beak the mystic flower, emblem of death and chastity, the white poppy. Allegorical figures also attracted attention. Burne-Jones was especially fond of them and Simeon Solomon, the most pallid of all Pre-Raphaelites, painted such subjects as *Dawn*, *Amor Sacramentum*, *Night and Love* and *Sleep of Remorse*. Madox Brown painted a young girl to represent the Protestant faith, while Woolner's projected monument to Wordsworth was desperately allegorical, with groups representing Control and Aspiration.[2] Rossetti, too, uses allegorical figures in *The House of Life* and in such paintings as *Sibylla Palmifera* and *Lady Lilith*.

But among Pre-Raphaelites maybe the most successful allegorical painter was G. F. Watts, of whom Symons wrote an appreciation in 1900. He over-values Watts's work, but his essay serves yet again to illustrate how the Pre-Raphaelite movement could properly be read by later critics in terms of their own enthusiasms. Symons emphasizes, quite rightly, the way in which Watts's allegorical figures show how unsure he was of the limits of pictorial expression—a perpetual difficulty with Pre-Raphaelite art. But he hails 'an evident meaning' beyond the figures' 'mere presentment of themselves', finding, specially, in the picture of *Psyche* 'a symbol made perfect in humanity'.[3]

[1] Hunt, I, 350–1. In contradiction of Hunt's disclaimer it is interesting to note the undeniable use of traditional types and emblems by the Pre-Raphaelite movement: see the talk on this by Ian Fletcher, *The Listener*, 25 May 1967.

[2] Respectively, *Pre-Raphaelite Letters and Diaries*, p. 87, and p. 296.

[3] *Studies in Seven Arts*, p. 96.

But Pre-Raphaelite art also offers examples of a symbolist vision of a more confident literary quality than those allegories, which both Yeats and Symons sharply distinguished, in theory at least, from symbolism.[1] Still concerned with accurate descriptions in their pictures, Millais, Rossetti and Burne-Jones nevertheless also managed to infuse an exterior scene or actual figure with more subtle suggestions, so that in many of their pictures our attention is quickly directed to the noumena.

Millais, for example, in *Christ in the House of his Parents* presents a prophetic glimpse of the crucifixion; both *Ferdinand and Ariel* and the pen and ink sketch, *The Ghost*, celebrate more than normal states of mind and experience. But above all in his *Blind Girl* and *Autumn Leaves* there is a deliberate evocation of more than the visible scene. In the first, the sensation of the blind girl's loss is made more poignant by the beauty of the radiant light and rainbow after a heavy shower; the second sounds an elegiac note, which Holman Hunt recalls Millais describing: 'To me nothing [better than the 'sensation' of burning leaves] brings back sweeter memories of the days that are gone. . . .'[2] It is these memories of the past that the canvas is intended to evoke. Andrew Lang noted that 'the *spiritual* note of the picture lies in the contrast between the carelessness of the young girls . . . and the serious *whisper* of the twilight'.[3] This work by Millais has little of the strange, compelling, dream-like work by his fellow Pre-Raphaelite brothers, for despite his technical proficiency he is already succumbing to the sentimentalism which dominates much later work. For Millais, sentimentality was close to and probably a legitimate development from symbolism. For Victorian sentimentality was a means of infusing into what was otherwise a purely materialistic, 'scientific' representation of the external world some spirit or suggestion which the phenomena do not contain.[4]

Instead of Millais's sentimentality or Hunt's moral symbolism,

---

[1] *Ibid.*, p. 97, and Yeats's *Essays*, p. 148.
[2] Hunt, op. cit., I, 286.
[3] Quoted Bate, *English Pre-Raphaelite Painters* (1899), pp. 35-6, my italics.
[4] A point made by Humphrey House, *All in Due Time*, p. 147.

Rossetti and Burne-Jones relied more upon dreams, trances and other forms of supernatural vision in their pictures.[1] At first Burne-Jones was influenced by Rossetti and his account of a proposed pair of pictures inspired by the Blessed Damozel suggests his symbolic interests:

In the first picture I shall make a man walking in the street of a great city, full of all kinds of happy life; children, such as he will never have, and lovers walking, and ladies leaning from windows all down the great lengths of street leading to the city walls; and there the gates are wide open, letting in a space of green field and cornfield in harvest; and all round his head a great rain of swirling Autumn leaves blowing from a little walled graveyard. And in the other picture I shall make lovely Heaven, where the lady stands at the edge of the garden and leans over, trying to count a thick flight of little souls in bright flames, and the garden of Heaven full of all flowers on every side of her and of lovers who have met again.[2]

Later Burne-Jones passed from Rossetti's influence to a more distinctive style based upon Mantegna and Botticelli. Yet his fondness for ultra-phenomenal worlds changed only in the quality of their expression. His *Aurora* shows an abstract, impersonal figure stepping lightly beside a still canal on which the wharves and trees and sunrise cast ethereal reflections. But the abstraction is strangely and even movingly modified by Burne-Jones's handling, which imparts to it a meaning that—by Symons's criterion for successful symbolism—cannot be detached 'entirely from the manner of its expression'.[3] A writer in *The Dome* defended his work in the same fashion that Yeats defended Blake: 'the unusual proportions and unusual colours of Burne-Jones's figures may not be those of Nature, but they are the colours and proportions which he found necessary for giving full expression to his thoughts' (V, 56).

[1] As Agnes Morgan says, 'Only Rossetti and after him Burne-Jones seem to have suspected that the accumulation of naturalistic detail and strict verisimilitude constrict rather than release the larger poetic truths of inspired perception' (Introduction to the Fogg Museum of Art catalogue, *Paintings and Drawings of the Pre-Raphaelites and their Circle* (Cambridge, Mass. 1946), p. 9).

[2] Quoted, ibid., pp. 23–4.

[3] *Studies in Seven Arts*, p. 97.

Other work brings figures, often allegorical, equally often supernatural, who are caught in a vast and spellbound silence, like those in his watercolour, 'The Magic Circle'. His *Helen of Troy* shows a golden vision of the nude figure apparently rising from the smoking ruins which are as evocative as Helen herself. *Angels of Creation*, each holding crystal spheres, gaze passionlessly beyond the viewer, all mutely expressive of wonder and praise. La Sizeranne found it, rightly, 'impossible to conceive a more graceful and less pedantic symbolism'.[1] Even the austere Holman Hunt liked these panels,[2] and I cannot help thinking that there was a secret fondness even in him for the occult and magic world of the other Brothers. This is suggested by his watercolour study at the Fogg Museum for one of the iridescent bubbles that float at the feet of the Spirit Children in *The Triumph of the Innocents*. The study represents the Woman running from the Red Dragon, and the handling of the prismatic colours creates a sensation of powerful fantasy. Later in *The Yellow Book* (XI) Patten Wilson offers a similar image in his drawing of a dragon menacing a knight and a lady crouched in separate crystal spheres. Only the power of Hunt's imagination has been replaced by Wilson's decorative ingenuity.

Rossetti provides the most interesting examples of symbolist vision in Pre-Raphaelite painting. It is significant that he left *Found* incomplete. For it reveals his lack of interest in contemporary scenes and mere anecdotage conveyed in a realistic manner. They allowed little scope for his instinct to explore the vague unreality of dreams, the divine world of ideal beauties, the inward dramas of the soul. His frequent choice of subjects from Dante was prompted perhaps by a wish to invoke a poetry which had itself many symbolic reverberations upon which he could rely. His habit of fixing sonnets to his paintings also helps to emphasize and articulate their allusions and symbolism. He told Mrs Morris he was thinking of producing a book of autotype portraits of her, each of which would have a sonnet attached, doubtless to spell out the private emotion and allusions it held

[1] *English Contemporary Art* (1898), p. 236.
[2] Op. cit., II, 364.

for him.[1] This is exactly the function of the sonnet for *Astarte Syriaca*, those for *Mary's Girlhood*, or these lines from that for *La Bella Mano*:

> O lovely hand, that thy sweet self dost lave
> In that thy pure and proper element
> Whence erst the Lady of Love's high advent
> Was born, and endless fires sprang from the wave. (I. 373)

They emphasize, to an extent which the picture cannot, the symbolic and allusive properties of the water, just as the sonnet further suggests that the lips of the lady are of 'music-measured speech / The fount, and of more bliss than man may crave'.

Rossetti was generally hospitable to a symbolist mode of expression. He said to Allingham that his *Hamlet and Ophelia* was 'deeply symbolical, *of course*'.[2] He altered the titles of the sonnets for *Sibylla Palmifera* and *Lady Lilith* to 'Soul's Beauty' and 'Body's Beauty'—obviously in an attempt to emphasize the symbolic, ideal significance of the two figures. The Llandaff triptych was not, he explained, 'a literal reading of the event of the Nativity, but rather a condensed symbol of it'.[3] At Hastings he loved to 'lie and symbolize till one goes to sleep, and that be a symbol too perhaps'.[4] It may well be that when in the same letter he says that all art is boring 'except when followed in the dozing style' he is expressing his preference for symbolism, which Yeats was later to describe in similar terms as a vision of truth 'in the depths of mind when the eyes are closed'.

Certainly the 'dozing style' is an appropriate description of many of Rossetti's pictures. In a letter of 1871 he talks of what he intends to suggest by his painting of the death of Beatrice:

It must of course be remembered, in looking at the picture, that it is not intended at all to *represent* death, but to render it under the semblance of a trance, in which Beatrice seated at a balcony overlooking

---

[1] British Museum MS. 52333 B, fol. 142.

[2] Quoted by Marillier, *Dante Gabriel Rossetti, An Illustrated Memorial of His Art and Life* (1899), p. 66, my italics.

[3] *Rossetti Papers, 1862–1870*, p. 51.

[4] *Ruskin, Rossetti and Pre-Raphaelitism*, p. 9. The lyric, 'Woodspurge', is presumably a result of such activity.

the city, is suddenly rapt. . . . She, through her shut lids, is conscious of a new world.[1]

Not only does the central figure of this picture 'doze', but we must ourselves respond to her trance and to the dreamy, evocative background if we are to appreciate it. For even after reading Rossetti's warning that *Beata Beatrix* is not intended to represent her death, the picture is rather unexpected. The physical appearance of the figure, as of many others, is emphatic enough to distract some attention from its supernatural implications. When Patmore complained once that a picture's symbolism was remote and unobvious, Rossetti replied that he wanted to make 'the symbolism inherent in the fact'.[2] But it is evident that often, as in the *Beata Beatrix*, the physical facts predominate and even obscure the symbolism.

Yeats certainly sensed the symbolic intentions in Rossetti's painting of women, as Symons did in those by Watts. In 'The Symbolism of Painting' Yeats notes how Rossetti used his favourite image of woman to suggest either certain emotional resonances or, by the use of traditionally symbolic properties, some divine essence:

> If you paint a beautiful woman and fill her face, as Rossetti filled so many faces, with an infinite love, a perfected love, 'one's eyes meet no mortal thing when they meet the light of her peaceful eyes' . . . but one's thoughts stray to mortal things, and ask, maybe, 'Has her lover gone from her, or is he coming?' or 'What predestined unhappiness has made the shadow in her eyes?' If you paint the same face, and set a winged rose or a rose of gold somewhere about her, one's thoughts are of her immortal sisters, Piety and Jealousy, and of her mother, Ancestral Beauty, and of her high kinsmen, the Holy Orders, whose swords make a continual music before her face. (p. 150)

Similarly Symons notices one particular portrait by Watts which 'gazes into our eyes with a triumphant sensuality of soul, implacable, amiable, interrogatory'; as his talent grows so Watts masters

---

[1] Pierpont Morgan Library MS., MA 1640(3). Swinburne also described the picture as 'wholly symbolic and ideal', *Notes on the Royal Academy Exhibition* (1868), p. 48.

[2] *Ruskin, Rossetti and Pre-Raphaelitism*, p. 139, and B. Champneys, *Memories and Correspondence of Coventry Patmore* (1900), II, 233.

the 'beauty of every symbol by which any divinity can be made visible', and the symbols he chooses are the features of ideal women and men.[1]

This Pre-Raphaelite symbolism of a beautiful woman is extensive and the following chapter is devoted exclusively to it. Here it is important only to stress that almost every Pre-Raphaelite painter uses such symbolism either to communicate the state of his soul or to focus some idealism.[2] In the words which Stephen Daedalus was to borrow from Aquinas to define his own, similar idealisms, the beautiful woman is 'a light from some other world, the idea of which the matter was but the shadow, the reality of which it was but the symbol'.[3] It seems then no coincidence that Yeats deliberately equates perfect symbolism with melancholy beauty (p. 185), one example of which he admired in Rossetti's paintings:

> Woman herself was still in our eyes . . . romantic and mysterious, still the priestess of her shrine, our emotions remembering the *Lilith* and the *Sibylla Palmifera* of Rossetti . . . and how could life be ritual if woman had not her symbolic place?[4]

For the Pre-Raphaelites and their followers the symbolic part that woman played was to remind them of a *sens mystérieux de l'existence*.[5]

When Rossetti uses a beautiful woman in his painting as the symbol of his varying emotions, he sometimes achieves a balance between her physical presence and the states of his soul she reveals; at other times he insists so much upon the woman's actual physical existence that she fails to suggest any spiritual meaning. The problem he faces is the difficulty of achieving the necessary 'fusion binding infinite and romantic associations to a

---

[1] *Studies in Seven Arts*, p. 90.

[2] See O. Doughty, 'Rossetti's Conception of the "Poetic" in Poetry and Painting', *Essays by Divers Hands*, XXVI (1953).

[3] *A Portrait of the Artist as a Young Man* (*Portable James Joyce*, The Viking Press, New York 1959), p. 479.

[4] *Autobiographies*, p. 302.

[5] The phrase is again Mallarmé's: see Michaud, *La Doctrine Symboliste* (*Documents*), p. 15.

limited object', of giving shape 'to a chaos of fleeting intuitions and psychic forces, lending them focus and direction'.[1] He confronts exactly the same problems in his poetry.

As the third chapter showed, the sonnets of *The House of Life* echo with transient and half-defined states of feeling—'wild images of Death, / Shadows and shoals that edge eternity' (XLI). Rossetti seems glad to lose himself in some great ulterior drama, where casual phenomena are keys to unknown places of the spirit, where 'sky-breadth and field-silence and this day / Are symbols also in some deeper way' (LXXIV). The clues which we seize in our interpretation are just those casual phenomena, and when they are missing or confused interpretation becomes precarious, as for instance in 'The Monochord' (LXXIX) or 'Heart's Hope' (V). The obscurity of the sequence is due to the poetic task Rossetti set himself—a visionary perception of the mysteries that lie at the heart of life. As Yeats said of Blake, 'he spoke of things for whose speaking he could find no models in the world he knew'.

Rossetti's best moments are when he does find models in the world he knew and where his Pre-Raphaelite fidelity to natural detail can be used to endow phenomena with precision as well as tremulous symbolic meaning. An excellent example is the lyric, 'The Woodspurge', or the use of dead leaves in

> How then should sound upon Life's darkening slope
> The ground-whirl of the perished leaves of Hope
> The wind of Death's imperishable wing? (IV)

or the visual image which suggests flawless peace in 'Silent Noon'—

> Deep in the sun-searched growths the dragon-fly
> Hangs like a blue thread loosened from the sky:—
> So this wing'd hour is dropt to us from above.
> Oh! clasp we to our hearts, for dauntless dower,
> This close-companioned inarticulate hour
> When two-fold silence was the song of love. (XIX)

[1] These phrases are from Professor Wilson Knight's definition of a symbol, *The Christian Renaissance* (revised American edition, New York 1962), p. 23.

or the bitterness of dead hope conveyed by the admonition—

> Nor stay till on the year's last lily-stem
> The white cup shrivels round the golden heart. (LXXXIII)

At times he is too deliberate about endowing a limited object with infinite and romantic associations, as in 'Sunset Wings' or 'Downstream'. He wrote to his mother about the latter poem that 'I doubt not you will note . . . the intention to make the first half of each verse, expressing the landscape, tally with the second, expressing the emotion, even to the repetition of phrases.'[1] He can occasionally use the device exceptionally crudely—

> Yet, Jenny, looking long at you,
> The woman almost fades from view.
> A cipher of man's changeless sum
> Of lust, past, present, and to come
> Is left . . .

But he can frequently avoid such conscientious and clumsy symbols. At his best they are still sharp and yet evocative. There is the image of Jenny's remorse—

> Round the long park, across the bridge,
> The cold lamps at the pavement's edge
> Wind on together and apart,
> A fiery serpent for your heart;

or that of lust, 'like a toad within a stone'; or Helen's breasts in 'Troy Town'—

> The sun and moon of the heart's desire:
> All Love's lordship lay between.

Rossetti's poetry is symbolic in a further way than its use of some object to provide an analogue to the 'certain secret thing he had to tell' (XLIX). He was sometimes unable to find models in the world he knew for the visions at the depths of his soul; then he is forced into more suggestive and shadowy images, like those of the sixty-second sonnet. But even these at their best offset complete vagueness with some sort of definition.

[1] *Letters*, III, 976.

> Then shalt thou see me smile, and turn apart
> Thy visage to mine ambush at thy heart
> Sleepless with cold commemorative eyes; (XCVII)

here 'ambush' allows the magnificent image of remorseful nostalgia to grip us by its brief concrete allusion. Similarly, the familiar image of a building by the sea clarifies without constricting the symbolic abstractions in 'The Dark Glass':

> Shall birth and death, and all dark names that be
> As doors and windows barred to some loud sea,
> Lash deaf mine ears and blind my face with spray.
>   (XXXIV)

Christina Rossetti's poetry also offers examples of symbolist vision. Her symbolism is both of the sort Yeats called 'traditional', like the lilies and roses by the Princess's head in 'The Prince's Progress', and a more subtle kind, as in 'An Old-World Thicket' (p. 64), where the beauty of the first view and the final sunset are visions of happiness and ultimate bliss for the poet. In his reminiscences of her Watts-Dunton wrote of the 'apprehension of the Noumenon underlying the phenomenon as evidenced by all her poetry'.[1] Her 'Birds of Paradise' (p. 242)—originally called 'Paradise in a Symbol'—describes the birds in such a way that they assume a significance above and beyond that explicitly assigned to them. Similarly in 'A Triad' (p. 329) the three women in love are presented by their physical appearances which serve to suggest the hidden aspects of their characters and emotions. Some of her earliest attempts at poetry reveal considerable symbolic power. In 'The Dead City', which her grandfather first printed for her privately in 1847, she asks 'What was I that I should see / So much hidden mystery?' (p. 103). Her most famous poems use parable and allegory to reveal hidden mysteries, as in 'Uphill' (p. 339) or 'Shut Out' (p. 320), or personification, as in 'The World' (p. 182). Less dream-like than her brother and usually less suggestive, she nevertheless recognizes the double existence of things which Lionel Johnson later saw as the tendency of English symbolism:

In English, *symbolisme* and its literature mean this: a recognition, in

---

[1] *The Nineteenth Century* (February 1895), p. 363.

things, of a double existence: their existence in nature, and their existence in mind . . . So, literature is the evocation of truth from the passing show of things . . . (*HH*. VI, 64)

IV

The Pre-Raphaelite movement's taste for a symbolist function for its imagination is confirmed by three writers in the middle of the second half of the century. Simeon Solomon, Swinburne and Walter Pater all acknowledged earlier Pre-Raphaelite efforts and drew upon them for their own symbolism.

Solomon's *A Vision of Love Revealed in Sleep* (1871) obviously owes much to other Pre-Raphaelites. His vague personifications come direct from *The House of Life*: Memory, sitting on grey sands by the sea and bearing on her head 'a light rain of faded autumn leaves' (p. 3), presides over Solomon's work as she does over Rossetti's. From the sonnets as well as from 'Hand and Soul' come Solomon's dream-wrapt visions, the 'mystical agony' (p. 7), the figure of the man whose 'lips trembled with the weight of myriads of visions he called forth' (p. 21). On the second page, after seeing the nude figure whom he recognizes as his soul, Solomon realizes that 'the visible images of those things which we know only by name were about to be manifested unto me', a sentence which refers adequately to parts of *The House of Life*. From Morris is borrowed the scenery of a symbolic landscape— 'we passed along a pleasant land that lay beneath the light of a great content' (p. 26)—as well as the faintly archaic vocabulary and lilt of the language. While Swinburne's influence is perhaps seen in the cloying and incantatory texture of the style, the tremulous generalities, a fascination for the sea, or the rich décor: '[he] clothed me with a vestment in colour like the heart of an opal, and over my left shoulder he laid a stole tinted like a flame seen through water'. The tone and rhythm of that sentence in particular are a remarkable anticipation of Wilde's *Salomé*.

Swinburne saw in Solomon's prose poem 'the mystery of all beauty',[1] where old forms rise again under his hand with 'the

---

[1] Swinburne's essay on Solomon is in *The Bibelot* XIV (Maine 1908). All references are to this edition.

shadow of a new sense, the hint of a new meaning'; 'they know of something beyond form and outside speech' (p. 294). This critical adulation is couched in language close to that used by Yeats and Symons in their definitions of symbolism.[1]

Pater's talent is of course superior to Solomon's and his work demonstrates a greater attachment to fact, to some reality by which the noumena may be delineated. Much of it traces in the phenomena of art or real life already existing cyphers which reveal the au-delà, the soul of things. In this search one can take as Pater's own method what he describes as Florian Deleal's 'instinctive . . . . way of receiving the world':

> that sensible vehicle or occasion became, perhaps only too surely, the necessary concomitant of any perception of things, real enough to be of any weight or reckoning, in his house of thought . . . a protest in favour of real men and women against mere grey, unreal abstractions; and he remembered gratefully how the Christian religion, hardly less than the religion of the ancient Greeks, [translates] so much of its spiritual verity into things that may be seen. . . .[2]

And Pater praises Rossetti for letting matter and spirit play inextricably into each other:

> if the spiritual attains the definite visibility of a crystal, what is material loses its earthiness and impurity. . . . Like Dante, he knows no region of spirit which shall not be sensuous also, or material.[3]

He praises Rossetti's 'delight in concrete definition' and the 'really imaginative vividness, namely, of his personifications' (p. 208). He stresses Rossetti's love of detail and his 'subtle and fine . . . imaginative hold upon all the secret ways of sleep and

---

[1] Compare further such phrases of Swinburne's as 'the graceful mysticism of a symbolic rhapsody in prose' (p. 295), 'music made visible' (p. 309), 'the subtleties and harmonies of suggestion' (p. 311), 'the Hebrew love of dim vast atmosphere and infinite spiritual range without foothold on earth or resting place in nature' (p. 301) and 'the spirit that watches in the depth of its crystal sphere the mutable reflections of the world' (p. 300). Solomon dabbled in Jewish mysticism, which Swinburne presumably recognizes in these remarks.

[2] 'The Child in the House', *Miscellaneous Studies* (1923), pp. 186–7.

[3] *Appreciations* (1913), p. 212. All further references by Pater to Rossetti are to this book and edition.

dreams' (p. 210). He sees in him 'some revival of the old mytho-pœic age' (p. 210) and the 'remote and mystic' use of his talent for pictorial description (p. 211). For Pater obviously the great attraction of Rossetti was that, because life was a crisis for him at every moment, the intensity of such crises sustained an 'impressibility towards the mysterious conditions of man's everyday life, towards the very mystery itself in it . . .' (p. 211). Rossetti was one who gave to 'art a new order of phenomena, in the creation of a new ideal' (p. 218). In such remarks as these Pater's enthusiasm takes on emphases and tones which anticipate Yeats's references to symbolism.[1] Later Rossetti is called the 'Interpreter' of his *House of Life* (p. 214), this time looking forward to Mallarmé's poet who was the *déchriffreur de l'univers*. Pater concludes his essay by acknowledging Rossetti's revelation of 'the ideal aspect of common things' and his 'imaginative creation of things that are ideal from their very birth' (p. 218).

The similarity between the visions of Pater and Rossetti can nowhere more interestingly be seen than in their interpretations of Giorgione. The sonnet for *A Venetian Pastoral* (I, 345) is an attempt to explain the significance of the silence which the picture presents. As in 'Silent Noon' (I, 186), where the 'inarticulate hour' makes visible the lovers' passion, the silent heat in Giorgione's painting reveals the *au-delà*. The phrase, 'brink of day', suggests the boundaries of reality as much as of evening. The silent essence of the picture is twice defined—first, as 'Sad with the whole of pleasure', and, second, as 'Life touching lips with Immortality'. After Pater's remark about Rossetti's revelation of the ideal aspect of things, the abstractions of that last line are particularly interesting. The line had originally read 'Silence of heat and solemn poetry', when the poem appeared in *The Germ*. The alteration indicates, I think, Rossetti's increased awareness

---

[1] In his Leonardo essay in *The Renaissance*, for instance, certain phrases recall Yeats: compare Leonardo's 'aiming at an impossible effect' (p. 117) with Yeats's comments on giving a body to something that moves beyond the senses; Leonardo's art of 'going deep, of tracking the sources of expression to their subtlest retreats' (p. 107), with the other's 'visions of truth in the depths of the mind'; or Pater's very Yeatsian praise of Leonardo for being 'clairvoyant of occult gifts in common or uncommon things' (p. 111).

of those invisible essences for which he was searching and his confidence in handling them.

Pater's essay on 'The School of Giorgione' makes an explicit reference to Rossetti's sonnet,[1] and his criticism is a close elaboration of the poet's interpretation. What Rossetti called the silent heat at brink of day Pater terms 'exquisite pauses in time, in which, arrested thus, we seem to be spectators of all the fulness of existence, and which are like some *consummate extract or quintessence of life*'.[2] Productions of the Giorgionesque school, says Pater, are painted poems of the sort 'which tells itself without an articulated story' (pp. 155–6). The inarticulate story is defined in terms which could apply to Rossetti's poetry as well:

profoundly significant and animated instants, a mere gesture, a look, a smile, perhaps—some brief and wholly concrete moment—into which, however, all the motives, all the interests and effects of a long history, have condensed themselves . . . (p. 156)

Both writers could also be described in the phrase Pater used of Pascal: they possessed a 'peculiar intuition of a world, prospective, or discovered below the faulty conditions of the present, in either case changed somewhat from the actual world'.[3]

Pater's position in the Pre-Raphaelite movement was considerably strengthened by his dual role as critic and original writer, for in his work are linked the interest in general discussions which were to be popular at the century's end as well as the creative talent which gave the Pre-Raphaelite movement its impetus. The latter may be seen in such a piece as 'The Child in the House', the critical interests in his essay on Botticelli. The symbolist tendency of both is the same.

Florian Deleal acquired a religious fervour based on a strange ability to see significance or symbolism in ordinary events. For him 'the acts and accidents of daily life borrowed a sacred colour and significance' (op. cit., p. 195). This rarified spiritual existence,

[1] *The Renaissance*, p. 151.
[2] Ibid., pp. 156–7, my italics. Symons quotes a similar passage which Pater omitted from his reprinted Giorgione essay in which he wrote of 'some messenger from the real soul of things' (*Walter Pater, a study*, p. 29).
[3] *Appreciations*, pp. 8–9.

this 'scheme of some higher and more consistent harmony' (p. 194), satisfied his 'mystical appetite for sacred things' (p. 193). Religion, in effect, was an ideal, transcendent representation of the familiar incidents of human life. Similarly, in Botticelli's religious paintings Pater finds 'an undercurrent of original sentiment, which touches you as the real matter of the picture through the veil of its ostensible subject' (op. cit., p. 53). Even in non-religious subjects Botticelli's 'alert sense of outward things' subserves his visionary purpose, which 'usurps the data before it as the exponent of ideas, moods, visions of its own' (pp. 55–6).

Pater's own apprehension of noumena is usually controlled and directed through his sense of outward things. His admiration for both Winckelmann and Michelangelo is important, because between them they provide examples of the two parts of the total vision which seems to constitute Pater's symbolism: Michelangelo's fascination for extra-phenomenal visions, and Winckelmann's love of finite images. For Michelangelo the world of natural things has almost no existence (p. 76). But Winckelmann, although withdrawn into a region of ideals (p. 186), possesses the talent of escaping 'from abstract theory, to intuition, to the exercise of sight and sound' (p. 194). Winckelmann learnt to concentrate upon the phenomenal world without losing touch with its supra-phenomenal implications; for him the Venus de Milo is 'in no sense a symbol . . . the mind begins and ends with the finite image, yet loses no part of the spiritual motive' (p. 217). Michelangelo, on the other hand, who believes in dreams and omens (p. 81), concentrates in his figures of *Night, Day, Twilight* and *Dawn* 'those vague fancies, misgivings, presentiments, which shift and mix and define themselves and fade again . . .' (p. 98). He always presses beyond the outward to apprehend the unseen and abstract form of beauty (p. 90); his sonnets are characterized by a

dreamy atmosphere in which men have things as they will, because the hold of all outward things upon them is faint and thin . . .

The sonnets represent a

lifelong effort to tranquillize his vehement emotions by withdrawing them into the region of ideal sentiment. (p. 88)

V

In France it was as late as 1891 that Mallarmé produced his famous *dictum* that 'Nommer un objet, c'est supprimer les trois quarts de la jouissance du poème qui est faite de deviner peu à peu.'[1] In England, on the other hand, such a theory seems to have been accepted as an unacknowledged principle for most of the Pre-Raphaelite movement. An increasingly prominent aspect of the symbolism I have been discussing is its tendency towards vagueness, its reliance, even, upon mere patterns of sound by which to articulate its insights. Imprecision and 'attenuation of detail', which Pater notices as characteristically modern,[2] are closely linked to a reliance upon 'music' to communicate symbolist vision. Yeats seems to suggest this, writing in *The Dome*, when he saw that 'Pattern and rhythm are the road to open symbolism, and the arts have already become full of pattern and rhythm' (I, 234). No discussion of the English contribution to a wider symbolist movement can ignore its ideas about music in the non-musical arts; these in turn involve an account of its addiction to vagueness.

It is possible to distinguish between a vagueness which is necessary and unavoidable and one which seems deliberately cultivated as an easy alternative to conscientious artistry. Indeed, there is a well-defined element in Victorian literature which invokes imprecision and suggestion to articulate an otherwise frustrated vision: 'language, even when it fails to state or describe, has a legitimate emotive power if it operates not independently, in a beautiful but empty mist, but by re-directing our attention to objects.'[3] The danger was that it is easy for a minor talent like Solomon, for example, to slip into beautiful and empty mists. His *Vision* lacks the sense of urgency and immediacy which Rossetti sometimes conveys in *The House of Life*, and he relied too heavily upon obscure, emotional abstractions: in Swinburne's words—'the latent relations of pain and pleasure, the subtle conspiracies of good and evil, the deep alliances of death and life,

---

[1] *Oeuvres Complètes*, p. 869.   [2] *The Renaissance*, p. 222.
[3] J. Holloway, *The Victorian Sage* (1953), p. 52.

of love and hate, of attraction and abhorrence'.[1] Solomon himself talked of *visible images* of things known only by name. But as Swinburne notices and extravagantly praises, Solomon usually refuses to be hampered by the phenomenal world and the control of the will.

The danger is only a little less obvious with some of Morris's prose romances. They provoke the same need to distinguish between a reluctant use of suggestion, viable nevertheless, because nothing concrete or definite lies to hand, and a reliance upon it as an easy means to symbolic resonance. As has already been shown, *The Hollow Land* can compel our attention by its careful control of suggestion. Its ending provides a good example:

Through the golden streets under the purple shadows of the houses we went, and the slow fanning backward and forward of the many-coloured banners cooled us. . . . We stopped before the gates and trembled, and clasped each other closer; for there, among the marble leafage and tendrils that were round and under and over the archway that held the golden valves, were wrought two figures of a man and woman winged and garlanded, whose raiment flashed with stars; and their faces were like faces we had seen or half seen in some dream long and long and long ago, so that we trembled with awe and delight. And I turned, and seeing Margaret, saw that her face was that face seen or half seen long and long and long ago; and in the shining of her eyes I saw that other face, seen in that way and no other, long and long and long ago—my face. And then we walked together towards the golden gates, and opened them; and no man gainsaid us. And before us lay a great space of flowers.

Rossetti's poetry at its best has this same sense of tremulous meaning. In his sonnet for 'Our Lady of the Rocks' he contrives a nervous balance between what Pater called an 'exaggerated inwardness' and some need for definition:

Mother, is this the darkness of the end,
    The Shadow of Death? and is that outer sea
    Infinite imminent Eternity?
And does the death-pang by man's seed sustained
In Time's each instant cause thy face to bend
    Its silent prayer upon the Son, while He

[1] Op. cit., p. 311.

Blesses the dead with His hand silently
To His long day which hours no more offend.

Mother of grace, the pass is difficult,
    Keen as these rocks, and the bewildered souls
        Throng it like echoes, blindly shuddering through.
Thy name, O Lord, each spirit's voice extols,
    Whose peace abides in the dark avenue
        Amid the bitterness of things occult. (I, 344)

The concrete details of the painted landscape become symbols in his response to the picture and control what might otherwise become mere atmosphere. Yet mood and atmosphere in the poem are skilfully handled through the 'open' and hesitant rhythms of the octet and the difficult progress through the short phrases of the sestet towards the evocative, but shadowy, satisfaction of the last two lines' smoother rhythm, where 'peace' and 'bitterness' are drawn ambiguously together.

Rossetti's symbolism is vague only for lack of precise cyphers in the real world; usually he is quite capable of offering some definition by means of a limited object. He would probably have been puzzled by Addington Symonds's remark that by its very vagueness description acquires 'a power of suggestion', or by Symons's notion that art is never statement, always evocation.[1] Rossetti criticizes Keats for the phrase, 'kisses four', in 'La Belle Dame Sans Merci', because it provided 'a suggestiveness of under-meaning which is no gain'.[2] Yet he is himself often guilty of just such hinted significances in 'The Blessed Damozel', for example, with her seven stars and three lilies. A greater reliance upon such effects is found in other members of the Pre-Raphaelite movement.

If Rossetti confines himself to the interpretation of Giorgione's silence as 'Life touching lips with Immortality', Pater committed himself only to 'some consummate extract or quintessence of life'. For him it is always *some* form, *some* tone in the hills, *some* mood of passion or insight. Rossetti tried to define his visions with sharper details and personifications, but Pater omits his

---

[1] *In the Key of Blue*, p. 16, and *Studies in Seven Arts*, pp. 95–6.
[2] D. G. Rossetti, *John Keats. Criticism and Comment* (Privately printed London 1919), see third letter.

abstractions and practises that 'attenuation of detail' already mentioned. He seems too complacent about Rossetti's 'predilection for minor tones' or Angelico's 'over-charged symbols, a means of *hinting* at an idea which *art cannot adequately express*, which still remains in the world of shadows'.[1] He himself is often seduced by similar shadows and minor tones. But it is not only that his symbolism is weakened by its vagueness, but it seems, in fact, as if vagueness *is* the symbolic method.

In his famous Gioconda passage the effect is based upon a calculated vagueness and a tenuous hold upon definite ideas. He says that Leonardo uses the subjects of his pictures as 'a symbolic language for his own fancies' (p. 128), which is what Pater also does. For neither of them is the picture 'crude symbolism' and the reason for this, although not expressed in these terms, is its vague suggestiveness. The smile is *unfathomable*, the presence beside the waters expressive of 'what in the ways of a thousand years men had come to desire' (p. 129). To the weariness of such a generality are added the *frissons* of equally 'strange thoughts', 'fantastic reveries and exquisite passions'. The grave, the deep seas and Eastern mysteries offer no further clues to her actual meaning. She 'might stand', Pater vaguely concludes, as 'the symbol of the modern idea' (p. 130). We are left, as I imagine was intended, to project our own fantasies into a symbolic language which Leonardo (*apud* Pater) leaves conveniently open. Pater admits as much about another Leonardo, the *Saint John the Baptist*, 'whose treacherous smile would have us understand something far beyond the outward gesture or circumstance' (p. 122); that something is explained only as the 'starting-point of a train of sentiment, as subtle and vague as a piece of music' (p. 123).

Pater occupies a crucial place in Pre-Raphaelite symbolism precisely because he connects music with the vagueness endemic to noumenous vision and because he recognized a symbolist imagination at work in earlier Pre-Raphaelites. He praised the *music* of Rossetti's poetry (op. cit., p. 47) and so alerts us to how sound and rhythm contribute to the total impact. But Rossetti

[1] *The Renaissance*, pp. 62 and 216, my italics.

himself also draws upon explicitly musical images to communicate
the mysteries of life:

> The music lives upon my brain
> Between your hands within mine eyes;
> It stirs your lifted throat like pain,
> An aching pulse of melodies.
> Lean nearer, let the music pause:
> The soul may better understand
> Your music, shadowed in your hand,
> Now while the song withdraws. (I, 253)

> those that haunt
> The vale of magical dark mysteries
> Where to the hills her poet's foot-track lies
> And wisdom's living fountain to his chaunt
> Trembles in music? (I, 299)

The second of these, although implying a precise statement, is
essentially vague and its vagueness is supported by incantatory
rhythms and a soft alliteration of 's' sounds.

A special technique which Swinburne shares with Rossetti is
to let his fancy play upon a striking concept and weave it into
an elaborate pattern. He provides, more obviously than Rossetti,
an example of music which seeks to suggest the *au-delà* by an
accumulation of harmonies. The passage about Iseult in 'The
Sailing of the Swallow' shows, like Rossetti's women, that the
face is a cypher of her soul; but, as the passage proceeds, the
evocation of her soul becomes less and less distinct among the
impressionistic kaleidoscope of images:

> Her gaze was glad past love's own singing of,
> And her face lovely past desire of love.
> Past thought and speech her maiden motions were,
> And a more golden sunrise was her hair.
> The very veil of her bright flesh was made 5
> As of light woven and moonbeam-coloured shade
> More fine than moonbeams; white her eyelids shone
> As snow sun-stricken that endures the sun,
> And through their curled and coloured clouds of deep
> Luminous lashes thick as dreams in sleep 10

Shone as the sea's depth swallowing up the sky's
The springs of unimaginable eyes.
As the wave's subtler emerald is pierced through
With the utmost heaven's inextricable blue,
And both are woven and molten in one sleight   15
Of amorous colour and implicated light
Under the golden guard and gaze of noon,
So glowed their awless amorous plenilune,
Azure and gold and ardent grey, made strange
With fiery difference and deep interchange   20
Inexplicable of glories multiform;
Now as the sullen sapphire swells toward storm
Foamless, their bitter beauty grew acold,
And now afire with ardour of fine gold.[1]   24

Precise description of Iseult's eyes (l. 7) is lost in the reverie of
the seventeen lines that follow. That they are 'unimaginable' (l. 12)
and 'inexplicable' (l. 21) in the first place seems the greater reason
to imagine explanations of them; yet the final effect is that we are
led away from the object of the passage, Iseult, into a rich vision
of evocation and musical suggestiveness. This is achieved mainly
by Swinburne's refusal to let an object be itself: superlatives out-
bid superlatives (ll. 1–2, 6–7 and 14), and explanations are explained to redundancy (ll. 8 and 10). When the passage draws to
a close in the calmer, less breathless rhythms of the last three
lines, our impression of Iseult is far from precise.

Swinburne frequently ignores or bypasses specific phenomena
and produces the reverberant generalities of 'Dolores', which he
himself described as a 'transient state of spirit' and 'so distinctly
symbolic and fanciful'.[2] The cumulative effect of his cadences in
'A Forsaken Garden' or the choric tribute to love in *Atalanta in
Calydon* would have been an impressive example of poetry's
music to later poets. Symons, certainly, was well aware of it
when he defended Swinburne's poems as 'harmonies' and said
that 'his record of things is *clouded over* with shining words'.[3]

Of earlier Pre-Raphaelites, Rossetti's and Swinburne's were,

---

[1] IV, 13–14: the numbering of the lines is my own.
[2] *Notes on Poems and Reviews* (1866), p. 12.
[3] *Figures of Several Centuries*, pp. 182 and 161, my italics.

then, the most emphatic examples of musical suggestion in symbolist writing. But the *Oxford and Cambridge Magazine* and the poetry of Christina Rossetti could also claim to have set some precedence for this particular aspect of symbolism. Christina, convinced as she was of the transience of all earthly things, was particularly prone to suggest this insubstantiality in her poetry. Consequently she relies upon nuance and musical cadence, in which she comes, of the English writers we have considered, closest to Verlaine:

> let a distant stream
> Of music lull me, languid as a dream,
> Soft as the whisper of a summer sea . . . (p. 293)

> A perfect sunlight
> On rustling forest tips;
> Or perfect moonlight
> Upon a rippling stream;
> Or perfect silence,
> Or song of cherished lips. (p. 312)

> She sat and sang alway
> By the green margin of a stream,
> Watching the fishes leap and play
> Beneath the glad sunbeam. (p. 290)

Equally musical and impressionistic is her evocation of the magic sea-scape of 'Sleep at Sea' (pp. 154–6), or of dream worlds where castles stand 'of white transparent glass / Glittering and frail with many a fretted spire' (p. 21). Even in her allegorical poems the precision of the parable is not maintained: the milk-maid in 'The Prince's Progress', with her green eyes, has the allure of a siren and, because of the snake image, the suggestion of Eve's witching power. In much of her poetry she is concerned with spiritual life beyond everyday circumstance and this is best invoked by imprecise suggestion, by such visionary, dream-like moments as that noted in *Speaking Likenesses*:

. . . in one moment the sky before her flashed with glittering gold, and flushed from horizon to zenith with a rosy glow; for the northern lights came out, and lit up each cloud as if it held lightning, and each hill as if it smouldered ready to burst into a volcano. Every oak-tree seemed turned to coral, and the road itself to a pavement of dusky carnelian.[1]

The *Magazine* of 1856 printed three articles on Tennyson which saw him as a great example of the poet as musician; the free, spontaneous flow of music characterizes his poetry, and his songs are music without notes. This was exactly the emphasis of Todhunter's dirge for Tennyson's burial which insists upon the music of the Laureate's poetry (*R*. II, 1–2). Further instances of the *Magazine's* inclination towards musical suggestion and vagueness are the impressionistic recreations of architecture. Morris's vision of Amiens is contrived to a large extent by the sound of the prose. The cathedral

rises up from the ground, grey from the paving of the street, the cavernous porches of the west front opening wide, and *marvellous with the shadows* of the carving you can only *guess at*; and above stand the kings, and above that you would see the twined *mystery* of the great flamboyant rose window with its thousand openings, and the *shadows* of the flower-work carved round it, then the grey tombs and gable, grey against the blue of the August sky, and behind them all, rising high into the *quivering* air, the tall spire over the crossing (p. 100, my italics)

In the musical imprecisions of the suggestion Morris comes close to the quality and tone of Pater's prose, especially a piece like 'Vézelay'.[2] Pater's contribution to this aspect of symbolism was decisive, for his essays perpetually use music to explain a symbolist vision in other arts. Leonardo's *St John the Baptist* starts 'a train of sentiment, as subtle and vague as a piece of music'; the Venetian painters use actual details of their native landscapes 'but as notes of a music which duly accompanies the presence of men and women, presenting us with the spirit or essence only of a certain sort of landscape—a country of the pure reason or half-imaginative memory'.[3] If he does not always

---

[1] *Speaking Likenesses* (1874), p. 94.
[2] In *Miscellaneous Studies*.
[3] *The Renaissance*, p. 142.

refer to music, his own prose takes on a musical quality, which may again be described in the terms that he uses of Florian Deleal:

So he yielded himself to these things, to be played upon by them like a musical instrument, and began to note with deepening watchfulness, but always with some puzzled, unutterable longing in his enjoyment, the phases of the seasons and of the growing or waning day, down even to the shadowy changes wrought on bare walls or ceiling—the light cast up from the snow, bringing out their darkest angles; the brown light in the cloud . . . the protracted light of the lengthening day . . . that beam of June sunshine . . . a way of gold-dust across the darkness . . . (op. cit., pp. 161–2)

This same watchfulness of the changing aspect of life and the attempt to catch its every modulation produce a style nervous in its control and characterized by the quality Pater identified in aesthetic poetry—'continual suggestion, pensive or persuasive, of the shortness of life' (op. cit., p. 227). Some of the best of Pater has that quality. When he regards Watteau's *Noblesse*, he finds himself involuntarily anticipating the coming rain:

The storm is always brooding through the massy splendour of the trees, above those sun-dried glades or lawns, where delicate children may be trusted thinly clad; and the secular trees themselves will hardly outlast another generation.[1]

Pater is able to suggest this transience with the same 'tact of omission' he praises in Watteau (p. 2) and the cadences of the prose have a consequently musical effect:

A sudden light transfigures a trivial thing, a weather-vane, a windmill, a winnowing flail, the dust in the barn door: a moment—and the thing has vanished, because it was pure effect; but it leaves a relish behind it, a longing that the accident may happen again.[2]

But not only is Pater master of his own music. He crystallizes another aspect of symbolism in the elaboration of his theory that 'All art constantly aspires towards the condition of music'.[3] The theory is based upon this notion that the arts

---

[1] *Imaginary Portraits* (1887), p. 34.   [2] *The Renaissance*, p. 185.
[3] *The Renaissance*, p. 141. The quotations in the discussion that follows are either from this essay on Giorgione or from that on Winckelmann.

correspond to a series of developments in the human mind. Thus architecture, 'which begins in a practical need, can only express by vague hint or symbol the spirit or mind of the artist'. Spiritual qualities only 'lurk' about architecture as 'volatile effects'. Sculpture like the *Venus de Milo* lends itself to a mind not unduly self-analytic, but which recognizes in finite form something of spiritual motive. It is an 'ideal art', because thought is exactly accommodated to the 'proper range of its sensible embodiment' and the spirituality 'takes up the whole given material, and penetrates it with an imaginative motive'. It is reserved to the complex modern movement to find its appropriate dialect in painting, poetry and music. Unlike sculpture, the spirituality and exaggerated inwardness of these modern arts need 'the utmost attenuation of detail' in order to translate 'every delicacy of thought and feeling, incidental to a consciousness brooding with delight over itself'.

Music becomes Pater's ideal modern art because it successfully evades the mere intelligence. In painting and in poetry we are reminded either of things—the starkly limited phenomena represented—or of concepts, both of which have a life and activity outside their artistic articulation. The best poetry and painting suppress mere subject, whether visual or conceptual. In lyric poetry we are least able to separate matter from form and it is thus the highest kind of poetry:[1]

And the very perfection of such poetry often appears to depend, in part, on a certain suppression or vagueness of mere subject, so that the meaning reaches us through ways not distinctly traceable by the understanding.

Similarly Venetian landscape paintings burden themselves little with precise details of the scenery. Music alone evades the bondage of the 'mere intelligence'. It realizes the perfect identification of matter and form and in

its consummate moments, the end is not distinct from the means, the form from the matter, the subject from the expression.

[1] George Moore was later to follow up this suggestion of Pater's by producing his anthology of *Pure Poetry* in 1924; see his introduction especially.

It is the chief function of the aesthetic critic, according to Pater, to estimate the degree to which each work of art approximates to this musical success.

Pater's theoretical encouragement for the arts' evasion of conceptual or merely descriptive language was congenial to the symbolist imagination of the Pre-Raphaelites, especially as it was confirmed by his own mode of vision and his own interpretations of other arts. His insistence on music as the most perfect dialect for the modern imagination made explicit what in the Pre-Raphaelites had been frequently assumed and practised. It also offered to a later figure like Yeats as thoughtful and persuasive an example as he could find among French symbolists.

To the major examples of symbolism among Pre-Raphaelites —to Rossetti, Swinburne and Pater—many French and English writers later looked. If the 1890's were attracted by Verlaine's advice—'rien que la nuance' and 'de la musique avant toute chose'— Verlaine himself, it must be remembered, saw at least one painting of Rossetti's, *Monna Rosa*, as a musical composition.[1] Another later symbolist, de Wyzewa, thought Christina Rossetti's poems 'chantants' and in *Monna Innominata*, especially, some of the most musical verses in English.[2] Arthur Symons's discussions of various members of the Pre-Raphaelite movement all stress the musicality of their writing. He suggests that Swinburne 'sees musically', and that Rossetti 'with no passion for music as music . . . gives one as actual a sense of it in a stanza of *The Bride's Prelude* as in the fixed eyes of his portraits of women'. And he also emphasized how Pater appreciated 'a kind of music in the very nature of things' and explained how 'thought moves to music'.[3]

A critic in *The Dome* saw *The House of Life* as strenuous, exotic and impassioned music. He also writes that in

these days of the association of Music and Literature, one instinctively links Paderewski with Walter Pater . . . (II, 33)

[1] See chapter one, supra p. 10.
[2] 'Une Femme-Poète Anglaise: Christina Rossetti', *Revue des Deux Mondes* (15 December 1908), p. 927.
[3] *Figures of Several Centuries* (on Swinburne) p. 191 and (on Pater) p. 317; *Studies in Strange Souls* (on Rossetti), p. 7.

Paderewski's playing

thrills our jaded senses with a breath of the Primeval, and the Pre-Raphael and most especially the Oriental . . . (II, 36)

And in a sonnet on Giorgione which looks back to Rossetti and Pater, Gordon Bottomley explains that the music of the concert gives place to 'the golden voice of silence', thus inferring that music is a means to ultimate vision. Obviously the Pre-Raphaelites offered a precedent and a point of reference in a discussion of musicality in literature, and it is as much to their work as to the French that Yeats and Symons appeal when they advocate the merits of pure sound over denotative language.

Symons constantly celebrates 'an art of vague, more indeterminate form, of more wandering cadences', in which 'all but what is most essential in outward form, in intellectual substance' has been refined away.[1] The dangers of such an art are obvious. A means to symbolism can in fact become an end in itself. To minds susceptible to easy effects, parts of Rossetti's sonnet sequence, for example, or Pater's writing offer obvious technical devices which can be copied without bothering with any of the intellectual ideas they serve. In the passages on Du Bellay or on Florian's preoccupation with the sensuous elements in human knowledge the most easy and obvious aspects of Pater's imagination are the most striking: on Du Bellay, the 'sudden light' that 'transfigures a trivial thing', the delight in 'pure effect', the 'relish' and 'longing' that it leaves; on Florian's vision, the yielding, the music, the deepening watchfulness of the minute variations of change and shifting light. And a later theorist like Yeats encouraged mere technical effects by his authoritative pronouncements:

The poet of essences and pure ideas must seek in half-lights that glimmer from symbol to symbol as if to the ends of the earth, all that the epic and dramatic poet finds of mystery and shadow in the accidental circumstances of life. (p. 87)

Yeats is more convincing about symbolism when he theorizes than when he discusses specific examples.[2] It sounds seductive and

[1] *Dramatis Personae* (1925), pp. 346–7.

[2] For instance, Yeats's discussion of the 'moving' and 'subtle' symbols in Blake, Nash and *Timon of Athens* is vague and tenuous (*Essays*, p. 156).

potentially interesting when Yeats urges the use of words as subtle as the body of a flower or a woman. But the practical difficulties of expressing the unknown and the silent, of representing the invisible *au-delà*, are beyond most imaginations. One result is that much poetry in the 1890's *talked* about the symbolist method rather than *used* it. For example, Francis Thompson—

> Within her eyes' profound arcane
> Resides the glory of her dreams;
> Behind her secret cloud of hair.
> *She sees the Is beyond the Seems.*

or Lionel Johnson's 'Magic'—

> Because I work not, as logicians work,
> Who but to ranked and marshalled reason yield:
> But my feet hasten through a faery field,
> Thither, where underneath the rainbow lurk
> Spirits of youth, and life, and gold, concealed:
>   . . . my thoughts turn
> To thoughts and things of an eternal fashion:
>   The majesty and dignity
>   Of everlasting verity.[1]

When writers were forced back on practice rather than theoretical talk about their symbolism, the result was usually a vagueness achieved by exquisite technical manipulation. This is true of Yeats's early poems. Those which A. J. A. Symons included in his *Anthology of Nineties Verse* are full of pale thrones, far-off valleys, wharves of sorrow, forgotten beauties, sad Roses, shadowy pools and the continual presence of the meaningful sea. All are incantatory and decorative, but remarkably vague.

If Yeats was to discover that this symbolist aesthetic was insufficiently concrete and vigorous, few of the other nineties poets made the same discovery. The lures of symbolist poetry, as Yeats describes them (p. 163), attracted superficial and lazy minds who saw an opportunity to avoid the description of uncongenial phenomena and the telling of tales. Instead, symbolist verse proved

---

[1] *An Anthology of Nineties Verse*, ed. A. J. A. Symons (1928), p. 155, my italics, and p. 95.

an excuse for vague, indefinite figurings forth, full of suggestion
and contrived nuance, 'vague scribbling, in obscure, stuttering
verses'.[1] Such things as Symons's 'Faint Love'—

> Colours that faint; dim echo far above
> The crystal sound, and shadow beyond sight;[2]

or Nora Hopper's 'Lament of the Last Leprechaun' (*YB*. III,
158–9) with its self-conscious use of sibilants and a veritable
banquet of symbolic suggestions from 'the red shoon of the shee'
to the 'dishonoured whitethorn tree'. 'The Fields of Dream' by
I. K. Lloyd merely weaves various tenuous notions around its
title, talking of 'the bright symbols of this grass'.[3] While Victor
Plarr thought that to be Celtic was to have an inherent mastery
of the occult and the arts of symbolism.[4]

No wonder that Ezra Pound wished to disclaim all connection
with the movement, 'because symbolism has usually been associated with mushy technique'.[5] Inexact and 'soft terminology',
Pound notes, is one sign of literary ill-health. Seizing upon a
characteristic phrase of 1890's symbolism he fixes on the major
anxiety of the Pre-Raphaelite movement:

Don't use such an expression as 'dim lands of peace'. It dulls the
image. It mixes an abstraction with a concrete . . . it comes from
writers' not realizing that the natural object is always the adequate
symbol.[6]

Some Pre-Raphaelites like Rossetti tried to use for symbols such
natural objects as the woodspurge or a woman's face; Pater, too,
admired Winckelmann's love of finite images. But, as Pound
sharply reminds us, the inclination towards abstraction, towards
makeshift attempts at capturing some transcendent notion not
fully perceived[7], dominated English symbolism from early in the

---

[1] Zola's judgment on symbolist poetry quoted *A*. I, 41.

[2] *An Anthology of Nineties Verse*, p. 137.

[3] *The Acorn* (1906), II, 270.

[4] See *In the Dorian Mood*, p. 3. Cf. Yeats's claim that Blake's Irish ancestry
has much to do with his visionary gift, *The Works of William Blake*, I, 3.

[5] *Fortnightly Review*, XCVI (September 1914), pp. 461 ff.

[6] *Literary Essays* (1954), p. 5.

[7] See on this topic Hugh Kenner, *The Poetry of Ezra Pound*, p. 98.

Pre-Raphaelite movement; it gradually came to represent by itself the symbolist method.

Pound's strictures on mushy technique are almost certainly justified. What perhaps they fail to do is recognize the spiritual distress of many Victorian imaginations. Appalled by the mechanic and exterior world and yet sustained by no 'truth of eternal outlines', they were forced, as Pater was keenly aware, back upon relative insights, back into 'a world of fine gradations and subtly linked conventions, shifting intricately'.[1] From among these they constructed noumenous and shadowy visions as an antidote to a world of hard and uncongenial phenomena.

VI

The Victorian nostalgia for more substantial and authentic visions than those permitted by the contemporary relativist spirit may be seen at its most poignant in the Pre-Raphaelite enthusiasm for William Blake.[2] Interest in his work was fostered first by a group of early Pre-Raphaelite Brothers and continued mainly by two later members of the movement, Swinburne and Yeats. What they write about Blake tends to reveal their own spiritual and artistic anxieties rather than display particularly secure readings of Blake's work. Late nineteenth-century symbolism found in Blake's writings and engravings both actual precedence for their own visions and the opportunity to formulate theories out of their readings. Their sense of how Blake is relevant to their own endeavours

---

[1] 'Coleridge's Writings', *Westminster Review*, LXXV, p. 108.

[2] Alexander Gilchrist's *Life of Blake with Selections from his Poems and Other Writings* (2 volumes) was issued first in 1863. In it Mrs Gilchrist acknowledges the help received from the Rossetti brothers in completing the work: Dante Gabriel was responsible for most of the second volume, namely the selections from Blake's work and the short introductions to them; he also made some additions to chapter 32 and wrote a supplementary chapter (no. 39) from notes Gilchrist had left. William Michael provided the Annotated Catalogue of the paintings and drawings. The *Life* was issued again in 1880 and several short pieces added at the end of the second volume, of which the most important for my purposes is the 'Essay on Blake' by James Smetham. All references are to this second edition, referred to as 'Gilchrist'. Other Pre-Raphaelite contributions were Swinburne's *William Blake. A Critical Essay* (second edition 1868), and W. M. Rossetti's Aldine Edition of the *Poetical Works of Blake* (1874).

produces unique, sometimes wayward, emphases. Yet what they say of his symbolist vision is an interesting commentary upon their own imaginative procedures.

. Both the early Pre-Raphaelite fidelity to nature and the inclination to intense noumenous vision found confirmation in Blake. James Smetham's essay quotes:

> To see a world in a grain of sand,
> And a heaven in a wild flower,
> Hold infinity in the palm of your hand,
> And eternity in an hour. (Gilchrist, II, 342)

They are lines which doubtless appealed to the Pre-Raphaelite love of intensely observed and resonant natural detail, a faculty which both Christina and Dante Gabriel Rossetti reveal and which Ruskin encouraged in the movement from its start. Blake's ability to embody his ideals and reveal them through a solid body of external truths is what Smetham singles out in the work of this 'great idealist' (II. 311). Blake learnt very early to project every idea into the sphere of the actual and to believe in and endow his own unique visions with concrete existence (II, 316 and 313). Referring to Blake's vision of angels among the suburban rooftops, Smetham says he merely took the further step of allowing his fancy to become veracious fact: 'What he thought, he saw', and, 'All thought came with the clearness and veracity of vision' (II, 323). William Michael Rossetti in his introduction to the Aldine edition similarly notes Blake's creative ability of seeing 'the visual semblance of the visionary essence' (p. lxiii).

Generally W. M. Rossetti's language is more confident than that of writers in the Gilchrist edition and he emphasizes more explicitly Blake's symbolist imagination, linking it with Dante:

Rapt in a passionate yearning, he realized, even on this earth and in his mortal body, a species of *nirvana*: his whole faculty, his whole personality, the very essence of his mind and mould, attained to absorption into his ideal ultimate —into that which Dante's profound phrase designates 'il Ben dell'intelletto'. (p. xi)

For Blake the spiritual was reality and the physical illusion, and his intuition 'catches at the *meaning* of the things through their appearances' (p. lxxiv). In support W. M. Rossetti quotes Blake's own affirmation that there 'exist in that external world (of the imagination) the permanent realities of everything which we see reflected in this vegetable glass of nature' (p. lxxix).

The main difficulty these early commentators experienced was his obscurity, which they tended to link with his supposed madness. For all his skill and the concrete turn of his mind Blake, Smetham admits, is far from lucid. For those who can 'only comprehend thought fully and perfectly elaborated in outward expression' (II, 313) Blake will not be completely congenial. W. M. Rossetti finds the prophetic books 'dark and chaotic . . . ponderous and turbid . . . replete with uncouth and arbitrary nomenclature—hieroglyphics sometimes seemingly void of demotic equivalents' (p. lxxxi). Smetham explains his obviously uneasy response to Blake by calling him a 'madman of superb genius' (II, 334), as if the second quality would palliate the first. W. M. Rossetti, cautious as ever, invokes the old meaning of 'enthusiast' to explain the mental irregularities he finds. At the same time he senses, as later Yeats was to emphasize, that this madness had some real connection with Blake's 'splendid, terrible, and daring imagination'.[1]

The madness and obscurity both intrigue these early commentators and make them rather nervous. Their own embattled conviction that their imaginations were basically hostile to the rest of Victorian culture helps the Pre-Raphaelites to see Blake as a fellow spirit. For he articulates ideal visions beyond the commonplace and mechanical phenomena of the practical world. Above all, his imagination is a private one to which only a few select spirits have access:

He can never be popular in the ordinary sense of the word . . . simply because the region in which he lived was remote from the common concerns of life. (Gilchrist, II, 351)

Yet they are also often puzzled and defensive in their claims for him, perhaps because they are presenting him, really for the first

---

[1] See Yeats/Ellis, *The Works of William Blake*, I, 96. All future references, unless otherwise stated, will be to this edition.

time, to an age that would not find in him a particularly sympathetic imagination. D. G. Rossetti laments the 'obscurities and darker mental states' which mar the poetry of *Songs of Experience*. But it is precisely such elements, as we have seen, that distinguish his own sonnet sequence. He reveals himself more accurately in his resentment of the 'commonplaces of social discontent' that creep into *Songs of Experience* (II, 27).

Swinburne, as might be expected, is less cautious and nervous in his advocacy. For him Blake is a man 'beautifully unfit for walking in the way of any other man'; a man 'born and baptized into the church of rebels' (pp. 1–3). This is the church of art and poetry, which is 'in no wise given for the sustenance or the salvation of men in general, but reserved mainly for the sublime profit and intense pleasure of an elect' (p. 36). Blake, in fact, serves Swinburne as an aggressive example of the artist's distaste for Philistine culture and morality. He joins Baudelaire as champion of 'l'hérésie de l'enseignement' and Swinburne uses his ostensible concern with Blake as the basis for an extended harangue on the independence of art.[1]

Once Swinburne has established the exclusive cult to which both he and Blake appeal, he moves on to explain Blake's symbolist vision. His imaginative life was not concerned with our earthly and materialist one:

To him the veil of outer things seemed always to tremble with some breath behind it . . . Flowers and weeds, stars and stones, spoke with articulate lips and gazed with living eyes. Hands were stretched towards him from beyond the darkness of material nature. . . . To him all symbolic things were literal, all literal things symbolic. (p. 41)

Blake fights on the side of an imagination which apprehends the spirit against the 'understanding which dissects the body of a fact' (p. 97). He rejects induction, science and external opinion, as Yeats was to reject will and the bondage of exteriority. He works rather by 'instinct', addressing himself often to children in the hope that they would be enfranchised from pietism and materialism (p. 28).

[1] See pp. 85 ff. Blake is here invoked to support what would be by the end of the century a dominant protest of art's independence.

But Blake also presented obscurities to Swinburne. The best claim he can make for Blake is that 'if he spoke strangely, he had great things to speak' (p. 46). Normal rules of communication had to be abandoned in order to talk adequately of matters removed from orthodox articulation. His dialect, Swinburne notes, was 'too much the dialect of a far country' (p. 47). When Swinburne comes to the prophetic books the obscurity troubles him, with some reason, much more:

But in these books there is not the substantial coherence of form and reasonable unity of principle which bring within scope of apprehension even the wildest myths growing out of unconscious idealism and impulsive tradition. (p. 194)

Blake degenerates into 'mere music', 'harmonies . . . perhaps not even musical to other ears than his' (pp. 194–5). What is interesting is that Swinburne invokes musical metaphors. Further, although he seems to resent his own incomprehension, he is at the same time hospitable to the vagueness he thinks is endemic to Blake's vision. *The Book of Ahania*, for example, holds for Swinburne 'dim and great suggestions of something more than our analytic ingenuities can well unravel by this slow process of suggestion' (p. 250).

The great culmination and confirmation of this Pre-Raphaelite revival of interest in Blake was the three volume *Works of William Blake*, which Yeats produced jointly with Edwin John Ellis in 1893. The dominant note of this vast work is that Blake's art represents not the confused exuberances of an eccentric mind,[1] but both an 'eddy of that flood-tide of symbolism which attained its tide-mark in the magic of the Middle Ages' and a symptom of the modern imagination: for 'as the language of spiritual utterance ceases to be theological and becomes literary and poetical, the great truths have to be spoken afresh' (I, x–xi). Blake announces a new era when poets would be the leaders of the race against science and materialism. Yeats's two major hostilities are canvassed here. The scientist's perfect intelligibility of

[1] Yeats expresses a certain impatience with earlier critics over their attitudes to this and their inabilities to read the symbolism correctly: see pp. 44 and 53–4.

statement is a result of his not being forced by 'the essential obscurity of truth to wrap his utterance about with symbol and mystery' (I, 237), while the materialist sees only what belongs to his 'contracted consciousness' (I, 243). The deficiencies of both are made good by the saving grace of the imagination, which—as Swedenborg announced to Blake—illuminates the path towards 'the Unlimited in the world of Eternity' (I, 407).

It is obvious, even from this brief account of a complex and strangely neglected area of the Victorian consciousness, that the Pre-Raphaelite movement found general support in Blake for its own imaginative activities. Both for his inwardness and his symbolist vision they welcomed his example.

Yeats specifically connects Blake and the Pre-Raphaelites on more than one occasion. Blake, he notes, hated the stereotyped formalism of Raphael's followers just like the Brotherhood of 1848.[1] Yeats also points out that Blake valued correct drawing as the Pre-Raphaelites had done (II, 320). But at the same time he admits that Blake also shared their reluctance to let an artist's technical expertise thwart his originality and inspiration: against this tendency 'the "Pre-Raphaelite Brothers" fought by allowing error and finish to go hand in hand and to be excused if poetic intention could be found in them' (II, 307). Both Smetham and Yeats comment upon Blake's early mediaeval enthusiasms and his work among the monuments of Westminster, a parallel with themselves which the Pre-Raphaelites would have been quick to appreciate. And Smetham's discussion of how Blake's poetry needs for its full understanding the support of engravings offered a sanction for the inter-dependence of the arts in the works of Rossetti or Morris.

Much of their criticism of Blake is frankly tendentious. They look to him for support of ideas and methods they have already tried or half-formulated, and their own interests and connections colour their reading of him. Both Swinburne and Yeats stress his

[1] P. 221. Cf. Swinburne who also noted how Blake hated another of the Pre-Raphaelites' particular *bêtes noirs*, Reynolds, under whose influence English art suffered as Italian did after Raphael, and against whom the Pre-Raphaelites originally directed their campaign (p. 3).

emancipation of dreamland as genuine literary material and obviously see him sanctioning their own interest in the landscape of dreams. Swinburne's version of the *Book of Ahania*, quoted above, makes Blake seem another Simeon Solomon; while his account of the poem entitled 'The Mental Traveller' reads like self-analysis or an allusion to Pater's Gioconda:

. . . the perversion of love; which having annihilated all else, falls at last to feed upon itself, to seek out strange things and barren ways, to invent new loves and invert the old, to fill the emptied heart and flush the subsiding veins with perverse passion. (p. 178)

And when he describes the *Visions of the Daughters of Albion* Swinburne seems to be conditioned by the dominant image of female beauty which his poetry and Rossetti's art celebrated (p. 228). Rossetti himself writes of 'Broken Love' much as if it were in fact part of his own *House of Life*: 'the agony and perversity of sundered affection' has never been more 'powerfully expressive' (II, 86). Another insistent impression from all their commentaries is their tendency to applaud in Blake, often where it is not appropriate, the success of a dim suggestiveness to which they themselves were prone. Yeats speaks, for example, of the 'shadowy multitudes' of *Jerusalem* and *Milton* (I, 50), and Swinburne has already been quoted on the musical and insubstantial harmonies of the prophecies.

Various elements in this revival of interest in Blake confirm those notions of symbolism which Pater contributed to the movement. Yeats especially echoes the Paterian emphasis on the peculiarly modern arts of poetry, painting and music, pointing out that Blake saw those three as the sons of Noah who survived the flood of rationalism. Yeats is quick to insist that music is no allusion for mere literary effect, but a substantial part of Blake's vision (I, 26). The man who has developed only his perception of thought can produce philosophic generalizations; but if 'he has developed his perception of mental sound it will give him music' (I, 243). We have also seen how Swinburne's uncertainty in face of the Prophetic Books suggested the image of vast and mysterious harmonies not susceptible to rational analysis.

One specific way in which Pater may even have *influenced* the reading of Blake occurs in Smetham's essay. Pater's essay on Winckelmann was issued in 1867 and it is in this that he first canvasses his notions about the various arts. Smetham's essay on Blake, which also discusses the technical effects and possibilities of the different arts, appeared nearly two years later in the *London Quarterly Review* for January 1869. Whether Smetham had seen the Pater essay we do not know, but certain echoes of it are striking. Smetham begins his discussion by noting the frequent but indecisive debates on the relations of subject-matter to form and style, of which Pater's essay must have provided one of the most recent and more incisive examples. Like Pater on the Venus de Milo, Smetham notes that probably the ideal art form 'unites in equal strength the forming and all-energizing imagination, and the solid body of external truth by which it is to manifest itself' (II, 313). But Blake belongs in Smetham's eyes to what Pater had called the more inward, modern arts which do not maintain this ideal fusion. For Blake appeals to those who 'look on the flaming inner soul of invention as being of far more importance than the grosser integuments which harbour and defend it, giving it visibility and motion to the eye' (II, 313). The sincere devotee of Blake would rank him with Michelangelo, in whose work 'thought is lost beyond the confines of sense, and he seems "in the spirit to speak mysteries" ' (ibid.). [Here, incidentally, Smetham appeals to a Renaissance figure who was to serve Pater in an essay of 1871 as a central example of the artist with a 'capacity for profound dreaming' (op. cit., p. 83), who was always pressing forward to apprehend delicate and fugitive details of almost unseen beauties.]

But Smetham again follows Pater in his account of the historical and psychological gradations of the arts. He encourages the student of Blake's plates not to fret over the inevitable limitations of painting and sculpture. He admits that poetry and literature are less frustrating as vehicles of the soul's visions (II, 314). If he seems to differ from Pater who admitted painting to the trinity of viable modern forms, he somewhat modifies his position a few pages later. Still a little defensive about what he sees as the limits of painting, Smetham suggests that colour adds to drawing what poetry gains by being set to music (II, 327). He is less concerned with the poetic part of the analogy, but in developing the ideas on colour he moves closer to Pater's position in the Winckelmann essay as well as anticipates other pieces in *The Renaissance* that were yet to appear. Smetham notes (II, 327) how certain melodies delight by themselves, just as colours may appeal without any communicative function. He discusses the 'hues and harmonies' among such natural effects as old brick walls covered with lichen and moss. He ends by claiming for certain landscape schools, much as Pater was to do for the Venetian school, a 'legality of magic' in which we do not question the tenuous and often apparently careless combination of tints and washes. In this way Smetham suggests how painting may still achieve a flexibility which brings it closer to the requirements of Pater's modern arts.[1]

The symbolism which these discussions of Blake document and support is perhaps the central mode of the Pre-Raphaelite imagination. It was an art which celebrated an alternative wisdom to materialism and the propositions of either science or Mr Gradgrind. As Smetham says of Blake (II, 323), it is a vision that leans towards imagery, not organized philosophy. It sometimes ignores the need to embody and substantiate and insists instead only upon an 'inward idea, which glimmers before the vision' (II, 317). Most of the Pre-Raphaelites shrank, as Pater said Angelico did, from the 'notion that what the eye apprehended was all' (op. cit., p. 217). Yet what the inward eye apprehended rarely had the confidence and definition that it did for romantics like Wordsworth and Coleridge. This was mainly because for Wordsworth the eye could still be the vehicle of phenomenal and noumenous vision. Even when he grew older and thought supplied charms more remote to the eye, the thoughts still focused themselves in exterior details. But later romantics, for whom vision, not sight, was all important, often grew impatient at the

---

[1] It is such discussions as these of Pater and Smetham that help to make sense of Symons's claim that symbolism and impressionism share the same intentions. See note 2, p. 124 supra.

'obstinate questioning of sense and outward things' by which Wordsworth's apprehension moved. Outward things seemed generally so uncongenial that they sought interests 'unborrowed from the eye'. Though the symbolist is dedicated to discover symbols by which his insight into mysteries may be made palpable, sometimes in the Pre-Raphaelite movement the urge to satisfy the spirit often frustrated the artist. Vagueness and a calculated impressionism took the place of the search for tangible equivalents of their visions.

PLATE 1. Rossetti, *Water Willow*. Samuel and Mary R. Bancroft Collection, Wilmington Society of the Fine Arts, Delaware Art Center, Wilmington, Delaware.

PLATE 2. Rossetti, *Beata Beatrix*. (1872 version of
the painting of 1863, now in the Tate Gallery).
The Art Institute of Chicago.

PLATE 3. Rossetti, *Mary Magdalene*. Samuel and Mary
R. Bancroft Collection, Wilmington Society of the
Fine Arts, Delaware Art Center, Wilmington,
Delaware.

PLATE 4. Rossetti, *La Pia de' Tolomei.* University of
Kansas Museum of Art, Lawrence, Kansas.

THE KISS OF
JVDAS

PLATE 5. Beardsley, *The Kiss of Judas*, from *Pall Mall Magazine*, July 1893.

PLATE 6. Photograph of Fanny Cornforth. Samuel
and Mary R. Bancroft Collection, Wilmington
Society of the Fine Arts, Delaware Art Center,
Wilmington, Delaware.

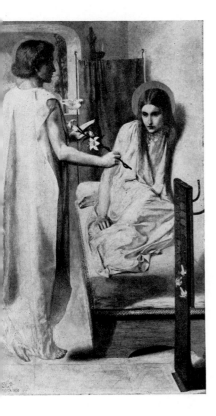

PLATE 7 (a). Rossetti, *Ecce Ancilla Domini* (later called *The Annunciation*). The Tate Gallery, London.

PLATE 7 (b). Beardsley, "The Mysterious Rose Garden", *The Yellow Book*, IV.

PLATE 8 (a). Beardsley, Headpiece from
Le Morte d'Arthur.

PLATE 8 (c). Beardsley, *The Woman in
the Moon* (detail), frontispiece to
Wilde's *Salom*é.

PLATE 8 (b). Beardsley, Headpiece fr
Le Morte d'Arthur.

PLATE 8 (d). Beardsley, "The Ascens
of St. Rose of Lima" (detail), *
Savoy*, II.

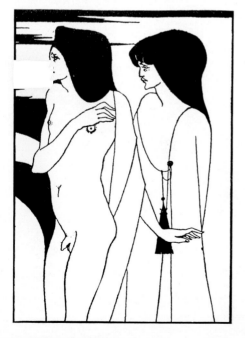

CHAPTER FIVE

'The Soul's Beauty':
The Pre-Raphaelite Image of Woman

Study only the beautiful and create only ideals
—Lafcadio Hearn

Yes, yes; but beauty is so difficult
—Aubrey Beardsley

I

ONE EXAMPLE of Pre-Raphaelite symbolism has been saved for separate consideration. It is the use of a beautiful woman as an image of the poet's introspection. The figure is a familiar one, especially in Pre-Raphaelite painting. A carefully observed version of her can be found in a letter Henry James wrote about Mrs Morris, in whom he recognized a 'grand synthesis of all the Pre-Raphaelite pictures ever made'. He exclaims:

she is a wonder . . . a tall lean woman . . . with a mass of crisp black hair heaped into great wavy projections on each side of her temples, a thin pale face, a pair of strange sad, deep dark Swinburnian eyes, with great thick black oblique brows, joined in the middle and tucking themselves away under her hair, a mouth like the Oriana in our illustrated Tennyson, a long neck . . .[1]

This Pre-Raphaelite ideal beauty has often been described as 'soulful'.[2] But the gibe contains an important truth: for Rossetti,

[1] The Letters of Henry James, ed. P. Lubbock (1920), I, 17–19.
[2] Even in 1878 The Monks of Thelma offers an aesthetic young lady who 'was not pretty, but she was full of soul'. Quoted Fletcher, 'Bedford Park: Aesthete's Elysium?', Romantic Mythologies, p. 182.

a beautiful woman *was* an image of his soul. This ideal beauty dominates his poems and paintings because much of his work, introspective at its best, seeks in her features an adequate mode of articulation.

The paradigm which best suggests the resonance Rossetti attached to the symbol occurs in his early story, 'Hand and Soul'. It is a story about a young artist, Chiaro dell'Erma, whose impulse is to search for 'a visible embodiment of his thoughts'. After some years of indecision as to how to conduct his artistic career and in a moment of despair because his large public paintings, allegorically depicting the virtues, have so little effect on social morality, he sees a vision of a beautiful woman. She calls herself the image of his soul and reassures him about his work. Henceforth he must be true to his own introspection and to the integrity of his own artistic imagination: 'Chiaro, servant of God, take now thine Art unto thee, and paint me thus, as I am, to know me . . . so shall thy soul stand before thee always, and perplex thee no more' (I, 394–5).

Two emphases emerge strongly from this tale. First, that a beautiful woman appears as a visible embodiment of his soul; second, that the artist should honour his soul, which means painting the images of his soul, the various moods of a beautiful woman. She becomes an ideal beauty because, as the story illustrates, her message reaffirms the ultimate sanctity of an artist's vision and the corresponding inadequacies of trying to accommodate his insights to contemporary realities. She is ideal too, for Rossetti, because in Dante he would have found the congenial idea that the contemplation of a beautiful woman would bring grace: 'Mirerol tanto fiso, / Ch'io diverrò beato, lei guardando.'[1] In one of his letters to Mrs Morris he exclaims how she had made known to him 'the fullness of wonder and worship'.[2]

What are for me two of his finest paintings, *Water Willow* and *Beata Beatrix* (Plates 1 and 2), both focus moments of his con-

[1] *Le Opere di Dante Alighieri*, ed. E. Moore, p. 182a. Rossetti's debt to Dante reminds us that the symbolic use of a woman was common in the Renaissance; its Pre-Raphaelite revival is another instance of a successful use of historical nostalgia.

[2] British Museum MS. letter, 52333A.53.

templation. In the first the desolation and sorrow suggested by the symbolic willow branches held in the woman's hand and by the melancholy landscape behind her are modified by a strange sense of recollected happiness. There is tenderness in the tilt of her head, while the eyes which at first perhaps conveyed only tearfulness suggest also a depth and warmth of emotion. It is much more than a portrait of Mrs Morris, it is a communication of Rossetti's state of mind.

So is his *Beata Beatrix*, which Swinburne described as 'wholly symbolic and ideal'.[1] Painted the year after his wife died, Rossetti gives her features to Beatrice and so, with metaphor borrowed from Dante, the picture commemorates their strange and intense relationship and Rossetti's own meditations upon death and the afterlife. Again the eyes, closed in this case, are the centre of the picture: for as Rossetti insisted, Beatrice, 'through her shut lids, is conscious of a new world'.[2] It is impossible to say that *Beata Beatrix* illustrates Dante or is just a commemorative portrait of his wife; our response to its considerable power must acknowledge that it offers a tangible equivalent of an intricate spiritual reality.

The various feminine figures who haunt both his poetry and his paintings have this, then, in common: they are a focus of Rossetti's idealism and specifically of his own introspective states. It has sometimes been the fashion to see in his work a divided impulse which makes him 'thrill to the appeal both of Mary Virgin and of Mary Magdalene, of Beatrice and of Jenny, of the Blessed Damozel and of Circe'.[3] What is important in this emphasis is that each of these two types serve as some different symbol in his work; but neither does he wish to maintain any strict distinctions between sensualist and idealist notions nor do his abilities permit it. I discuss elsewhere the slight and insufficient differences between Rossetti's presentations of Soul's Beauty and Body's Beauty.[4] The figures of Beatrice and Mary Magdalene (Plate 3)

[1] *Notes on the Royal Academy Exhibition*, p. 48.
[2] Pierpont Morgan Library MS., MA 1640(3).
[3] Introduction by F. L. Lucas to *Rossetti, Selections*, p. xxv.
[4] See supra pp. 143 ff.

have, after all, the same heavily sensual lips, the massive hair, the thick column of neck; only perhaps the eyes are different and it is with the eyes that Rossetti best communicates the special emotions that lie behind one particular picture.

No account of a divided impulse is taken either in Henry James' letter or by Hamilton in his description of the woman in *The Aesthetic Movement in England*:

a pale distraught lady with matted dark auburn hair falling in masses over the brow, and shading eyes full of love-lorn languor, or feverish despair; emaciated cheeks and somewhat heavy jaws, protruding upper lip, the lower lip being indrawn, long crane neck, flat breasts, and long thin nervous hands. (p. 24)

Facetiousness apart, Hamilton offers an image which is dominant-ly the same in all cases—*Aurea Catena, Lucretia Borgia, Pandora, Lady Lilith* (Plate 15*b*), *Veronica Veronese, La Bella Mano, Mnemosyne*. It is only in such early pictures as *Ecce Ancilla Domini* (Plate 7*a*) or *The Girlhood of Mary Virgin* that the central figure, modelled by Christina, is not immediately identified with the Pre-Raphaelite 'prototype'. But there are hints even here of the latter, more familiar figure. The little angel in the second has those penetrating eyes, and her counterpart in the other, the massive hair, strong chin and heavy neck; while the Virgin of the Annunciation has the characteristic droop of the head, eyes heavily focused on some point outside the picture and lips quite sensually parted. But by 1849 (*Il Saluto di Beatrice*) and 1851 (*Beatrice Denying Her Salutation* or *How They Met Them-selves*) there have evolved the distinctive features noted by Hamilton and James. While, as early as 1850, the Pre-Raphaelite Brotherhood had encountered Elizabeth Eleanor Siddal who was to be the first of a long line of models for Rossetti, all of whom seemed either to conform to the same ideal of beauty or, as Holman Hunt noted, were revised in order to do so. Hunt explains how Rossetti would ignore actual physiognomy:

Rossetti's tendency in sketching a face [was] to convert the features of his sitter to his favourite ideal type, and if he finished in these lines, the drawing was extremely charming, but you had to make believe a good deal to see the likeness, while if the sitter's features would not lend themselves to the pre-ordained form, he, when time allowed, went through a stage of reluctant twisting of lines and quantities to make the drawing satisfactory.[1]

This is confirmed by Rossetti who tells Mrs Morris in a letter that he is *adapting* her hair and neck for another Beatrice picture.[2] Indeed, it would be consistent with the symbolic intention if the beautiful woman, her eyes as 'lamps of his translucent soul', did not usurp the individual features of the models used to depict her.

Much more important than a discussion of the divided impulse in Rossetti is the swift progression from 'the sweet girlhood of Mary the Virgin to the claustrophobic *Pia* or the siren of the *Orchard Pit*.'[3] The mood of sweet girlhood did not last long and as Miss Siddal quickly replaced Christina as his model (and after Miss Siddal came Fanny Cornforth and Mrs Morris) so Rossetti's image of the beautiful woman soon changed to the one which both Hamilton and James identified as his; or which Swinburne saw in a study for *La Pia* (Plate 4):

her pallid splendid face hangs a little forward, worn and white against the mass of dark deep hair . . . the weak weary hands . . . In her eyes is a strange look of wonder and sorrow and fatigue . . .[4]

Yet, in Rossetti's poetry, this ideal figure had appeared very early. His painting of *The Blessed Damozel* (completed 1877) was anticipated by the *poem* of the same title thirty years before. Already his description of the lady emphasizes her piercing gaze, her eyes, 'deeper than the depth / Of waters stilled at even', the full ripe hair; the melancholy yearning is also in the poem, as are the betraying notes of sensuality. In other poems, like pieces of a jig-saw, can be found further elements of this ideal beauty, which,

---

[1] *Pre-Raphaelitism and the Pre-Raphaelite Brotherhood*, I, 341.

[2] British Museum MS. letter, 52332A.58.

[3] Evelyn Waugh, *Rossetti: His Life and Works* (1928), p. 212. F. L. Lucas also notes this transition from 'morning purity to the sultry heaviness of an autumn afternoon' (op. cit., p. xxii).

[4] Quoted W. D. Paden, '*La Pia dei' Tolomei* by Dante Gabriel Rossetti', *The Register of the Museum of Art*, The University of Kansas, Vol. II, no. 1 (November 1958), p. 43.

fitted together, constitute the one symbolic woman. The passionate eyes, 'that sometimes turned half dizzily beneath / The passionate lids' are also given to the Queen in 'The Staff and Scrip' ('Her eyes were like the wave within'), to 'The Card-Dealer' and to the lover whom Rossetti recalls in 'The Stream's Secret'. Rose Mary, Aloÿse of 'The Bride's Prelude' and the woman of 'The Sin of Detection' all have the pale complexion. And usually in conjunction with this, serving to frame the wan face, is heavy hair—'long tresses, full of musk and myrrh'; Aloÿse's jewel-decorated hair; the 'fall'n' and 'sheltering hair' of the lover in 'The Stream's Secret'; the 'fallen hair', again, of Rose Mary. Hair seemed to fascinate Rossetti so much (he buried his manuscript of poems in his wife's coffin between her hair and her cheek) that in his translation of Pugliesi's 'Canzone for his dead lady' occurs the line—'The soft fall of her hair'—which is not in the Italian. Jenny, the Card-Dealer and the siren of the Orchard Pit also have the emphatic heads of hair, although theirs are all golden rather than the usual auburn, which Rossetti presumably chose more often for its dramatic contrast with pale cheeks (see 'In the hair dark-waved the face lay white'). The 'thrilled throat', passionately stretched, of Rose Mary is given also to Aloÿse; but it becomes more insistent in the sonnets of *The House of Life*, as does the sensual insistence on 'her mouth's culled sweetness' (XXI). The physical image of his beloved in that sequence is remarkably forceful, occasionally more so than the various states of mind she represents: 'Sweet dimness of her loosened hair's downfall' (XXI), 'thrilling pallor of cheek' (XXXI), the 'sovereign face' (XVIII) with its 'warm lips' (XIV) above the 'round reared neck, meet column of love's shrine' (XXXI). Such descriptions might be multiplied. Where Rossetti is not explicit he implies as much: the 'wearied damsels' of 'Dante at Verona', who 'rest and hold / Their hands in the wet spurt of gold,' although scarcely described, suggest the same appearance.

Whether the ideal beauty is described fully (as in *The House of Life*, X) or merely apostrophized (XVII or XVIII) she is imbued with an intense significance, which, however vague, is extremely compelling. Her 'sovereign face' is musical with 'compassed mysteries', the greatest of which is the mystery of Love, and Rossetti was passionately concerned with penetrating that mystery. Brief and tantalizing glimpses of it are betrayed sometimes by the features of the ideal beauty.[1] The face of a woman has, he realizes, many 'moods of varying grace' (XVII); each mood reflects a different facet of his soul, and so of Love's mystery:

> Lady, in thy proud eyes
> There is a weary look
> As if the spirit we know through them
> Were daunted with rebuke
> To think that the heart of man henceforth,
> Is read like a read book.
>
> Lady, in thy lifted face
> The solitude is sore;—
> The true solitude follows the crowd.
> Will it be less or more
> When the words have been spoken to thee
> Which my thought is seeking for.
>
> Lady, can'st thou not guess
> The words which my thoughts seek?
> Perhaps thou deem'st them well to spurn
> And better not to speak.
> Oh! thou *must* know my love is strong,
> Hearing my voice so weak![2]

To realize how Rossetti's imagination was completely absorbed by this ideal figure and how effectively he could use its symbolic power, one has only to compare either his *Water Willow* (Plate 1) or one of his good studies of Miss Siddal and Mrs Morris (Plate 13b) with the woman in Hunt's *Awakened Conscience*, who is much less powerful. Or one has only to confront the gaze of his women or feel the quickening of the poetry in *The House of Life* when the

[1] Her eyes (III and XI) and her mouth (XLV) both 'betray her soul', and in 'The Stream's Secret' he apostrophizes with 'O soul-sequestered face'.

[2] 'A Prayer', MS. in the Samuel and Mary R. Bancroft Collection, The Wilmington Society of the Fine Arts, Wilmington, Delaware. This version has a few variant readings and is shorter than that printed in *The Works* (1911), pp. 267 ff.

woman dominates it, to realize how compelling a symbol she was for him.

II

Before we leave Rossetti's symbolic beauty and move on to see some of the changes that overcame her later there are two related concerns that need discussion: these are the sources of the image, and the relations between his imagination and real life which affect the image.

There had already been in poetry of earlier poets whom Rossetti read and admired descriptions which prefigure his own creation. Thus Tennyson's 'Spiritual Adeline':

> Mystery of mysteries,
>   Faintly smiling Adeline,
>   *Scarce of earth nor all divine*
> Nor unhappy, nor at rest,
>   But beyond expression fair
>   With thy floating flaxen hair;
> Thy rose-lips and full blue eyes
>   Take the heart from out my breast.
> Wherefore those dim looks of thine,
> Shadowy, dreaming Adeline?[1]

The mystery, the semi-divine presence and the dreaming eyes are all to be attributes of Rossetti's ideal beauties. Nor, with his fondness for Keats, is it likely that he would not have been attracted to the figure of Moneta in the second *Hyperion*, where the features of Tennyson's Adeline are confirmed but given greater point and intensity:

> Then saw I a wan face,
> Not pined by human sorrows, but bright-blanch'd
> By an immortal sickness which kills not;
> It works a constant change, which happy death
> Can put no end to; deathwards progressing
> To no death was that visage; it had past
> The lily and the snow; and beyond these
> I must not think now, though I saw that face.

[1] My italics.

But for her eyes I should have fled away;
They held me back with a benignant light,
Soft, mitigated by divinest lids
Half-closed, and visionless entire they seem'd
Of all external things.[1]

It is appropriate to Rossetti's use of these half-closed eyes, oblivious of all external things, that Moneta should have accused the poet in Keats's poem of being 'a dreaming thing, / A fever of thyself'. And another figure from Keats's poetry where Rossetti may have borrowed the properties of his women was the Belle Dame Sans Merci with her long hair and wild, wild eyes; she, too, was an agent of trance and sleep which released for the poet images he since wanders forlornly seeking.

But another source suggests itself. The young Pre-Raphaelite Brethren were much impressed with Ottley's series of reproductions in *The Italian School of Design* issued in 1823.[2] And here, in these incredibly poor renderings of work by Raphael, Leonardo and Michelangelo, are the various features of Rossetti's women. Leonardo's *Leda* (facing p. 20), although too plump in the cheeks for the real Pre-Raphaelite women, has the searching and passionate gaze Rossetti later used; Michelangelo's *Cleopatra* (facing p. 34) stresses the incredibly long neck, as does Raphael's *Head of an Angel* (facing p. 50) which also emphasizes the full lips; in another Raphael (between pp. 50 and 51) there are the heavy lips again, together with a heavy jaw; and in an anonymous study for *Heliodorus* (facing p. 53) the figure has the long neck, heavy hair, and in one study at least the chin thrown out.

These same characteristics, as already mentioned, dominated Rossetti's painting from early on. But while they originated in his imagination and maybe in his readings of Keats and Ottley they were soon to become part of his actual existence. Rossetti found his blessed Damozel in real life. First as his model, then as his mistress, then as his idealized Beatrice-figure and only finally and almost too late as his wife, Elizabeth Eleanor Siddal became the

---

[1] *The Fall of Hyperion*, canto 1, ll. 232–44.
[2] See F. G. Stephens in *The Germ* who lists Ottley among the sources of his essay on 'The Purposes and Tendency of Early Italian Art'.

living and actual exemplar of the ideal beauty Rossetti had evoked in his earliest pictures and poems. William Michael Rossetti described her as 'tall, finely formed, with a lofty neck, and regular yet somewhat uncommon features, greenish-blue unsparkling eyes, large perfect eyelids, brilliant complexion, and a lavish heavy wealth of coppery-golden hair'.[1] As much the same she appears in *Beata Beatrix* (Plate 2), painted by Rossetti in 1863, the year after his wife's death, in memory of her, whose features he gave to Beatrice.

Yet it is here that a speculation, which Henry James first suggested, becomes more interesting. In the letter, already quoted, in which he describes Mrs Morris he casually raises the problem:

It's hard to say whether she's a grand synthesis of all the Pre-Raphaelite pictures ever made—or they a 'keen analysis' of her—whether she's all original or copy . . .[2]

Holman Hunt certainly suggests that Rossetti altered a person's features to accord with his ideal beauty.[3] But the interesting question is how early did he start to do this. It is generally accepted that Millais's picture of Ophelia's death best captured Elizabeth Siddal's likeness; there she appears rather more *petite*, more of a naive Victorian Miss than in any drawing or painting from Rossetti's hand. It would appear that Rossetti saw even his future wife in the light of his increasingly definite vision of the ideal woman. To envisage real life in terms of the imagination is certainly possible for the man who placed his manuscript book of poems in his wife's coffin, a gesture Rossetti must surely have copied from his sister's *Maud*, where the heroine buries her locked book in her best friend's coffin.[4]

There are grounds, too, for suspecting that, like Rossetti, some later writers saw their own lives in artistic terms. When Oscar Wilde became engaged to Constance Lloyd he described her in words which echo the ideal beauty—'very grave, and mystical,

[1] *Dante Gabriel Rossetti. His Family-Letters, with a memoir*, I, 171.
[2] See note 1, p. 177 supra.
[3] See supra pp. 180–1.
[4] See *Maude, a story for girls* (1897), p. 78. In an introduction to the story William Michael Rossetti says that it was originally written in 1850.

with wonderful eyes, and dark brown coils of hair: quite perfect . . .'[1] One cannot help wondering whether Wilde chose her
because she approximated to the ideal, though photographs give
little support for that, or whether he enhanced her retrospectively
by viewing her in its light. In Beerbohm's *Zuleika*, it will be
remembered, the Duke did not quite like the arrangement of
clouds in the sky, and the Gods humoured him. The incident
could be a satiric comment on a late nineteenth-century tendency
to manufacture important and beautiful moments of existence.
The Duke was lucky to have obliging divinities who allowed
natural effects to be rearranged more aesthetically; but not all
aesthetes were as lucky. Much poor writing at the end of the
century arises from a Ducal reluctance to accept reality, followed
(seeing that no gods intervene) by deliberate manipulation of
realities which would thus be more congenial artistic material.

Rossetti also tried to achieve his ideal in photography as well as
on canvas. In the Bancroft Collection are two photographs, this
time of Fanny Cornforth, one of which represents her combing
her long hair and the other (Plate 6*b*) with her head tilted dreamily
back and eyes staring out of the picture, while a mirror behind
her reveals the other side of her face. This last, taken in the
garden at 16, Cheyne Walk was, she recalled, *posed* by Ruskin and
Bell Scott.[2]

So in painting, as well, maybe, as in photography, Rossetti
arranged the real world after visions of his ideal beauty. Which
explains why his various models—Elizabeth Siddal, Mrs Morris,
Fanny Cornforth, Alice Wilding, Marie Spartali (Mrs Stillman)—
all leave the impression of being the same woman, an impression
caused by Rossetti's constant attempts to bridge the gulf between
his ordinary existence and the ideal life of the imagination. The
connection between his ideal beauty and her real models seems one

---

[1] *Letters*, p. 155. A photograph of Constance Lloyd faces p. 158.

[2] According to a note in the MS. catalogue of the Bancroft Collection; both the
photograph and the details about it were given to Bancroft by Fanny herself.
There are two further photographs in the collection of Marie Spartali Stillman,
in one of which she is dressed in a copy of the garment depicted in Rossetti's
water-colour, 'Sidonia the Sorceress' (see Richard Ormond, 'A Pre-Raphaelite
Beauty', *Country Life*, 30 December 1965).

of the most illuminating aspects of that peculiar Victorian phenomenon to which Humphrey House drew attention:[1] namely, the realization of a cleavage between modern life and the deeper, spiritual purposes it was recognized that art should follow. House cites
Patmore's *The Angel in the House* as one example of an attempt to
bridge that gulf by trying to invest Victorian marriage with deep
spiritual and psychological significance. Rossetti's painting of his
various models is another; they interested him only as they could
be given a new existence as his ideal beauty, and his representation
of them was always an attempt to invest the woman he represented
with some spiritual and psychological meaning.

In ordinary life (and he seems to have been really attached only
to Elizabeth Siddal and Jane Morris) he again seemed to be
interested only when they could fulfil a deeper need in his
emotional existence. Thus his painting of Siddal as the *Beata
Beatrix* (Plate 2) and of Jane Morris as *La Pia* (Plate 4) represents
attempts to imbue his models with great significance as well as
to elevate his own life with them nearer his imaginative ideals. To
paint his wife as Beatrice meant that, first, Elizabeth Siddal
acquired the symbolical associations that Beatrice had for Dante
Alighieri and, second, that Dante Gabriel was trying to heighten
his own emotional existence by identifying himself and his wife
with another, more moving relationship.[2] Similarly, to invoke the
the image of Janey Morris in the story of *La Pia dei' Tolomei* was
perhaps an attempt to invest his own life and love with resonant
literary overtones of Dante's *Purgatory*. La Pia had been im-
prisoned by her husband in the Maremma and died eventually in
that deadly marshland from malaria or from poison; part of her
words to Dante were translated and placed upon the frame of
Rossetti's picture:

> Remember me who am La Pia; me
> Siena, me Maremma, made, unmade.
> This in his inmost heart well knoweth he
> With whose fair jewel I was ringed and wed.

[1] *All In Due Time*, pp. 154-5.

[2] William Gaunt has traced some of the psychological repercussions of such
identifications and 'adaptions' of reality in *The Pre-Raphaelite Tragedy*, pp.
40-7.

The canvas was begun in 1868, when it was relevant to his often repressed feelings about Mrs Morris, and taken up and completed in 1880, fraught now with feelings of agony and remorse. If the ideal work of art was an image of the artist's soul, as Chiaro dell'Erma was reminded in his vision, then a painting like *La Pia* was a resonant success. The picture is at once a record of a complex and often guilty relationship,[1] and a dramatic heightening of his private life by seeing it in the guise of Dantesque incident. It was an artistic and emotional device which occasionally lets Rossetti produce a compelling work. It was, however, to prove a disastrous precedent for later artists.

III

The symbolic beauty whom Rossetti first celebrated grew extremely popular as the century wore on. The varying purposes she served and the alterations they wrought upon her throw an interesting light on the course of late nineteenth-century art. Rossetti's own work shows that she became more and more an expression of his growing depression and bitterness, especially after his wife's death in 1862. Here the ideal beauty has been modified from within, as a result of real emotional stress. But she did not always have such a vital function. In *The Defence of Guenevere*, for example, her appearances are less functional than they are decorative and she prefigures the function she is to fulfil best by the end of the century. The volume was appropriately dedicated to Rossetti by William Morris, as a good deal of the inspiration, not least for the image of the woman, comes from Rossetti. In 'Praise of My Lady' Morris writes:

> My lady seems of ivory
> Forehead, straight nose, and cheeks that be
> Hollow'd a little mournfully.
> *Beata mea Domina!*
>
> Her forehead, overshadow'd much
> By bows of hair, has a wave such

[1] I am in debt for my discussion of this picture to W. D. Paden's monograph, already cited: see note 4, p. 181 supra.

As God was good to make for me,
Beata mea Domina!

Not greatly long my lady's hair,
Nor yet with yellow colour fair,
But thick and crisped wonderfully: . . .

Her great eyes, standing far apart,
Draw up some memory from her heart,
And gaze out very mournfully; . . .

Her full lips being made to kiss,
Curl'd up and pensive each one is;
This makes me faint to stand and see . . .

Of her long neck what shall I say?
What things about her body's sway,
Like a knight's pennon or slim tree
—*Beata mea Domina*!—

Set gently waving in the wind;
Or her long hands that I may find
On some day sweet to move o'er me?

The fourth stanza there certainly suggests that she may still serve a symbolic purpose, but the central impression of the poem as a whole is a consummate pattern of sound and mood. In 'Golden Wings' the insistent pattern absorbs colours as well, and could well be offered as an early English equivalent of the French symbolist taste for symphonies of colour and sound. Morris, I suggest, already reveals in these verses his talent for decoration and design:

Many scarlet bricks there were
    In its walls, and old grey stone;
    Over which red apples shone
At the right time of the year.

On the bricks the green moss grew,
    Yellow lichen on the stone,
    Over which red apples shone;
Little war that castle knew.

> Deep green water fill'd the moat,
>   Each side had a red-brick lip,
>   Green and mossy with the drip
> Of dew and rain......

Into this pattern the figure of the beautiful lady is readily absorbed:

> Stoop'd down a little she sat there,
>   With neck stretch'd out and chin thrown up,
>   One hand around a golden cup;
> And strangely with her fingers fair
>
> She beat some tune upon the gold;
>   The minstrels in the gallery
>   Sung: 'Arthur, who will never die,
> In Avallon he groweth old.'
>
> And when the song was ended, she
>   Rose and caught up her gown and ran;
>   None stopp'd her eager face and wan
> Of all that pleasant company.
>
> Right so within her own chamber
>   Upon her bed she sat; and drew
>   Her breath in quick gasps; till she knew
> That no man follow'd after her:
>
> She took the garland from her head,
>   Loosed all her hair, and let it lie
>   Upon the coverlit; thereby
> She laid the gown of white and red;

She is as decorative there as she is to be in a later production like the 'Orchard' tapestry.[1]

Swinburne's conception of woman was undoubtedly influenced too by the example of Rossetti.[2] The first series of *Poems and*

---

[1] In the Victoria and Albert and illustrated in a booklet of Morris's designs printed by H.M. Stationery Office for the Victoria and Albert Museum, 1958.

[2] Mario Praz has of course suggested this and much else about this *femme fatale* in *The Romantic Agony*. I am concerned in this chapter with a somewhat different aspect of her image.

Ballads came out in 1866 and its figures of women certainly mirror the physical aspects Rossetti had given them by then. There are Faustine's 'carved lips' and 'state of splendid hair that droops' (p. 106); or

> Feeling my love in all her limbs and hair
> And shed between her eyelids through her eyes; (p. 12)

> And ruinous lilies in thy languid hair . . . (p. 59)

> . . . thine eyes
> Blind me, thy tresses burn me; (p. 57)

or the 'throat of carven pearl' (p. 83). The queens that pass in 'The Masque of Queen Bersabe' (pp. 221 ff.) leave little doubt of the stimulus to Swinburne's imagination derived from Rossetti. But to the image of the other's woman Swinburne adds strange passions, lusts, sins and perversities:

some woman, real or ideal, in whom the pride of life with its companion lusts is incarnate. In her lover's half-shut eyes, her fierce unchaste beauty is transfigured, her cruel sensual eyes have a meaning and a message; there are memories and secrets in the kisses of her lips. . . .
She is the darker Venus, fed with burnt-offering and blood-sacrifice; the veiled image of that pleasure which men impelled by satiety and perverted by power have sought through ways as strange as Nero's. . . .[1]

Despite his insistence that Dolores's eyes hold a meaning and a message, he seems less interested in learning what they are than in the shock tactics he can achieve with her.

The additions to this female figure may have been suggested to Swinburne by hints in Rossetti's own work,[2] but what is interesting is that they become more pronounced in Rossetti's work after Swinburne's *Poems and Ballads* had appeared in 1866. Rossetti's later women, like the 1875 study for the Sphinx, or *La Donna della Finestra* (1870 onwards), or the siren of the 'Orchard Pit' (1869),

[1] *Notes on Poems and Reviews*, p. 12.
[2] Praz somewhat exaggerates Rossetti's 'conspicuous preference for the . . . cruel' (op. cit., p. 218). There are certainly hints of his fascination in 'Sister Helen' or *Lucretia Borgia*, but they are in no way as conspicuous as Swinburne's.

PLATE 9 (a). Beardsley, *Withered Spring*, ink drawing. National Gallery of Art, Washington, D.C., Rosenwald Collection.

PLATE 9 (b). Millais, *Autumn Leaves*. Manchester City Art Galleries.

PLATE 10 (a). Mucha, Poster for JOB cigarette papers.
Victoria and Albert Museum.   Crown Copyright.

PLATE 11. Margaret Macdonald Mackintosh, *Motherhood*, gesso panel. National Museum of Antiquities of Scotland.

PLATE 12.
Burne-Jones, *Aurora*.
Queensland Art
Gallery, Brisbane.

PLATE 13 (a). Burne-Jones, Head of young woman. Study for the *Hesperides*. Fogg Art Museum, Harvard University, Grenville L. Winthrop Bequest.

PLATE 13 (b). Rossetti, pen sketch of Mrs. Morris. The Pierpont Morgan Library.

PLATE 14. Burne-Jones, *Angels of Creation*, second and sixth panels. Fogg Art Museum, Harvard University, Grenville L. Winthrop Bequest.

Plate 15 (a). Anthea Gyles, *Lady Lilith*, illustrated in *The Dome*, I (new series).

Plate 15 (b). Rossetti, *Lady Lilith*. Samuel and Mary R. Bancroft Collection, Wilmington Society of the Fine Arts, Delaware Art Center, Wilmington, Delaware.

PLATE 16. Beardsley, *Arthur Glimpsing the Questing Beast*, from Malory's *Le Morte d'Arthur*.

seem closer to the figures of 'Laus Veneris' or 'Dolores'. It is likely then that Rossetti's image of the ideal beauty may have been modified by reading Swinburne's poetry, which may have accentuated in Rossetti his urgent and real sense of the futility of life and love—the sense of cruel waste that is described in his lines on 'Beauty', written in the same year as the fragments of the 'Orchard Pit':

> Like the wild hyacinth flower which on the hills is found,
> Which the passing feet of the shepherds for ever tear and wound,
> Until the purple blossom is trodden into the ground.[1]

Another contribution to the changing character of the Pre-Raphaelite woman comes from Walter Pater and, specifically, from his version of La Gioconda. There is little doubt that again her image owes much to Rossetti and Swinburne already, though Pater seems especially concerned with 'the fascination of corruption (which) penetrates in every touch of its (the Medusa's) exquisitely finished beauty'. A similar fascination held Rossetti, who shares with Pater an extraordinarily intense apprehension of the mutability of things and the corruption of the world's perfection. The face of the Gioconda, with its slightly 'sinister' smile, is seen as the image of Leonardo's *ideal lady*, embodied and beheld at last' (my italics). Pater considers her in much the same way as Rossetti did his images of ideal beauty: as 'clairvoyants, through whom, as through delicate instruments, one becomes aware of the subtler forces of nature'. And just as Rossetti's women served as images of his soul, so does La Gioconda for Pater. She is 'a beauty wrought out from within upon the flesh, the deposit, little cell by cell, of strange thoughts and fantastic reveries and exquisite passions' (p. 129); but her thoughts, reveries and passions are, in fact, Pater's own. La Gioconda is the 'revealing instance' of Pater's mode of thought and work, just as he says it is of Leonardo's.

Another member of the Pater–Swinburne circle to borrow the ideal beauty was Simeon Solomon. *A Vision of Love Revealed in Sleep* ends with the vision of 'the Very Love, the Divine Type of

<hr/>

[1] *Rossetti, a selection*, ed. F. L. Lucas, pp. 149–50. Cf. the 'Lines from The Roman de la Rose' (ibid., p. 107).

Absolute Beauty'; in both that and its misty world of symbolic, abstract figures *A Vision* seems to owe most to *The House of Life*. But like much else in this study the real qualities of a work are less important than what others thought of them, and Swinburne's essay on Solomon in 1871 is of more significance than *A Vision* itself.[1] For Swinburne finds in Solomon's work exactly those elements of Pre-Raphaelitism that have been considered in this chapter. He offers Swinburne an admixture of cruelty with beauty: 'the aftertaste of fierce weariness and bitter languor that corrodes the soul' (pp. 311–13). The features of Solomon's characters serve as symbolic revelations of states of soul: 'the deep alliances of death and life, of love and hate, of attraction and abhorrence' (p. 311). Yet it is obvious, I think, that Swinburne is reading into Solomon's work what he most wanted—'the Hebrew love of dim vast atmosphere and infinite spiritual range' (p. 301) or 'the subtleties and harmonies of suggestion' (p. 311). These visions of mysterious beauty were part of Swinburne's imaginative make-up and, like Pater, he sought them in others.

In the continuity of admiration between the Pre-Raphaelite Brotherhood and the 1890's Swinburne's part is again seen to be an active one. His reading of Solomon's work in 1871 links Rossetti's use of the ideal beauty to the later, *fade* versions of the 1890's. But here a further consideration is interesting: namely, that Pater's Gioconda may have coloured Swinburne's reading of Solomon. The Leonardo essay had appeared two years earlier in 1869 in the *Fortnightly*. The general implication of Pater's description is the same, as well as a striking similarity of certain key phrases—compare, for instance, her weary eyelids with Swinburne's 'fierce weariness', 'the soul with all its maladies' with Swinburne's corrosion of the soul, Pater's stress on the *suggestiveness* of La Gioconda with Swinburne's 'subtleties and harmonies of suggestion' (p. 311) and the *recherché* experiences Pater attributes to her with Swinburne's more abstract account—'we see the latent relations of pain and pleasure, the subtle conspiracies of good and evil' (p. 311).

---

[1] Swinburne's essay, which he never reissued, is reprinted in *The Bibelot*, Vol. 14. References are to that edition.

The most interesting and important interpreter of the ideal beauty was Burne-Jones, not least because he was a most accomplished draughtsman. His first work was inspired by Rossetti, while at the end of his career he had the young Beardsley under his tutelage. So that he spans the Pre-Raphaelite movement almost in its entirety.

The 1861 watercolour, *Clerk Saunders*, presents a simple version of Rossetti's beautiful woman in Maid Margaret: the pale face framed by the dark hair, the strong neck, the emphatic eyes and mouth. 'Green Summer' (1864) offers a whole collection of such ladies, all like Mrs Morris. By the 1870's Mantegna's influence can be detected in the figures of the *Perseus* paintings, but this is mainly in the manner of the drapery; the women who arm Perseus are the same Pre-Raphaelite beauty, though here too a heavier, more sensuous emphasis is given to their lips and gestures, and a more penetrating gaze to their eyes. A study for the Hesperides dated 1870 (Plate 13*a*) is emphatic about the lips and large, deep eyes, and the pose given to the woman also emphasizes the long neck; the main difference in Burne-Jones's image is the hair, which although usually thick has a less claustrophobic effect than in Rossetti. And as late as 1896 the allegorical figure of *Aurora* (Plate 12) stepping beside the canal and clashing her cymbals is still the same lady.

When Burne-Jones saw *Aurora* hanging in exhibition, he noted its paleness—'it most certainly cannot scream, its voice was like the faint sound of a flute that can hardly be heard among the cornets-à-piston'.[1] His particular role in this Pre-Raphaelite continuity of admiration seems to have been to etherealize, to make paler, the image of the beautiful woman. She no longer seems to have the sensual life and passionate warmth of Rossetti's creations; for Burne-Jones she may inhabit a world of mysteries, allegory and suggestion, as she does in his *Angels of Creation* (Plate 14), but she has discarded any real physical presence and reveals directly the noumenous world where she exists with no pretentions to any phenomenal existence.

[1] Quoted Ironside, *Pre-Raphaelite Painters*, p. 46.

IV

Those are the main accretions to the figure as she moves towards the 1890's where she has a ubiquitous if desultory existence. She now becomes a stock property, a second-hand, decorative device with some slight guarantee of suggestive power. She retains little of the symbolic, idealist force she had for Rossetti or Burne-Jones. Yeats spoke for all members of the Rhymers' Club in his Autobiographies when he said that they

praised a desired woman and hoped that she would find amid their praise her very self, or at worst, their very passion. . . . Woman herself was still in our eyes . . . romantic and mysterious, still the priestess of her shrine, our emotions remembering the *Lilith* and *Sybilla Palmifera* of Rossetti.

As his remark reveals, she offers only vicarious emotion ('our emotions remembering . . . Rossetti'). Charged with no personal feeling now, she merely points back to Rossetti, as Rossetti had pointed back to Dante. But Rossetti had some compelling reasons for taking his metaphors from Dante, while his followers later in the nineteenth century had little more to justify them than artistic and emotional laziness.

Indeed later artists and writers were frequently guilty of invoking the image of their Soul's Beauty in order to fake some profounder significance for their life. In 'Modern Beauty' Arthur Symons relies upon second-hand images from the Pre-Raphaelite imagination:

> I am Yseult and Helen, I have seen
> Troy burn, and the most loving knight lie dead.
> The world has been my mirror, time has been
> My breath upon the glass; and men have said,
> Age after age, in rapture and despair,
> Love's poor few words, before my image there.
>
> I live, and am immortal; in my eyes
> The sorrow of the world, and on my lips
> The joy of life, mingle to make me wise;

Yet now the day is darkened with eclipse:
Who is there lives for beauty? Still am I
The torch, but where's the moth that still dares die? (II, p. 150)

It will be noticed that he uses, in direct imitation of Rossetti, her eyes as a symbol of the world's sorrow, and the images are painstaking and exact. He is perhaps deliberately rehearsing the type in order to satirize the modern inhospitality to such heroines, but he barely disengages himself from the nostalgia which should be the object of the rather drab irony. Yeats's response is more straightforward: his lover celebrates a beautiful friend's 'Pale brows, still hands and dim hair', while the curlew's cry recalls to Yeats her 'Passion-dimmed eyes and long heavy hair'. The same woman is the cause of Dowson's 'Impenitentia Ultima' (*S.* I) and she is the inspiration of much of George Moore's volume, *Flowers of Passion*, which is filled with 'downward gazing eyes' and more lengthy descriptions of the familiar figure:

> Like trailing hyacinth, flows the clustering hair;
> And column-wise straight from her bosom grows
> The large full throat.[1]

She appears, too, in rather unexpected places like the beginning of Crackenthorpe's realist story, 'He Wins Who Loses', where the cliché of the Victorian novel is given specific Pre-Raphaelite colouring:

Rebellious masses of dark brown hair straggled on to her forehead, and her round, grey eyes had a dreamy, far-away look to them.[2]

On another occasion the irrelevance of her appearance—'her faultless throat', 'all her hair', 'My Beatrice, and my perfect love' —is laughably betrayed when we realize that the title of this piece by Herbert Horne is 'To ——, on returning a silk kerchief of Hers' (*HH.* II, 131–3). Generally one is forced to echo Francis

[1] *Flowers of Passion* (1878), pp. 69 and 84.
[2] *A.* I, 104. The woman figures in other realist stories, too; see 'The Fancy and the Fact' (*D.* I, 155), 'The Accursed Cordonnier' (*D* VII, 113) or 'The Penman' (*D.* IV, 179).

Thompson, through whose poetry, too, flickers that inevitable beauty:

> Still I see the dusked tresses—
> But the old angers, old caresses?
> Still your eyes are autumn thunders,
> But where are *you*, child, you?[1]

Lionel Johnson's 'The last Music' involves a 'lady of the spheres' who is unmistakably a close relation of the Blessed Damozel—

> hair in sombre braids
> With beauty overshades
> Her brow broad and serene—(*R*. I, 48)

but when it turns out that Johnson had once loved this creature, we recall Yeats's remark about his lack of lived experience to supplement that gained in the library. So with most of Johnson's contemporaries. In E. Nesbit's 'Day and Night' (*YB*. IV) the woman's face ('with mists of love her face seemed dim') seems to stare at us, not from Nesbit's own experience, but from Rossetti's *House of Life*. Too steeped in Pre-Raphaelite studies to look at life for themselves, their knowledge of beauty and of ideal woman is totally derivative. Sometimes writers would even rely upon their readers' identifying the figure of the beautiful woman from the merest hints. Dowson, especially, can summon her up innumerable times by the slightest reference to the 'prototype': 'The citadel of your sacred lips' conjures her in 'Ad Manus Puellae', 'swan's neck and her dark, abundant hair' in 'Epigram', 'deepening eyes' in 'Growth'.[2] And Cynara, to me at least, is always envisaged as the traditional Pre-Raphaelite beauty. Occasionally Dowson attempts to use her symbolically after Rossetti's fashion:

> And all her flower-like beauty, as a glass,
> Mirrors out hope and love; (p. 39)

but the symbol itself is stressed rather than its implications, which

---

[1] *The Poems of Francis Thompson* (Oxford Standard Authors 1948), p. 341.
[2] *The Poetical Works*, ed. Desmond Flower (Cassell's Pocket Library 1950), pp. 50, 87 and 49 respectively.

also happens in Osborn's 'More bright than goblets are thine eyes / Through which thy soul doth shine . . .' (*D.* VII, 66).

Although a writer in *The Yellow Book* explained that 'someone painted you one day / Perchance to ease his soul' (II, 177), the soulfulness that is insistent in Rossetti hardly survives the meaningless if dutiful manipulation of the beauty's stock properties in such images as Todhunter's 'Voluptuous Lilith' (*R.* I), Lionel Johnson's 'Dark Angel' (*R.* II), *Psyche* or *Sphinx* (*P.* I) or Graham R. Tomson's 'Vespertilia':

> I found her straying by that barren bower,
> Her fair face glimmering like a white wood-flower
> That gleams through withered leaves:
> Her mouth was redder than the pimpernel,
> Her eyes seemed darker than the purple air
> 'Neath brows half hidden—I remember well—
> 'Mid mists of cloudy hair. (*YB.* IV, 49)

She acquires, if anything, only an exaggerated melancholy. 'There is no Excellent Beauty', wrote Francis Bacon, 'that hath not some Strangeness in the Proportion.' But by the end of the nineteenth century the strangeness had grown out of all proportion: in Symon's 'Mundi Victima' for instance—

> Consuming eyes consenting to confess
> The extreme ardour of their heaviness,
> The lassitude of passionate desires . . .
>   . . . purple eyelids bent
> Towards some most dolorous accomplishment
>   . . . the carnal mystery of the eyes,
>   . . . the burning pallor of the cheeks. (*S.* VIII, 15)

Wilde's poem, 'The Sphinx', partly because it is so obviously derivative, provides a useful synthesis of all previous strange beauties. The subject itself had been handled by Rossetti and the various physical aspects emphasized in both the Sphinx and her lover, Ammon, are those already noted as characteristic features of Rossetti's ideal beauty; but here they are made solemnly bizarre and perverse. The 'curious cat' which 'Lies crouching on the Chinese mat with eyes of satin rimmed with gold' recalls the cat with 'splendid circled eyes' of Swinburne's 'Félise'. And the 'thousand weary centuries' she has known and her 'subtle-secret' smile are borrowed from Pater's famous passage on La Gioconda. In his other poems where the figure is wholly woman, rather than half woman and half cat, Rossetti's influence especially is marked, as in 'Madonna Mia':

> A lily-girl, not made for this world's pain,
>   With brown, soft hair close braided by her ears,
>   And longing eyes veiled by slumberous tears
> Like bluest water seen through mists of rain:
> Pale cheeks whereon no love hath left its stain,
>   Red underlip drawn in for fear of love
>   And white throat . . .
>   . . . whose wan marble . . .

And the Blessed Damozel's ripe hair is stolen to grace 'La Bella Donna della Mia Mente'. But these details are decorative in Wilde, and the increased emphasis on strangeness has little function.

v

Decoration is, then, the new role the Pre-Raphaelite ideal beauty acquires during the 1890's. No longer used as a tangible equivalent for inarticulate spiritual realities or as a private myth often conjoined with public myth as in Rossetti's *Lilith* (Plate 15*b*), she comes to exist, hackneyed and reduced to a few token features, an end in herself and no longer a means of revelation, as in the *Lilith* of Althea Gyles (Plate 15*a*) which Yeats admired.[1]

Her life in the 1890's is, in fact, vital only when she is used deliberately as decoration. Her features are employed frequently by Beardsley in his illustrations for the *Bon-Mots* series,[2] where the craning neck, sensuous lips, staring eyes and massive head of hair offer visual patterns alongside but incidental to the verbal

---

[1] *The Dome*, I, 33. The image has a wide visual currency in the period: Laurence Housman especially exploits the thick neck, massed hair and prominent chin in 'The Reflected Faun' (*YB*. I) or the illustrations to his own story, 'The Troubling of the Waters' (*D*. old series II). See also the 'Lady of Shalott' (*YB*. IX), Nellie Syrett's work (*YB*. X) and George Thompson's lithograph (*YB*. III).

[2] The *Bon-Mots* series were published by J. M. Dent, London, 1893-4.

gems of Lamb, Jerrold or Sydney Smith. Similar marginal illustrations in which the Pre-Raphaelite beauty also figures are the decorative initials and chapter headings in Malory's *Le Morte-D'Arthur* (Plates 8*a* and 8*b*). It must be an extraordinary experience trying to read Malory's stories among a décor which re-creates the special enthusiasms of the Pre-Raphaelite imagination. But as far as Beardsley's use of the ideal beauty is concerned she is justly celebrated in her new decorative function by his trenchant blacks and whites. Her modified image is used similarly to decorate the covers of *The Yellow Book* (II and III) or *The Savoy* (I) or to illustrate Gautier's *Madamoiselle de Maupin*.[1]

Other artists, such as Charles Ricketts, Walter Crane or Margaret Macdonald, also involve the features of this woman in their designs. The woman in Ricketts's *Bacchanalian Scene* has a sharper face but is still recognizably derivative. Crane in his tapestry designs and book illustrations and Macdonald in her marvellous gesso panels (Plate 11) are eminently successful in integrating her features into their décor. The latter especially seems to be inspired by the massive sweeps of hair to execute similar arabesques of lines over the full panel.[2]

Another artist who used the ideal beauty was William Thomas Horton, whom Yeats also admired. The rhetoric of the essay Yeats prefaced to Horton's volume, *A Book of Images* (1898), is more convincing than Horton's actual work. This seems crude beside either his Pre-Raphaelite predecessors or a contemporary like Beardsley and, indeed, he usefully serves to bring out their strengths. Yeats chooses to stress in Horton's dream-like drawings both the *patterns* of formal shapes and images and such symbolism as 'the woman of *Rosa Mystica* and *Ascending into Heaven*, who is the Divine womanhood'. But despite Yeats's enthusiasm, later perhaps regretted,[3] Horton's images are a central example of a

---

[1] 'The Lady at the Dressing Table'. No. IV of six illustrations to *Mademoiselle de Maupin* by Théophile Gautier, published in portfolio by Leonard Smithers, London, 1898.

[2] For Walter Crane, see Italo Cremona, *Il Tempo dell' Art Nouveau* (Florence 1964), figs. 75–7.

[3] Yeats omitted the last section of his introduction and all mention of Horton when he reprinted it as 'Symbolism in Painting' in *Ideas of Good and Evil* (1903).

meagre decorative talent not quite content to allow the image of the ideal beauty to lose its symbolic functions. So his *Dawn* of 1897 is a rather unhappy conjunction of Blake's 'Ancient of Days' and Burne-Jones' *Aurora*, having neither the strange and electric energy of the first nor the ethereal presence of the second. In *A Reminiscence* sixteen years later a feeble Dantesque allusion is attempted with the traditional image of Dante in close-fitting cap and a Rossetti-like Beatrice; its title is sadly all too just.[1]

One might conclude this account of the decorative function of the Pre-Raphaelite beauty by mentioning briefly three rather distinct and famous artists who absorbed her more authentically into their work. Whistler, for example, invokes her in his *Femme en Blanc* where, as George Moore noted, 'the type of woman is the same—beauty of dreaming eyes and abundant hair'.[2] Here she is absorbed, as she is again in such pictures as *La Princesse du Pays de la Porcelaine* and *The Little White Girl*, into the texture and pattern of Whistler's colours. Her function is at last rightly and only visual.

In the same way, though with less *finesse* and delicacy of tone as befits a more public art-form, she achieves what is perhaps her most decorative apotheosis in the designs and posters of Alphonse Mucha. Her naked figure leans through a mass of tangled hair in Mucha's poster for the *Salon des Cent*; a less intense and more jaunty version is still recognizable advertising Ruinart champagne. She briefly assumes an ornate and more gaudy symbolism as *Été* in 1896 and as *La Poésie* two years later. Her long, naked neck and linear swirling hair occupy all our attention again in the title page design for *Le Pater*.[3] What is for me the most ironic of her appearances occurs in Mucha's poster for Job cigarette papers (Plate 10*a*): here from under Beatrician eyelids she gazes in mesmerized approval at the swirling smoke from her cigarette, which curls almost in parody of her own hair into the background

---

[1] Both are illustrated in *W. T. Horton. A Selection of his Work*, with a biographical sketch by Roger Ingpen, (London n.d.), pp. 27 and 143.

[2] *Modern Painting* (1893), p. 20.

[3] All examples mentioned are illustrated in B. Reade, *Art Nouveau and Alphonse Mucha*, catalogue of exhibition at Victoria and Albert Museum (H.M. Stationery Office), 1963.

of the poster and in its folds engulfs both the image of Pre-Raphaelite idealism and the symbol of the New (smoking) Woman.

In 1898 Mucha was sharing a studio with Whistler who was then in Paris. Two years later Picasso arrived in Paris on his way, so the artist himself declares, to England, where he was lured by images of the ideal woman which had come to Barcelona and had apparently an active life in certain of the artistic magazines. Picasso himself had produced copies of the ideal beauty, but seems soon to have moved towards a satire of her intense poses, for 'La Fille au Café' (Plate 10*b*) offers a grotesque caricature of her thrusting chin, long neck, massive hair and staring eyes.[1] This movement in Picasso from copying towards parody is a similar feature in the last English artist to whom we turn—Aubrey Beardsley.

VI

The focus of our interest in Beardsley must be upon his intelligence and its strenuous application in his art. The ideal Pre-Raphaelite beauty which has been traced through a variety of conditions prospered again in Beardsley's work. In contrast to the flaccid and unoriginal handling of her image by some of his contemporaries she achieves in his drawings a fresh and remarkable vigour. This entailed little modification of the original image as it appeared in Rossetti or Burne-Jones; rather it involved a thoughtful analysis of its contemporary significance and a brilliant, often witty explanation of the thoughts in visual terms.

Beardsley's decorative use of the feminine beauty has already been discussed. What is significant here is his just appreciation of her new decorative role and his ability to absorb her into his intricate pattern of black and white without diminishing or changing her. In his work for the illustrated Malory there is acknowledgement of her Pre-Raphaelite provenance—a fitting gesture, after all, in illustrations to a quintessential Pre-Raphaelite 'source-book'—and yet she is totally at one with the specific pattern into

[1] These early enthusiasms of Picasso are plotted in Phoebe Pool, *Picasso. The Formative Years* (1961), to which I am indebted.

which she is fitted. She never seems out of place, as she does often in other of her appearances during the 1890's. In one chapter heading (Plate 8*a*) she is more obviously a Burne-Jones figure and her hair which is particularized after Burne-Jones's fashion assumes the curves and decoration applied also to the scenery around her; the lute recalls perhaps the *Angels of Creation* or, at the least, the ethereal harmonies to which many Burne-Jones figures allude. But another, more Rossetti-like model (Plate 8*b*), with heavy mass of hair and intense gaze and surrounded by flowers (perhaps an allusion to a favourite symbolism of Rossetti's) suggests the more appropriate decorative pattern of large opposed masses of black and white which surround her.

A final example might be the cover for the third volume of *The Yellow Book*. The young woman administering the powder puff at her dressing table has something of the pertness and vulgarity of the music hall to which the Pre-Raphaelite ideal never pretended. Yet the craning neck, heavy upper lip and massive sweep of hair (made stronger by a corresponding movement in her black robe) recall her lineage. There is, I feel, a genuine wit in using the Pre-Raphaelite image in this context. A similar wit is involved in the famous design for the invitation card for the opening of the Prince's Ladies Golf Club at Mitcham: nothing more daunting could perhaps be imagined than this massive beauty gazing with mystic abstraction down the fairway, and the little lively pierrot-caddy throws her other-worldliness into gentle ridicule.

Beardsley's ridicule of the Pre-Raphaelite beauty is the main area in which his intelligence exercises itself. Pater had praised Rossetti for making the spiritual visible and sensual;[1] but often of course all that he achieved was a cloying physical presence, which Beardsley is quick to notice. He annotates it mercilessly in his designs for Wilde's *Salomé* which he mocks by using exaggerated images of the Pre-Raphaelite beauty for Herodias, the stomach dancer and even John the Baptist himself. In the watching figures in *The Woman in the Moon* (Plate 8*c*) he makes us aware of their intense gaze, almost goitrous necks and solid bulk of hair—the

[1] See supra p. 149.

hair especially Beardsley can always parody fluently with his mass of black ink on white paper. In 'The Kiss of Judas' (Plate 5) the beauty who reclines against the tree is exactly Rossetti's *Pia de' Tolomei* in which Swinburne noticed and Beardsley was to exaggerate the 'pallid splendid face (which) hangs a little forward, wan and white against the mass of dark, deep hair . . . In her eyes is a strange look of wonder and sorrow and fatigue.' To stress the satire Beardsley provides her with a grotesque, dwarfed attendant.

His drawings seem constant allusions to a wide variety of Pre-Raphaelite paintings. An early one, *The Litany of Mary Magdalen*, recalls Rossetti's *Girlhood of Mary Virgin*; the headpiece for the Malory title-pages alludes to the Burne-Jones series, *The Legend of the Briar Rose*; while generally throughout the illustrations in the Malory are barely concealed references to such other Pre-Raphaelite pictures as *The Beloved, Dante's Dream* or *Aurora*. In some cases the allusions have gentle undertones of satire, though Beardsley's admiration of 'the Immortal E B J'[1] would perhaps have precluded anything more than a gentle distortion of the draughtsmanship, stylized already in Burne-Jones by his affection for Mantegna. More savage satire is reserved for other figures: thus a grotesque drawing called *Withered Spring* (Plate 9b) alludes with more firm derision to Millais' *Autumn Leaves* (Plate 9a); the closed eyes of the eponymous figure in *The Ascension of St Rose of Lima* (Plate 8a) echo the shut eyelids of Rossetti's Beatrice.

Rossetti's draughtsmanship, much inferior to Burne-Jones, is a more obvious target for Beardsley. The satire on the intense bodily presence of many Rossetti beauties is one form his comments take. Among the *Salomé* drawings, 'A Platonic Lament' mocks the languor of many Rossetti figures (while another irreverent dwarf crouches under the bier to point the irony). The face he gives to Salomé as she kisses the mouth of John the Baptist is a massive exaggeration of features in *Veronica Veronese* or *The Roman Widow*, and the fall of Herodias' hair, of that in Mary Magdalene; in each case Beardsley's own drawing serves as

---

[1] Letter quoted in Brian Reade and Frank Dickinson, *Aubrey Beardsley*, the catalogue for the Exhibition at the Victoria and Albert Museum, item 138.

an implicit criticism of Rossetti's extravagant and oppressive colouring and draughtsmanship.

This also is the case in his *Mysterious Rose Garden* (Plate 7*b*), which was taken at the time of its publication in *The Yellow Book* to be a satire on Rossetti's version of the Annunciation, *Ecce Ancilla Domini* (Plate 7*a*). (Although the hair of the two figures seems more of a reference to Burne-Jones, the intricately worked backround and flowers suggest some of Rossetti's favourite motifs and the general subject is certainly an allusion to him.) In Rossetti's picture an intense, rather emaciated Virgin Mary crouches awkwardly on her bed before the large and apparently formidable presence of the visiting angel. In Beardsley the rather naive anatomy of Rossetti's painting is caught in the elongated 'Mary' and her nervous gestures, while her visitor's hands and feet emerge—amusingly far apart—from within his great enfolding cloak. The relationship between the two figures is rendered with a rather sinister mockery, especially in the 'Angel' who mutters dramatically behind raised hand and who is given both the trailing Pre-Raphaelite hair *and* a slim moustache.

Beardsley's mockery of Pre-Raphaelite idealism as expressed through images of this ideal beauty is not, however, a simple derision. I feel about many of his designs what Pater felt about Leonardo's: they are

full of a curious beauty, that remote beauty apprehended only by those who have sought it carefully; who, starting with acknowledged types of beauty, have refined as far upon these, as these refine upon the world of common forms. But mingled inextricably with this there is an element of mockery also; so that, whether in sorrow or scorn, he caricatures Dante even.[1]

It is in both sorrow and scorn that Beardsley revisits the ideal Pre-Raphaelite beauty.

He mocks his own evident fondness for Wagner or Wagnerian themes (a European manifestation which had, of course, much in common with impulses of the Pre-Raphaelite imagination). The drawing, 'The Wagnerites' (*YB*. III), provides as audience for a performance of *Tristan und Isolde* a regiment of Pre-Raphaelite

---

[1] *The Renaissance*, p. 108.

women with thick lips and heavy, be-flowered hair, whose intensity is conveyed by areas of black relieved only by the white of their enormous shoulders. Or the 'Siegfried' illustration for the Malory blends elegant memories of Burne-Jones with a diabolical landscape.

In his smaller marginal designs for *Le Morte D'Arthur* it is ultimately difficult to distinguish between his use of the ideal beauty as décor and his ironic celebration of her new activity, between—that is to say—his sense that she provides a useful shape to manipulate in his illustrations and his implied comment that this is all she now can aspire to. But in some of the larger drawings for the Malory, the satire seems more insistent and obvious. The face of Arthur glimpsing the Questing Beast (Plate 16) is a sinister redaction of all the ideal beauties Rossetti painted in his Arthurian pictures. Arthur's rather languorous inclination in face of the beast is heightened by the startled satyr at the top. Or the stylization of Merlin and Nimue, in which the craning neck is given equally to both characters, seems to ridicule at the same time as it delights in the myth.

This dual response of Beardsley's may best be seen in his handling of the theme of the hermaphrodite. The myth of the ideal union of male and female in one person had absorbed the Pre-Raphaelite imagination, no doubt because it provided a certain erotic fascination. Swinburne deploys the myth in a poem which invokes all the properties—the weary lips and eyes, the 'folds of all thy hair'—of Rossetti's beautiful women. As the movement grows her features are used indiscriminately and often without real purpose for male and female alike.[1] The two figures who listen to the pipes in *The Garden of Pan* by Burne-Jones are identical, and in his study of Sir Galahad, the knight's head is really the same as the female ones thronging the background. Simeon Solomon's soul appears to him in *A Vision of Love* as a

---

[1] Rossetti himself cannot be absolved of all blame for this later blurring of the female and male image. The triptych he designed for Llandaff Cathedral gives David almost feminine features, while the unused design for his Italian translations shows a man kissing a woman who is indistinguishable from him (see H. C. Marillier, *Dante Gabriel Rossetti An Illustrated Memorial of His Art and Life* (1899), pp. 74 and 107).

nude man, while the allegorical figure of Sleep has a masculine pronoun but the familiar features of Rossetti's women:

his eyes were not covered by their lids, yet it seemed as if slumber had fallen upon them; . . . mystic gaze . . . his locks were softly lifted by the air, and his lips trembled . . . his bent face was over-shadowed by the exceeding sadness . . . (p. 21)

By the 1890's this ambiguous or hermaphrodite figure was as familiar as the more certain image of the woman. Only syntax identifies the figure who, in attitudes reminiscent of the Blessed Damozel, bends over a pool to gaze at his reflection in J. Addington Symonds's 'Narcissus Flower':

A youth of mystic loveliness, inclined
Face-forward o'er the hurrying streamlet's gloom,
Bending dark brows of yearning, dim surmise,
To search time's turbid flood with prescient mind. (*HH.* II, 121)

Beardsley certainly follows the fashion. His treatment of man and woman in most of the *Salomé* drawings is identical, while in Malory, the drawing of Sir Tristram drinking the love potion offers a stylized confrontation between a man in the likeness of Rossetti's women and an Iseult after the Burne-Jones model. But Beardsley seems to share with Swinburne an ambivalent attitude towards the myth of Hermaphroditus. Swinburne wrote—

the sad and subtle moral of this myth, which I have desired to indicate in verse, that perfection once attained on all sides, is a thing thenceforth barren of use and fruit; whereas the divided beauty of separate woman and man—a thing inferior and imperfect—can serve all turns of life.[1]

Beardsley shares this paradoxical response to achieved perfection. He can mock the absurd rhetoric of Pre-Raphaelite idealisms and introspection at the same time enjoying the manipulation of their symbolism to which he reponds lovingly and intricately.

The drawing with which to end is not a particularly obvious

---

[1] Quoted Lafourcade, *La Jeunesse de Swinburne*, II, 453. For a learned account of the hermaphrodite image in France see 'The Image of the Androgyne in the Nineteenth Century', *Romantic Mythologies*.

one. But in *D'Albert in Search of his Ideals* much of Beardsley's complex response to the ideal Pre-Raphaelite beauty is allowed to mingle with another contemporary taste for the eighteenth century. D'Albert has the familiar massive head of hair, great intense eyes and the sensual mouth. The drawing suggests that while Beardsley is hospitable to the perfection of beauty and the quest for ideals yet he cannot refrain from mocking either their naivety or their ultimate sterility.

VII

The second half of the nineteenth century has been noted for 'its hectic cult of beauty', a beauty which was moreover 'very narrow and exclusive'.[1] The extravagant pronouncements on the subject evince wide range but little coherence and are sustained by no formal aesthetics.[2] Writers seemed content sometimes to talk of the vague abstraction, presenting it with a capital 'B', anonymous but absolute, enshrined in a careful but empty technique—

> To fight with form, to wrestle and to rage,
> Till at the last upon the conquer'd page
> The shadows of created Beauty fall.[3]

Beauty was virtually compulsory, as Beerbohm notices in *The Yellow Book* (IV, 281), and accordingly robbed of its chief charm.

The dominant image to emerge from this 'strange passion for beauty'[4] was that of the beautiful woman and here Rossetti's example encouraged a considerable following. Arthur Symons

[1] René Wellek, 'Walter Pater's Literary Theory and Criticism', *Victorian Studies*, I (1957), p. 46. Beerbohm discusses the cult of beauty and its original 'shy artificers' among the Pre-Raphaelites in *The Yellow Book*, IV, 278.

[2] *Inter alia*: 'In the light of that star he walked ever in a divine surety. It was the star of beauty' (*Dome*, old series, V, 42); 'Beauty is a Queen and must be served as a Queen' (quoted Cazamian, *Le Roman et les Idées en Angleterre* (Paris 1935), II, 367); 'in our desire for beauty in all things we are one' (Wilde, *Letters*, p. 147); 'Sometimes even now I think that there are sins more beautiful than anything else in the world' (*The Chameleon*, I, i, 41). Beerbohm notes that 'Beauty was sought in the most unlikely places' (*The Works*, 4th edition, 1921), pp. 46–7.

[3] *An Anthology of 'Nineties' Verse*, p. 43.

[4] *The Works of Oscar Wilde*, ed. G. F. Maine (1949), p. 225.

remarked how Rossetti 'stimulated the sense of beauty' and how its 'supreme embodiment' was in the 'beauty of women, and chiefly in the mysterious beauty of faces'.[1] The symbolic beauty was the focus for much otherwise inarticulate idealism. Her most impressive and compelling appearances may be justified in that way. But progressively she dwindled into a decorative device, used either to sustain a paucity of original emotion or, more legitimately, to display her ample presence in design and illustration. Fortunately, I think, her image survived derivative handling by lesser talents and found fresh life in the work of Beardsley or the later love poems of Yeats. Robartes, whose daily bread is truths, asks Aherne whether he has not always known that

> All dreams of the soul
> End in a beautiful man's or woman's body.[2]

Ideals are essentially remote. 'Beauty seems always something remote from the stress of common life,' wrote Max Beerbohm. 'Though it may exist in such life, it can be conceived only as at a distance.'[3] It was a paradox that the Pre-Raphaelite imagination at its best had celebrated for an age not easily convinced. What is probably the last appearance of the Blessed Damozel in the nineteenth century illustrates this. A story in *The Dome*[4] shows a girl acting the Blessed Damozel in a *tableau vivant*: for the hero she represents the poetic, the romantic and the beautiful—'a languishing maiden to sigh to me on moonlight nights.' His friend, a curate, counsels him to 'leave all those ridiculous Rossetti affectations' in favour of 'a wholesome, sensible, good-looking, good-tempered English girl.' Here is the full confession of that gulf between reality and art which vitiates so much of late nineteenth-century work.

---

[1] *Figures of Several Centuries*, pp. 202 and 205, and *Dramatis Personae*, p. 129.
[2] *Collected Poems*, p. 186.
[3] Quoted J. G. Riewald, *Sir Max Beerbohm, Man and Writer* (Brattleboro, Vermont 1953), p. 54.
[4] Old series, II, pp. 29 ff.

CHAPTER SIX

Realism and the 'Larger Latitude'

I want to deal with the essentially unheroic, with the day-to-day
life of that vast majority of people who are at the mercy of paltry
circumstance

       —Harold Biffen in *New Grub Street*

There are moments when I desire squalor, sinister, mean surroundings, dreariness and misery

       —Reggie Hastings in *The Green Carnation*

I

AFTER THE TRANSCENDENT VISIONS of the symbolists the
realism of the nineties seems more substantial and far less dangerous in the hands of minor writers. Realism[1] looked for its subject
matter to ordinary circumstances and events which writers could
find everywhere around them. In the magazines of the nineties
it produced a quantity of short stories, notable for their artistry
and genuine concern for their subjects; some of these compel
more attention than they have perhaps received. The main danger
of the realistic method is that it could elicit dull, pedestrian cata-
logues of exteriority quite as unsatisfactory as the symbolism
which had rejected the same surfaces for being meaningless and
insecure. As Waugh wrote in *The Yellow Book*, 'the natural
inclination of frankness, the inclination of the virtue in the rough,

---

[1] I use this term to refer to all the English work discussed in this chapter. In
France the terms *realism* and *naturalism* represented different approaches and
creative methods, but with their importation into England the distinction was
blurred and becomes less useful. *Esther Waters*, for example, has the heavy
deterministic emphasis of Zola's naturalism and at the same time Flaubert's
detached and elegant description of reality.

211

is to blunder on resolutely with an indomitable and damning sincerity, till all is said that can be said, and art is lost in photography' (I, 204). But in the work of some of the best realists—Crackanthorpe, Harland, D'Arcy, George Moore, Dowson—art does not succumb to photography.

Realist fiction at the end of the century had various, closely connected aims. There were careful descriptions of the exterior world, used to give as great an immediacy and sense of actuality as possible. The same thoroughness was also shown with the interior world of a character's mind, and here a growing interest in psychology was exploited by the realist writer. Further, it required a treatment of the most moving and characteristic incidents of modern life. But it seemed to seek out those incidents which either went unmentioned among middle-class readers or were found at a lower social level than the reader or author inhabited, what one writer called 'this proletarian exclusiveness' (*YB*. V, 178). It was as if to make any depiction of an actuality 'real' for the reader, it had to be especially brutal in its impact upon his cosseted sensibilities: realism seemed to begin at the point where the writer was able *épater le bourgeois*. Hence the premium upon risqué subjects, prostitution, sex, failed marriages;[1] on louche and forbidden places, music-halls, brothels, madhouses, even cabmen's coffee stands;[2] on urban nostalgia, slums and cityscapes. Hence also the bleak pessimism, the emphasis on the inevitability of degeneration, despair and disaster.[3]

Much of all this had been inherited from foreign writers, Ibsen or Verhaeren, but above all from France. The determinism, the bleakness of subject, the outspokenness on certain topics, the tough or exotic emphasis placed on instruments of destruction from drugs and alcohol to tuberculosis and prostitution—all these

[1] A writer in *The Albemarle* explained the normal reaction to marriage: 'If the matrimonial yoke proved irksome, neither party dreamt of lightening it by discussing the failure of marriage . . .' (II, 3).

[2] Symons was introduced to cabmen's coffee stands by a friend who was a taker of hashish and a lover of the sordid (*S*. IV, 92).

[3] This emphasis is reflected in such titles as Egerton's *Discords* (1894) or Crackanthorpe's *Wreckage* (1893). The *Sketch* remarked that the more sombre and depressing the nearer art was to truth (cited Frierson, *L'Influence du Naturalisme Français sur les Romanciers Anglais de 1885–1900* (Paris 1925), p. 236).

the nineties would have found in the contemporary French novel and short story. Indeed, English writers had all done their French homework and were scrupulous in demonstrating so. Le Gallienne's line, 'Within the town, the lamps of sin are flaring', recalls too closely for coincidence Baudelaire's 'La Prostitution s'allume dans les rues';[1] if it is not a deliberate echo, it certainly reveals an attempt at very similar effects. George Moore, in particular, explains his French debts and enthusiasms in his *Confessions*, and when the *Spectator* reviewed his *Esther Waters* in 1894, it observed that 'one is made aware by certain passages that Mr Moore would fain imitate the methods of Zola and his odious school'.[2] It did add, however, that Moore's faith as a Christian and his instincts as a gentleman prevented a successful imitation.

Despite a good deal of affectation, realism does seem to have been, as *The Yellow Book* claimed, the 'most interesting and suggestive development in the poetry and fiction of our time' (I, 212). George Moore was filled with wonder by 'the idea of a new art based upon science, in opposition to the art of the old world that was based on imagination, an art that should explain all things and embrace modern life in its entirety, in its endless ramifications, be, as it were, a new creed in a new civilization . . .'.[3] Even through Crackanthorpe's guarded article on reticence in literature there shows an enthusiastic acceptance of the novel's supremacy 'in a time of democracy and science' (*YB*. II, 259).

Those two words are of immense significance. 'Democracy' implies the broadening scope of subject matter, the increasing artistic interest in all types of people and circumstances. The second implies the new techniques suggested to writers by the sciences. Both democracy and the advance of science, together with the progress in Positivism, were the aspects of the late nineteenth century which Zola stressed in an interview given to *The Albemarle* in 1892.[4] Zola was himself praised by Havelock Ellis for drawing our attention to 'the latent artistic uses of the

---

[1] *English Poems* (4th ed., 1895), p. 89, and 'Le Crépuscule du Soir', *Les Fleurs du Mal*, XCV.

[2] Quoted I. Gregor and B. Nicholas, *The Moral and the Story* (1962), p. 98.

[3] *Confessions of a Young Man* (Travellers' Library Ed., 1928), p. 75.

[4] 'Realism in France and in England. An Interview with Zola', I, 39–43.

rough, neglected details of life' and for extending language's usefulness in the scientific description of reality (*S.* I, 74–7). In another piece on Nietzsche, Ellis vindicates the 'immoralist' who lawfully opens up 'any region for free cultivation' (*S.* IV, 60). Again, Hardy's *Jude the Obscure* is said to have dealt 'very subtly and sensitively with new and modern aspects of life' (*S.* VI, 48).

In *The Yellow Book* Crackanthorpe's hero, Haselton, is new and modern in his psychological insight into the 'play of his own personality' (V. 134). Crackanthorpe himself, through the mouth of one of the speakers in a critical dialogue, confesses that the psychological interest of literature is the most powerful for him (*A.* I, 217). Many short story writers in other magazines of the time seemed to have shared that psychological curiosity, and it becomes as much a feature of the realistic writer's repertoire as what Waugh called 'the fidelity of the kodak' (*YB.* I, 217). An initial puzzlement as to why *The Savoy* (II) printed Havelock Ellis's translation of Lombroso's 'A Mad Saint' is resolved if one recalls this literary interest in psychology, to which Lombroso's analysis and discussion of the inspired woman and his impartial, scientific inquiry presumably appealed.

Attitudes among realist writers varied as much as Harold Biffen's does from Reggie Hastings's in the mottoes quoted at the head of this chapter. There was the superficial one, typified by Hastings, whom Hichens satirizes; he was one of those who have been described as tourists rather than explorers in Bohemia.[1] The languid, affected desire for cheap and easy thrills in the alien (and hence alluring) world of slum and squalor is betrayed usually by a sentimentality that is totally at odds with the realism. This is the fault into which Symons falls with the 'delicious shame' for his Juliet of a night; or it is revealed by such phrases as the 'romance' of London in its poorer quarters (*YB.* II, 121), or the frequent appeals to the 'poetry of the city'. Symons's review of Henley's poems, which are also said to be instinct with a sense of the poetry of cities, diagnoses this particular danger when he complains that 'to be modern in poetry . . . and yet poetical is perhaps the most difficult as it is certainly the most interesting of

[1] V. de S. Pinto, *Crisis in English Poetry*, p. 27.

all artistic achievements'.[1] Although the danger was especially acute in the large amount of verse on modern subjects, even prose like Crackanthorpe's *Vignettes* talks of 'the mysterious, sumptuous splendour of a murky London night'.[2]

While much of the realism is not as obviously sentimental as the London poet who wrote—'That's the great town at night: I see her breasts',[3] some of it skirts close to sentimentality. This is the case with Symons's piece in the final *Savoy*, 'The Childhood of Lucy Newcome', which shows the girl's existence as poverty and death advance and overtake first her mother and then her father. Or those 'Three Stories' (*YB*. II) which present in turn a mis-marriage, the despair and despondency of the girl wishing to escape a wearisome life looking after her father, and a bare, cold and filthy room containing a man's corpse. Or the exoticism of Le Gallienne's 'A Ballad of London': 'Men die and rot deep out of sight / To keep this jungle-flower bright.'[4] For although many of such pieces seem intended to be what Moore called 'a dagger in the heart of the sentimental school'[5] the despairing and sordid circumstances are handled with an unnecessary fondness or fascination. The delineation of murky details of London in George Egerton's 'A City Mood' is too loving; she is indeed one of those who betray themselves with the phrase, 'poetry of the city' (*YB*. I, 192).

It is only the assured and careful treatment which Ella D'Arcy gives to 'Irremediable' (*YB*. I) that saves it from this fault. In the story of the inevitable decline of a potential writer married to a Whitechapel slut with a drunken father, all aspects of realism occur: the determinism (hence the title), the fascination for lower classes, the intricate details of the poor quarters, the analysis of

---

[1] *Fortnightly*, LII (August 1892), p. 184.

[2] *Vignettes* (1896), p. 55. What is most distressing perhaps is the discrepancy between the rhetoric and the insight rather than the general notion. Whistler in such pictures as *Old Battersea Bridge* or Sickert in some of his Music Hall paintings could celebrate the poetry of the city with the necessary technical assurance to convince one of the vision.

[3] *Anthology of Nineties Verse*, p. 35.

[4] *The Eighteen-Nineties, A Period Anthology in Prose and Verse*, chosen by Martin Secker and with an introduction by John Betjeman (1948), p. 226.

[5] Quoted Gregor and Nicholas, *The Moral and the Story*, p. 98.

the man's mental and spiritual reactions to his situation. They are handled well, I think, and the story is a fine one. But the danger is when such details, methods and ideas were handled with the mentality of a Reggie Hastings. Then they are sentimental or sensational at their worst, at their best mechanical.

A great deal of the realism does appear rather mechanical, like the etchings of the Clyde and the Glasgow slums in *The Yellow Book* (XIII). Especially mechanical seem the despair and pessimism which were an almost inevitable part of the realism: for instance, the unrelenting decline of the useless and unhappy dweller in the Temple, or the ailing girl, given a few months to live, racked with coughing fits as she tries to keep warm by the fire.[1] The pessimism seems even more colourless when it is expressed by itself, as in Dowson's 'Vanitas' or Johnson's 'Nihilism'.[2]

Because they required little imagination, 'the gospel of ugliness' and the 'cheerlessness of modern literature'[3] were relied upon as central motifs in realist work. The décor especially leans heavily upon such clichés: the 'distant rumour of feverish London';[4] the dark dirty staircase leading to the Paris studio (*YB.* X, 266); 'all the sin of the city seemed crushed to listlessness; vacantly wistful, the figures waited by the street corners' (*YB.* V, 147); the 'tangle of slummy streets' with garish cafés where harlots dance with drunken sailors (*YB.* III, 71). The climax of a very typical story by Lionel Johnson is an anthology of all such ideas: in 'A Commentary on Love' the two partners in the love affair decide to postpone getting married, but the girl tires of waiting and marries somebody else, then meets her former lover to say goodbye. The squalid street they choose for their meeting is 'an appropriate scenery for their passion':

[1] Respectively, the second of Harland's 'Two Sketches' (*YB.* I) and Crackanthorpe's 'Modern Melodrama' (ibid.).

[2] Such was the extent of this stress on determinism that it may be taken for granted for ironic purposes: see 'The End of the Episode' where the Squire's wife 'had read some modern novels, and therefore did not talk of Providence' (*YB.* IV, 256).

[3] Accusations against contemporary literature which are acknowledged by Crackanthorpe (*YB.* II, 265).

[4] Crackanthorpe, *Vignettes*, p. 55.

the dingy street changed into a flaring market, where another street ran across it; a scene of very vulgar commerce, full of sordid sights; the rough barrows and tressels crowded the pavement, discovering, under gross gas jets and naphtha lights, piles of rotting fruit and dirty vegetables; the road was littered with banana skins and broken baskets; unpleasant women with fat red faces kept up a chorus of harsh cries; grimy children sprawled about the place. (*A.* II, 40)

But some of the work transcends such desperately realistic *mis-en-scène* and provides interesting and even moving explorations of the human predicament.

In contrast to Reggie Hastings's affectation is Harold Biffen's earnest interest in the essentially unheroic lives of ordinary people; for, as one of Evelyn Sharp's characters remarks, 'it is all nonsense to pretend that working hard for one's living is rather an amusing thing to do'.[1] Gissing confirms that sentiment convincingly enough in 'The Foolish Virgin' (*YB.* VIII). Two stories by John Gray in *The Pageant*[2] deal very effectively with marriages where one partner's mind hovers unsteadily near insanity and the circumstances of life are poor and quite unheroic. In *The Albemarle* Alice Fleming's story of the girl who steals to save her husband from a pauper's funeral and finally commits suicide is also told without hysteria, sensationalism or sentimentality (I, 66–70). Often the best stories have no particularly strong emphasis on poverty and lower-class life, yet still seek the essentially unheroic actions of human beings in whatever station of life. Crackanthorpe's 'When Greek Meets Greek' (*S.* II) or D'Arcy's 'The Pleasure Pilgrim' (*YB.* V) may both deal with more or less wealthy people, but their interests lie in exploring carefully the minds and actions of these people. D'Arcy especially exhibits a delicacy of treatment that recalls without being derivative the contemporary work of Henry James:

Campbell's embarrassment began to wear off. Now that he was getting accustomed to the girls, he found neither of them awe-inspiring. The red-haired one had a simple child-like manner that was charming. Her strange little face, with its piquant irregularity of line, its warmth

---

[1] *YB.* VIII, 184; the story is significantly entitled 'In Dull Brown'.
[2] 'Niggard Truth' (I) and 'Light' (II).

of colour, began to please him. . . . When she suddenly lifted her red-brown lashes, those queer eyes of hers had a velvety softness too. Decidedly, she struck him as being pretty—in a peculiar way. He felt an immense accession of interest in her. It seemed to him that he was the discoverer of her possibilities.

In Crackanthorpe's story Pearl is curious about the activities of her husband and about their constant progress around fashionable resorts with abrupt alterations in the quality of their accommodation, for none of which she is offered real explanations.

Now, since the solitude of her life caused every trivial incident to assume the proportions of an important event, this change in his habits inflamed her curiosity to fever heat. Seated on the bed, or standing in the doorway of the bedroom she would wait listening. Presently a scraping as of the gentle turning of a key. Then for a long while, sometimes an hour, sometimes two hours—nothing—only the movements of the other inmates of the house as they retired for the night. At last the scraping sound again and his tread in the passage.

One night she had worked herself up into such a state of nervous excitement concerning this mystery that she stole out in her stockinged feet to listen at his door. All was still. What could he be doing? She put her eye to the key-hole. Yes, there he was sitting at the table. There was no one else in the room. He was muttering to himself . . . He was lifting (cards) from a heap in the middle of the table and was scattering them over the table. . . .

The story continues to explore the effects of his gambling (and cheating) on them both. It is work that represents, as Henry James wrote of Crackanthorpe, a 'reaction against the smug and the superficial' treatment of human behaviour.[1]

Before I come to trace the Pre-Raphaelite contribution to this realism, there is one further aspect of it that needs particular attention, because the Pre-Raphaelites will be shown to have contributed considerably to it. It is what Henry James wittily called the 'permissibility of the larger latitude' (*YB.* I, 20), the use of subjects not customarily chosen for fictional treatment. In

---

[1] James's essay in appreciation of Crackanthorpe in the latter's *Last Studies* (1897), p. xix.

James's gentle satire, 'The Death of the Lion', an authoress who thinks it too indelicate to publish such a book under her own name has used a pseudonym for her *Obsessions*:

'Oh yes, a mere pseudonym; but convenient, you know, for a lady who goes in for the larger latitude. "Obsessions, by Miss So-and-So", would look a little odd, but men are more naturally indelicate. Have you peeped into "Obsessions"?' Mr Morrow continued sociably to our companion.

The emancipation of subject matter was an important part of realism, which was both its vehicle and its product. The new freedom of artistic expression attracted both the Biffens and the Hastings among writers.

George Moore seemed able to play both rôles. *Esther Waters* is an honourable and moving essay in realism. Yet in *Literature at Nurse or Circulating Morals* (1885), where he is telling, not doing, he is rather more easily satisfied with shock tactics. He hates Mrs Grundy and Mr Mudie, he says, because 'you dare question the sacred right of the artist to obey the impulses of his temperament; I hate you because you are the great purveyor of the worthless, the false and the commonplace' (p. 16). As a consequence of their narrow vigilance 'the paradise of the English novelist is in the school-room' (p. 19).

Sometimes the spirit of revolt got out of hand. In revealing what decorum and prudery had formerly concealed writers forgot their artistic responsibilities: art got lost, not this time in photography, but in sensationalism. Much of this seems to us now naive and jejune, like the sexual passion in 'Theodora' when the 'currents of madness seemed to mingle with my blood' (*YB*. IV, 187); or the fantastically shocking properties which absinthe seemed to have;[1] or the poet of 'In the Streets', wandering 'evilly-idle' under the glare of the lights and burning for a flower woman until he is put off by seeing the child in her arms;[2] or 'On our sleeves we wear our sexes / Our diseases, unashamed' (*YB*. IV,

---

[1] Hichens, with his keen perception of contemporary fads, makes Reggie Hastings drink absinthe when his mind is in its Whitechapel rather than West-End mood (*The Green Carnation* (1894), p. 11).

[2] *The Dome*, old series V, p. 31.

284). The writer of such work felt impelled to remind the reader of his larger attitudes (to paraphrase Henry James) and to demonstrate that 'I am no Puritan' (*S.* I, 40) or that

> there are souls of coarser grain,
> Or else more flexible, who find
> Strange, infinite allurements lurk,
> Undreamed of by the simpler mind,
> Along these streets, within the walls
> Of cafés, shops, and music-halls.[1]

But in contrast to such immaturity, there was writing that made its emancipation from the school-room a profitable and interesting advance. It was, indeed, thanks to such campaigners as Moore that literature was able to choose its subjects more freely, presenting them with none of the inhibitions of morality or middle-class decorum with which Dickens, for example, could colour his pictures of poverty. Work such as Conrad's 'The Idiots' (*S.* VI) and Fiona Macleod's 'Morag of the Glen' (*S.* VII) offer accurate and sensitive records of events and surroundings; Conrad's deals with the lower classes, madness, murder and suicide; MacLeod's has a harsh rugged quality, suitable to its setting. At their best such stories evince the two masteries for which Symons praised Zola: 'mastery of what might be called the atmosphere of character, as well as of surroundings' (*S.* III, 101).

One of the most interesting aspects of this increasing scope for subject matter was the exploration of the privacies of marriage; as with the rest of nineties work it attracted the Hastings and the Biffens. *The Dome* published four stories by Arthur H. Holmes which have this for their theme;[2] parts of Holmes's stories are tautly told, parts succumb to sentimentality. 'Elsa' (*S.* VI) is especially good, as in Crackanthorpe's 'Anthony Garston's Courtship' (*S.* III), a powerful and compelling tale of a Cumberland shepherd courting the parson's niece against his mother's fierce opposition, or Dowson's 'Apple Blossom in Brittany' (*YB.* III) with its extremely sensitive analysis of the hero's mind. And

---

[1] 'Urbanus Loquitur', *HH.* V, 107 ff.
[2] 'The Fancy and the Fact' (I), 'The Sixth Finger' (III), 'The Triumph of Ruth' (III) and 'Major Kay Lemming' (V).

from this new extension of artistic territory the novel and the story did not look back. 'Whatever comes next', Gosse was quoted as saying,

we cannot return, in serious novels, to the inanities and impossibilities of the old well-made plot, to the children changed at nurse, to the madonna-heroine and the god-like hero, to the impossible virtues and melodramatic vices. (*YB.* II, 268)

II

Professor Gombrich has demonstrated that before an artist can embark upon a 'copy' of the exterior world he needs a 'vocabulary' with which to express himself.[1] The nineties found much of their vocabulary as well as an encouraging precedent for using it in contemporary French fiction. But the affectation with which they proclaimed their discipleship to men like Zola and Balzac and their tendency to shock the bourgeois with French enthusiasms tend to conceal their debt to the Pre-Raphaelites. For while the Pre-Raphaelites may have lacked the radical enthusiasms which Symons or Moore learnt from Baudelaire or Zola, they nevertheless managed to pioneer new territory for the arts, thus allowing the Nineties the benefit of their experience to build upon and exploit. Waugh, for instance, in his article on 'Reticence in Literature' sees the tendency of his age towards literary freedom starting with Swinburne (*YB.* I, 213). If one remembers that Rossetti as well as Swinburne was attacked as the 'Fleshly School', the tendency may be seen to start even earlier.[2]

But in more than the controversy over what poetry might take as its legitimate province did the Pre-Raphaelites offer a precedent and a 'vocabulary'. There is, of course, their concern over the minute particulars of realistic vision. Then their interest in contemporary subjects has been too often forgotten by those who remember them only for their mediaevalism; particularly

---

[1] *Art and Illusion* (1961), p. 87.
[2] N. St John-Stevas sees the poetry of Rossetti and Swinburne as foreshadowing the open revolt of later writers against the Victorian conscience and its laws (*Obscenity and the Law*, especially chapter 3 and p. 74).

neglected are stories in the *Oxford and Cambridge Magazine* and Christina Rossetti's volume, *Commonplace*. One thinks also of Rossetti's 'Jenny' or *Found* anticipating Dowson's harlots or Symons's Juliet of a night; Christina's pessimism leading to 'Vanitas' and 'Nihilism'; Hunt's *Awakened Conscience* maybe prompting some *Yellow Book* or *Savoy* story about sexual misdemeanours and unhappy marriages.

III

As early as *The Germ* Tupper suggested that contemporary subjects should not be discarded in favour of those from the past. In his insistence that modern subjects could acquire 'romantic attractions' he even appears to be anticipating the 'poetry-of-the-city' emphasis of later in the century. So does F. G. Stephens, who comments upon the neglect of contemporary subjects and adds that the 'poetry' of the industrial scene has more mystery than is supposed.[1]

Later, in the *Oxford and Cambridge Magazine*, the emphasis is stronger. Heeley warns his readers against assuming that 'what was best in the sixteenth century is therefore best in the nineteenth' (p. 134). The author of 'The Work of Young Men in the Present Age' (pp. 558–64) urges meditation on social wrongs, on 'ills of our great cities' and, further, suggests that those who pored over chronicles in some Gothic nook 'must learn to . . . go down to the busy city, to mingle with the common herd'. Lushington found that Brown's *The Last of England* had set itself 'to represent the most moving and characteristic incidents of Modern Life' (p. 488). Most important, a handful of stories in the *Magazine* took their material or décor from what Fulford described as the 'huge masses of unutterable misery and degradation . . . gathering in the midst of our vast and ugly cities' (p. 190).

One of these tales, 'The Cousins', is perhaps surprisingly by Burne-Jones. Set in a strike-bound north, amid 'the pestilence of

---

[1] Tupper, 'The Subject in Art' (in two parts, vols. 1 and 3); F. G. Stephens (under pseudonym of 'Laura Savage'), 'Modern Giants', vol. 4.

huddled crowds, and all the untold horror of cities' (p. 20), it allows the author to exercise his social conscience, which he does energetically ('see the woe of the great city', etc. [p. 19]). But Burne-Jones comes closer to a more nineties manner in his emphasis upon the *angst* of city life (the death of the women, and the drunken street scene), just as he comes coincidentally closer to Rossetti's 'Jenny' when the hero leaves the contents of his purse in a whore's hand. A similar industrial setting is used by Dixon in his story, 'The Rivals'. The narrator was brought up in a manufacturing town—the 'half-filled pools of the brick field' (p. 34), the gas lights of the suburb, the fog, the mire and thawing snow; in the graveyard, where the heroine is buried after the numb misery and frustration of the action, the 'long row of poplars turned in sickness from the reeking smoke that was withering them' (p. 42). 'The Two Partings' concerns a quite typically nineties plot of somebody 'married to another, when her heart was mine'.[1]

These stories of 1856 represent an interest among Pre-Raphaelites which anticipates much of the realism in the nineties tales I have examined. By the end of the century, certainly, the notes of their 'muscular Christianity' and the occasionally explicit moral indignation at the lot of the oppressed, starving and sick have disappeared. But already in 1856 is being formed within Pre-Raphaelite circles a 'vocabulary' of urban description and the accompanying chorus of grief and pain; there is also an emphasis upon commonplace circumstances and the essentially unheroic.

Perhaps the most important and interesting Pre-Raphaelite contribution in this respect is Christina Rossetti's *Commonplace and other stories* (1870), which was in fact compared by one review of the time to modern French fiction.[2] Christina's title, *Commonplace*, could well match such later ones as D'Arcy's *Monochromes* or Street's *Episodes* for its suggestion of dull and fragmentary existence. As she wrote herself, 'I am so sorry you do not like the title "Commonplace"—for what else to name the

---

[1] P. 115. Cf. Crackanthorpe's 'He Wins Who Loses' (*A.* I) or Holmes's 'A Timely Hint' (*D.* VI).

[2] *The Sunday Times*, 12 June 1870.

everyday story I know not'.[1] Crackanthorpe actually echoes her title in two 'Commonplace Chapters' of *Sentimental Studies*.

Christina concerns herself with the day-to-day lives of ordinary people and seems, above all in the title story, to *emphasize* that aspect of her narration. 'Commonplace' begins in a 'monotonous row' of houses (p. 3). The following hundred and forty pages provide a not unabsorbing account of a dull, chastened and, despite occasional humorous touches, unsmiling account of courtship, marriage and enforced spinsterhood. The general tone is deliberately unheroic and even dreary: 'he answered commonplace remarks by remarks no less commonplace . . .' (p. 42), or 'People exchanged commonplaces, and took their seats; having taken their seats they exchanged more commonplaces' (p. 78). But even such wry irony is not able to brighten the tale. The mismarriage of James and the engagement of his sister in the sombre aftermath of Dr Tyke's death are presented as the meagre consolations of an awkward and vain existence; the spiritual unease of Lucy and the glib superficiality and worldliness of Jane make it an even bleaker story. There is little of Christina's usual stress upon the disadvantages of earthly life with the result that the incidents seem presented for their own value. The dogged details of the three spinsters' careers, if less neatly handled, are worthy of Crackanthorpe's listless, commonplace 'Sunday Afternoon' in *Vignettes*.

Christina's 'Commonplace' is also curiously like Arthur Moore's 'Second Thoughts' (*YB*. III) in both its matrimonial concerns and the motif of the man's return from the East in a second attempt at obtaining his lady's love; only Moore's story is superior in its tauter, more perceptive analysis of feeling and thought, as in the scene where Margaret thinks about the proposal of marriage (pp. 130–1). Equally, Christina's picture of the elder sister's obligations in looking after her sisters provides a similar sense of despondency as the second of the 'Three Stories' in *The Yellow Book* (II), where the girl is tied to her widowed father.

A further scene highly reminiscent of nineties realism is that

[1] *The Rossetti-MacMillan Letters*, ed. M. L. Packer (Berkeley and Los Angeles 1963), p. 82, note 76.

of the arrival of the Charlmonts at London Bridge Station and their cab drive into the city. The station, itself a symbol for the whole metropolis, was vast, confused, busy, dirty; and the city

> looked at once dingy and glaring; dingy with unconsumed smoke, and glaring here and there with early lighted gas . . . Along the Edgeware Road dirt and dinginess re-asserted their sway . . . (pp. 34–5)

Yet, while it seems to be intended as a depressing vista, certainly a 'commonplace' one, there is a certain ambivalence in the careful description and the delight in such detail as the early lighted lamps.

Flaring gas jets were an inevitable part of the nineties urban décor, yet they had been so in much Pre-Raphaelite work: Christina's story, Hunt's *London Bridge on the night of the Marriage of the Prince and Princess of Wales*, Dixon's story in the 1856 *Magazine* or Rossetti's 'Jenny' where the lamps become a brilliant symbol of the prostitute's remorse:

> Round the long park, across the bridge,
> The cold lamps at the pavement's edge
> Wind on together and apart
> A fiery serpent for your heart. (I, 87)

Two other stories in *Commonplace* are close to nineties realism in using as background the poor fishing quarter at Hastings. In 'Vanna's Twins' the man eeks out his livelihood 'by picking up and preparing marine oddities, pebbles, or weeds' (p. 220), while the detail of the narrator's return to London upon some 'legal question . . . touching my small property' (p. 225) is obviously intended to underline the social and economic distance between the narrator and the poor family with whom she stays. In 'The Waves of this Troublesome World' there is the fisherman's impoverished household, the bare-legged children in the fish market, the tyrannical and insensitive mother, an itinerant preacher and photographer, and Sarah's 'wasted form and frequent hacking cough' (p. 300). The ominous, telltale cough was to be another obvious and frequent leitmotif in nineties fiction.[1]

---

[1] See Crackanthorpe's 'Modern Melodrama' (*YB.* I) or 'Major Kay Lemming' (*D.* V).

IV

The rare use of contemporary subjects and settings by Dante
Gabriel bring him nearer than they did his sister to the realism
of the nineties. There are, in fact, only two examples of his
realism which I want to discuss, but both 'Jenny' and *Found*
offered exciting examples to the nineties. When *The Spirit Lamp*
reviewed Symons's *Silhouettes* it suggested that his studies of
boulevards and music halls more closely resembled 'Jenny'
than anything which had been written since Rossetti died.[1]

Both 'Jenny' and *Found* have a prostitute as the central figure.
In neither does Rossetti avoid a mawkish manner, which was
generally eliminated by later writers. An early sketch for the
picture bears the significant quotation, 'I remember thee; the
kindness of thy youth, the love of thy betrothal';[2] what we have
of the canvas suggests the man's anguish over lost innocence
and the girl's rather melodramatic refusal to confront him. He
surrounds Jenny with a similar, sometimes evasive sentimentality:
she is the 'Poor flower left torn since yesterday' (I, 83), her 'silk
ungirdled and unlac'd //And warm sweets open to the waist'
(p. 84). But there is more to the two pieces than a superficial
layer of cheap pathos. What is most striking in the picture is his
dramatic presentation of the incident—the cart obviously left in
a hurry when the former girl friend tries to slip away; the contrast
between his farmer's smock and the tawdry clothes of her trade;
the bleakness of the early hour.

The poem is even more interesting in this respect. The most
insistent part (and also the part where the poetry carries most
conviction) concerns Jenny's urban surroundings, which are contrasted with the rural innocence she had once known. The evoca-

---

[1] *The Spirit Lamp*, II, no. iv (Oxford 1892), p. 118. Similarly, in *Studies in
Strange Souls* (1929), pp. 41 ff., Symons argues that Rossetti was well acquainted
with the seamy side of London and adduces evidence from Watts-Dunton's
edition of Rossetti's letters in 1871. Obviously the Pre-Raphaelite example was
not unique (Symons might have looked to the drawing of the fallen women in
David Copperfield as well as to *Found*); but in their general response to Pre-
Raphaelitism the Nineties were alert to all precedents afforded them by the native
tradition.

[2] Ironside, *Pre-Raphaelite Painters*, pp. 32–3.

tion of 'A Lethe of the middle street' (p. 87) has several features which would later be typical of nineties writing. The gas lamps I have already mentioned; they are used again when the early-morning streets are described and the market produce is brought in at dawn:

> And the old streets come peering through
> Another night that London knew,
> And all as ghost-like as the lamps, (pp. 91–2)

which was a favourite setting of Symons or Dowson. The real distastefulness of Jenny's life is caught sharply as Rossetti describes the London children seeing

> your lifted silken skirt
> Advertise dainties through the dirt. (p. 87)

'Dainties' achieves considerable bitterness. It is generally this 'broil and bale' of city life that elicits Rossetti's most intense and successful lines; especially where, with his usual command of psychological insight into distressed or troubled minds, he suggestively equates the streets she walks with the shabby confusions of her mind:

> For is there hue or shape defin'd
> In Jenny's desecrated mind,
> Where all contagious currents meet
> A Lethe of the middle street? (p. 87)

A further similarity to Nineties' attitudes is the *frissons* that Rossetti experiences in the alien world of a whore's room, which he contrasts with his own study; equally the obvious titillation he expects to induce in a reader with such remarks as 'Love's exuberant hotbed' (p. 83) or

> It was a careless life I led
> When rooms like this were scarce so strange
> Not long ago. (p. 84)

There is, finally, a sense of the speaker's barely disguised superiority, which is often latent in Nineties work with ostensibly a more

'objective' approach.[1] The golden coins left in Jenny's hair and
the superficially pitying—

> Yes, from the daily jeer and jar,
> From shame and shame's outbraving too,
> Is rest not sometimes sweet to you? (p. 85)

—both leave an uncomfortable sense of Rossetti's confidence in
his own ability to be uncontaminated by Jenny's world.

Rather obviously, because of its determined morality, the attitude of Holman Hunt's *Awakened Conscience* is also superior.
But his treatment of the kept-woman theme provides another
anticipation of Nineties' realism, most emphatically in its sense
of the dramatic situation. For what makes the stories and sketches
of *The Yellow Book* and *The Savoy* often the most readable of
the contents is their authors' stress on the drama, the action (if
only mental) of their episodes, monochromes or wreckages. Hunt,
too, catches the woman at an *epiphany* of great intensity, as the
title indicates; the whole picture attempts to support that dramatic moment, even down to the startled cat under the table! When
Ruskin wrote to *The Times* about the picture his main concern
was to spell out the drama of the scene.[2] The fault of the picture
is, perhaps, that it does require its drama to be spelt out; but I
am concerned with the potential example that it offered the
nineties—in its dramatic emphasis, its subject and the details
which support the central theme. Hunt writes of it himself in
these terms, explaining how it was to be 'a *material* interpretation
of the idea' of *The Light of the World* by showing 'how the still
small voice *speaks* to a human soul in the *turmoil of life*'.[3] Of
Ruskin's remarks on the painting, two are in this respect of
great interest: he stresses the *common, modern, vulgar* objects in
the room, and, in expounding the whole story, ends on a heavily
deterministic note, which is not particularly moral:

nay, the very hem of the girl's dress, at which the painter has laboured
so closely, thread by thread, has story in it, if we think how soon its

---

[1] See Frederick Wedmore's 'The Deterioration of Nancy' (*S.* III).

[2] A modern critic who has offered a vigorous defence of the picture also
stresses its drama: see Robert Rosenblaum in *Partisan Review*, 24 (1957), pp.
97–8.

[3] *Pre-Raphaelitism and the Pre-Raphaelite Brotherhood*, I, 347, my italics.

pure whiteness may be soiled with dust and rain, her outcast feet failing in the street.[1]

And with that, the woman of the painting seems to join Jenny among those who dance in the Harlot's House of Wilde, walk the streets with Symons, or, to a background of mad music and strong wine, seduce Ernest Dowson. Nor, as a final note, did such subjects attract only Rossetti and Hunt; for according to the latter, Millais executed two or three designs illustrating 'unconsecrated passion in *modern life*'.[2]

v

Ruskin admittedly says that the woman of *The Awakened Conscience* 'may' be turned on the streets, but the forcefulness with which he describes her probable predicament does not allow much hope of its being only a possibility. A similar sense of inevitable decline and degeneration among sordid surroundings is an integral part of the realism of the nineties and resulted in moods of pessimistic determinism, as in 'Irremediable' or 'The Deterioration of Nancy'. There is nothing of exactly the same kind in Pre-Raphaelite work, but hints of similar ideas are there if later writers had wanted to find them.

Just as Ruskin emphasizes the moral decline of the woman in Hunt's picture, so Rossetti has certain suggestions of determinism and ominous inevitability about Jenny's fate. She is a flower plucked yesterday and left until 'tomorrow leave you bare' (p. 83). The acute sense of transience which permeates *The House of Life* also intrudes its pessimism here:

> What, Jenny, are your lilies dead?
> Aye, and the snow-white leaves are spread
> Like winter on the garden-bed.
> But you had roses left in May,
> They were not gone too. Jenny, nay,
> But must your roses die, and those
> Their purfled buds that should unclose?

---

[1] Quoted Ironside, op. cit., p. 31.

[2] Quoted ibid., pp. 32–3. See also Catalogue for the Millais Exhibition (at Walker Art Gallery and the Royal Academy, 1967), pp. 9 and 88 (item 328).

Even so; the leaves are curled apart,
Still red as from the broken heart,
And here's the naked stem of thorns. (I, 86)

Later in the poem, with the image of the potter's power over the clay, Rossetti muses on the fate at work in making Jenny what she is.

Despite her explicit morality, Christina Rossetti's bleak pessimism and resignation also offer an interesting precedent. I have already discussed her evident fondness and fascination for 'dead hope and paralysed effort';[1] while she obviously felt much of her despair, she sometimes seems to be relying on it as an automatic response, which she even rather enjoys.

In a similar emphasis upon the futility and bleakness of unheroic circumstance the nineties also made it rather a cliché. Later writers may have found in such a theme as Christina's eagerness for the grave where she would be untroubled by 'all that irked her from the hour of birth' (p. 293) an example of unremitting gloom in the face of life's tribulations. And *Commonplace*, while it does not emphasize any inevitable decline among its characters, lays considerable and even resentful stress upon the bleakness of their lives. There is, for example, the needless and, from the plot's point of view, irrelevant death of Dr Tyke in 'Commonplace'; the incredible and improbable tale of woe, distress and financial catastrophe in 'A Safe Investment'; the death of Vanna's twins, caught in a sudden and unlikely snowstorm[2]; the pinched circumstances and sorrows of the fisherman's family in 'The Waves of the Troublesome World'. True, Christina uses all such dire events to further some moral or devotional end; but there is a deliberation in their telling which draws attention to them for their own sakes, and it was an emphasis which her poetry repeatedly confirms.

[1] See supra, chapter three, pp. 103 ff.
[2] Swinburne complained of the unnecessary cruelty involved in this incident: *Letters*, II, 116.

VI

It has already been mentioned that a writer in *The Yellow Book* looked back to Swinburne for the beginning of his contemporaries' interest and success in achieving literary freedom. Swinburne, it is said, 'scrupled not to revel in sensations which for years had remained unmentioned upon the printed page' (I, 213). It is undeniable that he pioneered much of the ground, though maybe a difficult claim to appreciate in the age of *The Tropic of Cancer* or *Lady Chatterley's Lover*. His wish to celebrate one of the seven deadly sins each day of the week cannot shock Kensington today as much as it presumably did or was meant to then. Yet we must remember, as Ezra Pound says, that he wrote 'a great deal of his poetry to tear the pants off the Victorian era and to replace the Albert Memorial by Lampascus'.[1] It is this historical perspective that is important here; not that we may find *Poems and Ballads* uninteresting, but that Ruskin counselled against its publication, as he did that of 'Jenny'.

An insistent aspect of Swinburne's early poetry is its frank sensuality, its excessive passion:

> I knew the beauty of her, what she was,
> The beauty of her body and her sin,
> And in my flesh the sin of hers, alas! (I, 22)

It appears rather naive nowadays—

> That I could drink thy veins as wine, and eat
> Thy breasts like honey! that from face to feet
> Thy body were abolished and consumed (I, 60)

—but we must not underestimate its shock tactics, which become more deliberate when Swinburne confesses a satiety:

> I am weary of all thy words and soft strange ways,
> Of all love's fiery nights and all his days,
> And all the broken kisses salt as brine
> That shuddering lips made moist with waterish wine. (I, 58)

[1] *Literary Essays*, p. 204.

That is reminiscent of Rossetti's account of his 'careless life' to which he confesses in 'Jenny', and because Swinburne is less reticent (albeit imprecise) the *frissons* of his readers would be stronger. For the frank sensuality, the obvious statements of sexual passion ('Her beauty . . . Made my blood turn and swoon' [I, 1]), were highly sensational, simply because they were unconventional poetry and morality. That was exactly John Morley's verdict when he reviewed them for *The Saturday Review*; Swinburne's mind, he said, was 'aflame with the feverish carnality of a schoolboy over the dirtiest pages of Lamprière'.[1] His sensationalism anticipates a similar vogue in the nineties which I have already discussed, although Swinburne's is more wild and extravagant—

> Kiss me once hard as though a flame
> Lay on my lips and made them fire. (I, 192)

By the end of the century the shrillness has been lost, but lost precisely because Swinburne had pioneered the way for somebody like Dowson or Symons to travel in a slightly more relaxed manner: it is only slightly more relaxed, because the reading public in the nineties does not seem to have been educated for Cynara even by having known Dolores, and writers' awareness of this still made them self-conscious.

What makes Swinburne's early poetry important for the growth of a freer and franker realism later in the century is that he challenged conventional restraints upon a writer. Often some of the nineties realists convince one of their much firmer grasp of the realities they describe than Swinburne does: even Dowson had apparently found harlots cheaper than hotels, which it is doubtful if Swinburne had discovered for himself. But in this context Swinburne's insincerity is irrelevant. When he wrote 'Hermaphroditus', when he confessed to have reached 'the shrine where a sin is a prayer' (I, 158) or to finding that 'love is more cruel than lust' (I, 159), when he confused all sense of morality ('lilies and languors of virtue' versus 'the raptures and roses of vice' [I, 156]), he was indirectly claiming an artist's right to

---

[1] Quoted St John-Stevas, *Obscenity and the Law*, p. 61.

freedom of expression in the face of a Victorian like Ruskin's sense of its impropriety. In his reply to Buchanan's attack, Swinburne posed the same problem that Moore was to do nineteen years later in *Circulating Morals*; he asked 'whether or not the domestic circle is to be for all men and writers the outer limit and extreme horizon of their world of work'.[1]

Swinburne's zeal in this cause was complicated by his obvious wish to shock, by his perversity and by his flamboyant atheism. When he sings 'The burden of bought kisses' (I, 125) he is close to Symons or Dowson, but more frequently his manner suggests a boisterous and irreverent undergraduate seeing how far he can flaunt a *risqué* subject. While the 1890's still retained something of this urge to *épater le bourgeois*, it often became subservient to the desire for art to explore a greater range of subjects: they were often, in fact, settling down to use the legacy of Swinburne's efforts. So his flouting of popular conventions does not seem irrelevant to the later realism: the flamboyant atheism of the 'Hymn to Proserpine' made more possible the strongly *a*religious tone of *The Yellow Book* and *Savoy*; his joyous cultivation of 'the sullen savour of poisonous pain' (I, 34) helped the examination of the macabre, unheroic, and miserably commonplace; and when he admits to adulterous thoughts, 'Flesh of his flesh, but heart of my heart' (I, 37), and to a rejection of conventional morality in 'Dolores'—

> Time turns the old days to derision,
> Our loves into corpses or wives;
> And marriage and death and division
> Make barren our lives. (I, 159)

—he was doing very little more than provide the texts for such Nineties stories as 'Countess Marie of the Angels' (*S.* II), 'A Timely Hint' (*D.* VI), 'Elsa' (*S.* VI) or 'A Mere Man' (*S.* II).

Nor was Swinburne alone in his clashes with Victorian orthodoxy. At least one member of that orthodoxy, Robert Buchanan, associated him closely with Rossetti in the attack on 'The Fleshly School of Poetry'. And some years before Buchanan's attack,

[1] *Notes on Poems and Reviews*, p. 20. Compare his jibe in *Under the Microscope* (1872), p. 6: 'We see Harlequin Virtue make love to the goddess Grundy.'

Swinburne himself wrote of Rossetti's paintings in terms which would have underlined their association: 'idea incarnate of fault-less fleshly beauty and peril of pleasure unavoidable'.[1] Earlier still in 1850 the *Athenaeum* abused Pre-Raphaelite work at the Royal Academy with such remarks as 'disgusting incidents of unwashed bodies' and the 'loathsome reality' of decaying flesh.[2]

Buchanan's article, with Rossetti as its main target, appeared originally in *The Contemporary Review* for October 1871. His poetry and his painting are said to combine 'the same morbid deviation from healthy forms of life, the same sense of weary, wasting, yet exquisite sensuality'; they spread 'the seeds of dis-ease' in extolling 'fleshliness as the distinct and supreme end of poetic and pictorial art'. He considers 'Nuptial Sleep' 'shameless' for 'putting on record . . . the most secret mysteries of sexual connection . . . with so sickening a desire to reproduce the sexual mood, so careful a choice of epithet to convey mere animal sensations'. Similarly, Buchanan condemns the shamelessness of exposition in Solomon's picture of *Love Dying by the Breath of Lust*. What is most interesting is that Buchanan's remarks are directed against the artists' choice of subjects and against their verisimilitude in the depiction of them. Buchanan thus takes up the same attitude towards Rossetti as later guardians of Victorian morality adopted towards more outspoken writers such as Hardy, Moore or Wilde. He also, incidentally, accuses Rossetti of aims which these later writers were proud to have achieved: the re-cording of the secret mysteries of sex and the careful realism of their presentation. The defence that Vizetelly offered for himself after his trial in 1888 could well be offered on Rossetti's behalf: 'Is actual life to be no longer described in fiction simply because the withdrawing of the veil that shrouds it displays a state of things unadapted to the contemplation . . . of the young person of fifteen?'[3] Certainly Rossetti's descriptions do not convince us

[1] *Notes on the Royal Academy Exhibition*, p. 46.

[2] *The Athenaeum* (1 June 1850) p. 590.

[3] Quoted Stevas, op. cit., p. 82. Dr Enid Starkie also draws a parallel between the attack on Swinburne and Rossetti in 'The Fleshly School' and the latter prosecution of Vizetelly (see *From Gautier to Eliot: The Influence of France on English Literature, 1851–1939* (1960), p. 79).

today that they bear much relationship to 'actual life'. But whether they are convincing or not, Buchanan's outrage makes Rossetti seem a pioneer of the 'larger latitude'. Certainly Hamilton sees him as a pioneer in *The Aesthetic Movement* and the previous year Harry Quilter had expressed among his divided feelings about Pre-Raphaelitism an admiration for its early members who had 'laid open to artists . . . new phases of thought and feeling'.[1]

Rossetti's contributions to the emancipation of art from the schoolroom and to the possibility of larger latitudes are less obvious than Swinburne's; mainly because he was primarily concerned with other things as well, I think, as being rather cautious about this aspect of his poetry.[2] But the frank sensuality of Swinburne prevails, if more covertly, in Rossetti's work. 'The Blessed Damozel', it has already been noted, is marked by an insistence upon the sensual aspects of the lady in heaven. This insistence colours many sonnets of *The House of Life* and also emerges, in the form of mild eroticism, in such verses as these from 'The Staff and Scrip':

> She sent him a sharp sword, whose belt
> About his body there
> As sweet as her own arms he felt.
> He kissed its blade, all bare,
> Instead of her. (I, 77)

Because too many critics have tried to minimize the sensual element in Rossetti's work in the interests of other emphases, it is worth stressing how considerable it is.[3] Rossetti's susceptibility to the physical allures of the woman whom he uses as a symbol in his poems often intrudes upon her symbolic meaning:

> Her set gaze gathered, thirstier than of late,
> And as she kissed, her mouth became her soul; (XLV)

[1] 'The New Renaissance; or, the Gospel of Intensity', *MacMillan's Magazine*, XLII (September 1880), pp. 393–4.

[2] For one thing Rossetti was more disturbed by Buchanan's attacks than Swinburne; he also omitted sonnets from the final version of *The House of Life*, I imagine because they erred too much towards the sensual and erotic (see infra, p. 237).

[3] See Elton, *A Survey of English Literature 1830–1880* (London 1920), p. 8, where he thinks Rossetti a great ethical poet; Megroz, *Dante Gabriel Rossetti*,

or—

> Or when in the dusk hours, (we two alone,)
> Close-kissed and eloquent of still replies
> Thy twilight-hidden glimmering visage lies,
> And my soul only sees thy soul its own? (IV)

The way in which this sensuality assumes a disproportionate emphasis can best be seen even in sonnets which champion a spiritual love known only through the physical. In *The House of Life* XXI—'Love-Sweetness'—the exposition of the spiritual epiphany is vague ('the confident heart's still fervour') and bewildering in its metaphorical trappings ('the swift beat / And soft subsidence of the spirit's wing', etc.). The sestet does nothing to transcend the more immediate sensuality of the octet, where Rossetti insists upon the loosened hair and the 'mouth's culled sweetness by the kisses shed / On cheeks and neck and eyelids . . .'.

This uneasy conjunction of idealist and sensualist in Rossetti has been frequently noted and the exact significance or extent of this divided impulse is not important here. What is important is that just as Buchanan could ignore Rossetti's 'mystic' or 'spiritual' intentions and attack him for his part in the Fleshly School, so others towards the end of the century would have been attracted by his apparent interest in the physical; indeed, Buchanan would have called attention to it. Many observers would, anyway, have failed to see much difference between the two Rossetti pictures entitled *Lady Lilith* and *Sibylla Palmifera*, which were intended to represent the two beauties of Body and of Soul respectively. They are different women, certainly, but the latter still has many traits of her earthly counterpart. Her gaze may be less self-consuming, more public in its vision directed straight out of the frame; and her shoulders and bosom are covered. Yet the rich hair, the full lips and the thick neck are equally insistent.

---

painter poet of Heaven in Earth (London 1928), p. 171, where he says that 'The Blessed Damozel' is an 'ideal of love spiritualized'; see also P. F. Baum in his introduction to his edition of *The House of Life* (Cambridge, Mass., 1928), p. 24, who suggests that sonnets nos. XXI and XXVIII are examples of Rossetti's 'simple mysticism'.

Swinburne and Rossetti offered a welcome example of artists not afraid of exploring those parts of existence which were excluded from the Victorian experience. When Moore's deliberately shocking verses, *Flowers of Passion*, appeared in 1878, its inspiration could be traced to Rossetti and Swinburne as much as to French writers. Even if Pre-Raphaelite explorations of sex and physical passion are vague and unreal, their work pointed to such areas of reality as new and fruitful ones for the artist. If Rossetti seemed reluctant to pioneer too energetically—he omitted, this, for example, from *The House of Life*:

> This hour be her sweet body all my song . . .
> Her arms lie open, throbbing with their throng
> Of confluent pulses, bare and fair and strong;
> And her deep-freighted lips expect me now,
> Amid the clustering hair that shrines her brow
> Five kisses broad, her neck ten kisses long[1]

—if such 'frankness' was too much for Rossetti, those passages he did allow to stand must have tempted others to go further in their search for larger latitudes. Swinburne's and Rossetti's was an enticing example, suggesting the intensities and dramas for which later writers seemed particularly eager.

VII

Finally, and most obviously, there is the legacy of the Pre-Raphaelite determination to paint exactly what they saw in front of them and to neglect none of its details. One smiles at some of the consequences: 'the Pre-Raphaelite painter who was doing a twilight scene but rowed across the river in day time to see the shape of the leaves on the further bank, which he then drew in with full detail';[2] or Rossetti writing to Miss Boyd to ask for some details to put in his poem, 'The Stream's Secret',[3] or refusing

---

[1] Quoted in *Catalogue to the Ashley Library*, IX, p. 115.

[2] Ezra Pound, quoted Kenner, *The Invisible Poet: T. S. Eliot* (New York 1959), p. 152.

[3] *Letters*, II, 818. A series of letters in the Pierpont Morgan Library addressed to Mrs Temple reveal him worrying over magnolias to copy for *Fiammetta* and *The Lady at the Window*.

to provide bedclothes for the Virgin Mary in the *Annunciation* because Palestine's climate would not have called for them.[1] Slightly less absurd perhaps are Millais's painting a hedge, twig by twig, even to a bird's nest,[2] or Madox Brown borrowing some pictures of Italy from William Michael Rossetti from which to paint the background of his *Romeo and Juliet*,[3] or Rossetti's Dürer-like execution of the calf in *Found*,[4] or his brother's objection to an Academy picture of Duncan, because the head should have lain *deeper* in the pillows.[5]

They might well have abandoned such impracticable principles had not Ruskin actively encouraged them. He says he will subscribe to a work of Rossetti's, provided 'proper studies are made first' for the flower border.[6] And in his famous letters to *The Times* in defence of the Pre-Raphaelites it is their exact depiction of nature that he supports, saying there had been nothing like them in the way of drapery and detailed drawing since Dürer.[7] Again in his 1851 pamphlet on Pre-Raphaelitism he prophesies that they will found a new school in England if they 'adhere to their principles, and paint nature as it is around them, with the help of modern science. . . .'[8] It is doubtful whether the realists of the nineties represented the new school for which Ruskin hoped, but his words closely anticipate later writers who championed the realist school.[9] And thirty-six years after Ruskin's pamphlet, *The Hobby Horse* published his memorial notice of the engraver whose 'precision of facsimile' (II, 51) in reproducing specimens for Ruskin is still the object of his praise. His insistence upon the importance of laborious and careful copying of nature was certainly an influence upon the early Pre-Raphaelites: Millais's *The Waterfall*, for example, gives an immensely accurate geological account of the rocks beside the stream. Although it is not possible

[1] *Pre-Raphaelite Diaries and Letters*, p. 235.
[2] Ibid., p. 212.
[3] *Rossetti Papers 1862–1870* (1903), p. 226.
[4] *Ruskin, Rossetti and Pre-Raphaelitism*, p. 21.
[5] *Notes on the Royal Academy Exhibition*. p. 17.
[6] *Ruskin, Rossetti and Pre-Raphaelitism*, p. 123.
[7] *Works*, XI, p. 323.
[8] *Works*, XII, p. 358n.
[9] Cf. remarks by Crackanthorpe, Ellis and Zola quoted above.

for an artist to select nothing and reject nothing, many Pre-Raphaelite canvasses try very hard to prove that it is, with a relentless mass of detail in foreground, middleground and background, all seen with equal clarity.

Details count above all in explorations of new subjects, and here the nineties inherited the example of the Pre-Raphaelite Brotherhood. Far more important than their actual *cri de guerre* ('select nothing . . .') was the determination to evade stereotyped responses to a subject and, further, to evade them best by avoiding conventional subjects; the Nineties continued and enlarged this determination. Herein lies the real importance to later realism of Pre-Raphaelitism's emphasis on detail. For directing an artist to look closely at what he represents makes him either see new aspects of old subjects, or else realize that there are fresh areas of experience which have never been explored. And in either he will presumably support his observations by new details, which is how 'Jenny', *The Awakened Conscience* or Christina's *Commonplace* stories make such impression as they do. The same interest in careful 'scientific' observation successfully informs Nineties writing about commonplace or unheroic matters, like the absorbing particulars of gambling in Crackanthorpe's 'When Greek Meets Greek'.[1]

Just as the Pre-Raphaelites were concerned with details of the exterior world, so too they provide some examples, although neither so many nor so deliberate, of explorations of the mind, which are interesting anticipations of the vogue for psychological description in the nineties. In Christina's poem, 'The Lowest Room' (the 'modern vicious style' of which her brother disliked),[2] there is an analysis of a mind to a contemporary background of ladies' embroidery, marriage and garden walks. A similar use is made of psychological analysis within a realistic framework in her 'Waves of this Troublesome World'.

[1] Later writers seem to have picked up the Pre-Raphaelite fault of masses of unsorted, unselected detail where the eye wanders rather helplessly trying to pick out what is relevant: see the opening of Moore, *A Mummer's Wife* (1885), pp. 11–12. But Moore can of course make a magnificent use of details, as in the racing background of *Esther Waters*.

[2] See W. M. Rossetti's note in Christina's *Poetical Works*, p. 460.

The introspection of Christina, Dante Gabriel and Swinburne resulted in elaborate, if not always accurate or convincing, demonstrations of their minds' troubled complexities and visions: for instance, Swinburne's excited proclamation of his excessive affections—

> I have loved overmuch in my life; when the live bud bursts with the blossom,
> Bitter as ashes or tears is the fruit, and the wine thereof shame.
>   (I, 176)

or Rossetti's continuous variations upon the state of his soul—

> How should all this be told?—
> All the sad sum of wayworn days;—
> Heart's anguish in the impenetrable maze;
> And on the waste uncoloured wold
> The visible burthen of the sun grown cold
> And the moon's labouring gaze? (I, 100)

They lack the realistic framework of much of the Nineties' psychological descriptions, just as they lack the assurance and deliberation of, say, Crackanthorpe's analysis of the main character in 'The Haseltons'. Yet if they were not the actual inspiration for later work, the Pre-Raphaelites offered at least an example to improve upon: Rossetti, by his insistent probing of intense states of mind and by the claustrophobic anguish and thoughtfulness of many of his poems, like the storm and torment in the mind of Rose Mary or the sick obsessions of Sister Helen. His fascination with this last mental situation was to be a major enthusiasm of the Nineties, with their absorption in unusual, even insane mental states. Thus Laurence Housman's story of the idiot 'wizard', Eyloff,[1] shares with Rossetti, with at least a couple of writers in the 1856 *Magazine* and with Havelock Ellis, this interest in the human mind *à outrance*.

The *Oxford and Cambridge Magazine* also provides examples of this enthusiasm. There is Burne-Jones's 'The Cousins', a strange and forceful piece, which combines a realistic background with a picture of the narrator's distracted mind. Psychological analysis

---

[1] 'The Troubling of the Waters', *The Dome*, new series II.

or description occurs most usually in the *Magazine* when the minds *are* distracted: the crowded mental world of the mason in 'The Story of the Unknown Church'; the tormented thoughts mixed with biographical fragments in 'Frank's Sealed Letter'.

But the most interesting story is Fulford's 'Cavalay, a chapter of a life'. It ends:

And such is the story I now commend to you, dear reader,—simple and ordinary, with little incident, with no adventure, yet not devoid of thought and feeling, as the life of no man, though it seemed the most monotonous and commonplace, has ever been. The spiritual worth of a life is not always in proportion to the noise and bustle it has made. . . . Its most precious part may have been the unacted feeling and the unspoken thought.

This particular passage comes after Fulford has compared stories to different buildings—cathedrals, palaces, castles and 'mere dwelling houses'. Both in his comparison of the tale to a mere dwelling house and in his description of its ingredients and merits, Fulford gives a surprising summary of much nineties fiction. Just as the spiritual worth of a life is not judged by its noise and bustle, so he, as well as many later writers, would have said we cannot judge its artistic interest. Despite the moral earnestness and the 'dear reader-ing', Fulford's story anticipates many of the characteristics of later stories: the interest in the trivial and ordinary events of a life, the gloom, even morbidity shed over the tale by the sudden death of a character, Cavalay's visits to the poor in a friend's urban parish and, above all, the continuous use of unspoken thoughts. There are few passages of conversation or external description, for the narrative is told mostly through what happens in the mind of the main character, laboriously and painstakingly detailed. And if the point of the story is that Cavalay eventually learns the values of Duty and Patience, the 'sore trial' through which he passes to that knowledge affords Fulford considerable exercise in psychological exploration.

VIII

'Pre-Raphaelite Brethren', said Holman Hunt, 'were never realists'.[1] They were not, it is true, thorough-going realists like Moore, Crackanthorpe, D'Arcy, Dowson or Hardy. They had less of the deliberate pioneer in them and less urge (Swinburne excepted) to shock the average Victorian reader. They were also less overtly programmatic than writers in the 1890's and absorbed in rather more diversified concerns. Such anticipations of later realism as have been explored in this chapter were frequently incidental to Pre-Raphaelite intentions: Christina's pessimism subordinated to her devotions, Holman Hunt's realism subservient to his moral symbolism.

But it cannot be denied that elements central to Nineties realism are evident in the Pre-Raphaelite movement from its inception. Their use of contemporary subjects, of urban settings, of concentrated description of mental processes; pessimism, which if a characteristic of Christina alone is not unconnected with the dominant sense of transience in her brother or Pater and of life's consequent disappointments; their enlargement of the scope of poetry, either by Swinburne's immature revolts or by Rossetti's fascination for the sensual and, by Victorian standards, unusual experiences—he emphasized the *sin* of Launcelot, for example, in his painting at the Oxford Union;[2] their apparent extolling of 'fleshliness' and sex as suitable subjects for art; and in most of these aspects their careful devotion to detailed description. At the least, one can point to the way such elements anticipated later fashions. But it also seems possible to suggest that the Pre-Raphaelites provided both some English precedent for nineties enthusiasms and part of a 'vocabulary' for expressing them effectively.

[1] 'The Pre-Raphaelite Brotherhood: A Fight for Art', *The Contemporary Review*, May 1886, p. 740.

[2] *Ruskin, Rossetti and Pre-Raphaelitism*, p. 200. But it is worth noting that as late as 1893 George Egerton was still encountering editorial censure of her 'appeals to the sexual sense' which are similar to Buchanan's reaction to Rossetti and Swinburne. The editor of *The Weekly Sun* asked her, 'why speak of the lady's milk white limbs rounding off into pearl-grey shades (or whatever it is)? This is a direct appeal to sense' (quoted *A Leaf from the Yellow Book*, ed. de Vere White (1958), pp. 23–4).

Postscript

THE IMAGINATIVE ENERGIES of Pre-Raphaelitism seem exhausted by the century's end, dissipated often by the uncritical imitation of flatterers. A writer in *The Atlantic Monthly* summarized this sense of decline when in 1882 he said that Dante Gabriel Rossetti

has lived long enough to see the school and spirit which he, together with Mr Morris and Mr Swinburne, exemplifies ascend from faint beginnings to notable power, and then finally undergo the burdensome honor of travesty.[1]

These declensions of imitation, as well as the less disagreeable tributes of the 1890's of which he could not have known, have been rehearsed in the preceding chapters. Yet Pre-Raphaelitism did not altogether fail as an anti-scientific movement, as is sometimes reckoned.[2] Our sense of its often dispiriting decline has frequently to be modified by the apprehension of how Pre-Raphaelitism continued to stimulate the imagination even as it offered the wrong means to satisfy it. The stimulus came not merely from the re-introduction of the dragon into nineteenth-century poetry, but rather from the most eloquent reminder of the Carlylean dynamisms which the age often chose to neglect.

It seems a movement with many right instincts and concerns but unable to liberate itself from inadequate or inappropriate vocabularies. Holman Hunt observed, not altogether fairly, that Rossetti is absorbed less in the actuality of a poetic subject than in the 'finished phraseology, the mode of delineation'.[3] With more justice, *The Quarterly Review* suspected that in Swinburne

---

[1] *The Atlantic Monthly*, XLIX (1882), p. 119.

[2] See the motto from Cleanth Brooks used for my first chapter; it is taken from *Modern Poetry and the Tradition* (New York 1965), p. 241.

[3] Holman Hunt, *Pre-Raphaelitism and the Pre-Raphaelite Brotherhood*, I, 149.

remains only the 'phraseology of Republicanism'.[1] Both remarks elect to ignore the subject matter of Pre-Raphaelitism, but are right to emphasize how its dialects could distract writers from central issues. Their mediaeval enthusiasms are a crucial example of the tendency to be engrossed in the wrong vocabularies at the expense of genuine, personal concerns which do not as a consequence receive the attention they need.

When the Pre-Raphaelite imagination rejects or surpasses the inadequate languages with which it is hampered by its atavism, we see its more genuine and compelling qualities. Instead of *escape* through words—like those stunning verbal gems which Rossetti hoped to pitch upon in Froissart—they *act* through words. They explore both the resonant recesses of personality and what Blake calls 'portions of eternity, too great for the eye of man'. Pre-Raphaelitism enacts in its introspective and symbolist visions a wisdom that is antithetical to the Victorian world, and has the courage to preserve the integrity of those visions. It still experiences difficulties of articulation, which is why jokes can continue to be contrived at its expense:

The English soul possesses an extraordinary faculty for poetic reverie, capable of attaining the highest spheres of spiritual music, but also liable to run riot in an extraordinary Christmas calendar art suitable for retarded maiden ladies, as was the case with the Pre-Raphaelites.[2]

This reductive quip is fortunately not the complete account. The Pre-Raphaelites maintained that peculiarly English faculty for poetic reverie, satisfying the instincts which were rejected in Gradgrind's academy:

'They would be pictures of what was very pretty and pleasant, and I would fancy . . .'
'Aye, aye, aye! But you mustn't fancy,' cried the gentleman, quite elated by coming so happily to his point. 'That's it! You are never to fancy.'[3]

[1] *The Quarterly Review*, 132 (1872), p. 64.
[2] J. Casson, E. Langui and N. Pevsner, *The Sources of Modern Art* (London 1962), p. 12.
[3] *Hard Times*, chapter 2, 'Fact Versus Fancy'.

As long as such injunctions dominate, the Pre-Raphaelite imagination is a reminder that areas of spirit to which Mr Gradgrind denied authority must be honoured. In even a negative fashion Pre-Raphaelitism is an important counter in the intellectual scheme: as Holman Hunt said, Rossetti 'provokes the common sense of the world'.[1] More positively, he is a supreme English instance of a dedicated and serious artist, oblivious, if not actually hostile, to society's demands upon the arts. He provided an example of an artist who discovered, like Davidson, that the world was 'unadapted to reconstruct my own image', yet forged an art where it could be reconstructed. He offered an encouraging precedent for the two aspects of the 1890's which A. J. A. Symons notes in his *Anthology*: the superiority and the consolation of art, and the cultivation of the poet's personality.

These new emphases on art and the passions, particularly the ecstasy of love, were part of the development of new mental conditions, which Walter Pater recognized as the story of the nineteenth century, 'especially as exemplified in France'.[2] But they were equally, if perhaps less aggressively, exemplified in England. Pre-Raphaelitism continued as an energy in the last fifty years of the century because it grappled most consistently and uncompromisingly with those conditions. And the reason it merged sympathetically with French symbolism by the end of the movement was that they each constituted parallel solutions to peculiarly acute spiritual and artistic anxieties.

Nor was their joint inspiration ineffective after 1900. The work of Yeats and Pound and Ford Madox Ford, to name only three obvious figures,[3] rather than dismissing the Pre-Raphaelite imagination, maintains a dialogue with its essential notions. The life and contacts of Hugh Selwyn Mauberley as of Christopher Tietjens are not entirely hostile to Pre-Raphaelitism. They salute its presence in a landscape of the spirit even as they bid it a distinct farewell.

[1] Holman Hunt, op. cit., I, 217.

[2] *Miscellaneous Studies*, p. 13.

[3] I have tried elsewhere to argue in the same fashion about a less obvious figure, E. M. Forster: see my 'Mystery and Muddle in *A Passage to India*', *E. L. H.*, 33 (1966), 497–517.

The Burne-Jones cartons
Have preserved her eyes

. . . .

The thin, clear gaze, the same
Still darts out faun-like from the half-ruin'd face,
Questing and pensive . . .
'Ah, poor Jenny's case' . . .[1]

[1] Ezra Pound, 'Yeux Glauques', *Personae*, p. 201.

Select Bibliography

[An asterisk before an item in the bibliography denotes those works which treat of the influence of French upon English literature during the later nineteenth century: see Chapter One, p. 12, n.3.]

The Acorn, 2 vols., 1905 and 1906.

AGRESTI, A., 'Dell'Arte di Dante Gabriel Rossetti', the introduction to *La Vita Nuova*, illustrated with drawings by D. G. Rossetti, Turin 1911.

The Albemarle, a monthly magazine, edited by W. H. Wilkins and Hubert Crackanthorpe, 8 nos., 1892.

ARCHER, WILLIAM, *Poets of the Younger Generation*, 1902.

BATE, P., *English Pre-Raphaelite Painters*, 1899.

BEARDSLEY, AUBREY, *A Book of 50 Drawings*, with an iconography by Aymer Vallance, 1892.

A Second Book of 50 drawings, 1899.

The Early Work of Aubrey Beardsley, with prefatory note by H. C. Marillier, 1899.

The Later Work of Aubrey Beardsley, 1901.

Aubrey Beardsley Exhibition at the Victoria and Albert Museum. Catalogue of the original drawings, letters, manuscripts, paintings; and of books, posters, photographs, documents, etc., by Brian Reade and Frank Dickinson, 1966.

BEERBOHM, M. E., *The Works of Max Beerbohm*, 1896.

More, 1899.

The Poets' Corner, 1904.

Yet Again, 1909.

Zuleika Dobson, or an Oxford Love Story, 1911.

Rossetti and his Circle, 1922.

Seven Men and Two Others, 1950.

BLAKE, WILLIAM, *The Works of William Blake*, ed. Edwin John Ellis and W. B. Yeats, 3 vols., 1893.

The Poetical Works of William Blake, ed. with a prefatory memoir by W. M. Rossetti (Aldine edition), 1874.

BLUNT, A. and POOL, P., *Picasso: the Formative Years*, 1961.

BROWSE, LILLIAN, *Sickert*, 1960.

BUCKLEY, J. H., *The Victorian Temper: a study in literary culture*, Cambridge, Mass. 1952.

The Triumph of Time. A Study of the Victorian Concepts of Time, History, Progress, and Decadence, Cambridge, Mass. 1966.

BURDETT, OSBERT, *The Beardsley Period. An essay in perspective*, 1926.

BURNE-JONES, E. C., *Drawings of Burne-Jones*, with an introduction by T. Martin Wood, 1906.

BURNE-JONES, GEORGIANA, *Memorials of Edward Burne-Jones*, 2 vols., 1904.

*CAZAMIAN, M. L., *Le Roman et les Idées en Angleterre*; vol. II, *L'anti-intellectualisme et l'esthétisme 1880–1900*, Paris 1935.

The (Century Guild) Hobby Horse, a quarterly, ed. by A. H. Mackmurdo and H. Horne, 7 nos., 1886–92; new series, 3 nos., 1893.

The Chameleon, a quarterly, 1 no., 1894.

CHARLESWORTH, BARBARA, *Dark Passages, The Decadent Consciousness in Victorian Literature*, Madison and Milwaukee, 1965.

CHIARI, JOSEPH, *Symbolisme from Poe to Mallarmé: the Growth of a Myth*, with a foreword by T. S. Eliot, 1956.

*COLLET, GEORGES-PAUL, *George Moore et la France*, Paris 1957.

CONNOLLY, THOMAS E., *Swinburne's Theory of Poetry*, Albany, N.Y. 1964.

CRACKANTHORPE, HUBERT, *Wreckage*, 1893.

Sentimental Studies, 1895.

Vignettes, 1896.

Last Studies, with an appreciation by Henry James, 1897.

CRANE, WALTER, *The Claims of Decorative Art*, 1892.

The Work of Walter Crane, with notes by the artist, 1898.

William Morris to Whistler, 1911.

*DALE, HILDA, *La Poésie Française en Angleterre: 1850–90. Sa fortune et son influence*, Paris 1954.

D'ARCY, ELLA, *Monochromes*, 1895.

Modern Instances, 1898.

DAVIDSON, J., *In a Music-Hall, and other poems*, 1891.

Fleet Street Eclogues, 1st and 2nd series, 1893 and 1895.

Ballads and Songs, 1894.

New Ballads, 1897.

The Last Ballad and other poems, 1899.

*DECKER, C. R., 'Zola's Literary Reputation in England', *P.M.L.A.*, XLIX, 1934.

'The Aesthetic revolt against Naturalism in Victorian Criticism', *P.M.L.A.*, LIII, 1938.

DE LA SIZERANNE, ROBERT, *English Contemporary Art*, 1898.

The Dome, a quarterly, old series, 5 nos., new series, 7 nos., 1897–1900.

DOUGHTY, O., *A Victorian Romantic: Dante Gabriel Rossetti*, 1960.

'Rossetti's Conception of the "Poetic" in Poetry and Painting', *Essays by Divers Hands*, XXVI, 1953.

DOUGLAS, LORD ALFRED BRUCE, *Collected Poems*, 1919.

DOWSON, ERNEST, *Dilemmas, Stories and Studies in Sentiment*, 1895.

The Poetical Works, ed. with an introduction by Desmond Flower, Cassell's Pocket Library, 1950.

DUNN, H. T., *Recollections of Dante Gabriel Rossetti and his circle*, 1904.

EGERTON, GEORGE (MRS GOLDING-BRIGHT), *Keynotes*, 1893.

Discords, 1894.

A Leaf from The Yellow Book, the correspondence of George Egerton, ed. Terence de Vere White, 1958.

ELLMANN, RICHARD (ed.), *Edwardians and Late Victorians*, New York 1960.

*FARMER, A. J., *Le Mouvement Esthétique et 'Décadent' en Angleterre (1873–1900)*, Paris 1931.

FLEMING, G. H., *Rossetti and the Pre-Raphaelite Brotherhood*, 1967.

FLETCHER, IAN, *Walter Pater* (Writers and their Works, 114), 1959.

(ed.) *Romantic Mythologies*, 1967.

FREDEMAN, WILLIAM E., *Pre-Raphaelitism. A Bibliocritical Study*, Cambridge, Mass., 1965.

*FRIERSON, W. C., *L'Influence du Naturalisme Français sur les Romanciers Anglais de 1885 à 1900*, Paris 1925.

'The English Controversy over Realism in Fiction, 1885 to 1895', *P.M.L.A.*, XLIII, 1928.

'Realism in the 1890's and the Maupassant School in England', *French Quarterly*, X, 1928.

*GARBÁTY, THOMAS J., 'The French Coterie of the *Savoy*', *P.M.L.A.*, LXXV, 1960.

GAUNT, WILLIAM, *The Pre-Raphaelite Tragedy*, 1942.

The Aesthetic Adventure, 1945.

The Germ (1850), a facsimile reprint, introduced by W. M. Rossetti, 1901.

GHOSE, S. N., *Dante Gabriel Rossetti and Contemporary Criticism (1849–1882)*, Dijon 1929.

GILCHRIST, ALEXANDER, *Life of William Blake, with Selections from his Poems and Other Writings*, 2 vols., (2nd ed.), 1880.

GORDON, D. J., 'Aubrey Beardsley at the V & A', *Encounter*, 27, 1966.

GORDON, D. J., FLETCHER, IAN and others, *W. B. Yeats: Images of a Poet*, catalogue of exhibition at University of Manchester, 1961.

GRAY, JOHN, *Silverpoints*, 1893.

GREENAN, MARGARET R., *William Morris. Mediaevalist and Revolutionary*, New York 1945.

HAMILTON, W., *The Aesthetic Movement in England*, 1882.

HARLAND, HENRY, *A Latin Quarter Courtship and other stories*, 1890. *Mademoiselle Miss and other stories*, 1893.

*HARTLEY, K., *Oscar Wilde: l'influence française dans son oeuvre*, Paris 1935.

HICHENS, ROBERT, *The Green Carnation*, 1894.

HOARE, DOROTHY M., *The Works of Morris and Yeats in Relation to Early Saga Literature*, Cambridge 1937.

HOUGH, G., *The Last Romantics*, 1947. *Image and Experience*, 1960.

HUNT, WILLIAM HOLMAN, *Pre-Raphaelitism and the Pre-Raphaelite Brotherhood*, 2 vols., 1905. 'The Pre-Raphaelite Brotherhood: A Fight for Art', *The Contemporary Review*, 1886.

IRONSIDE, R. and GERE, J., *Pre-Raphaelite Painters*, 1948.

JACKSON, HOLBROOK, *The Eighteen-Nineties*, 1913. *Dreamers of Dreams*, 1948.

JOHNSON, LIONEL, *The Complete Poems*, ed. Ian Fletcher, 1953.

KERMODE, FRANK, *The Romantic Image*, 1957.

LAFOURCADE, G., *La Jeunesse de Swinburne*, 2 vols., Paris 1928.

LE GALLIENNE, R., *English Poems* (4th ed.), 1895. *Retrospective Reviews*, 2 vols., 1896. *The Book-Bills of Narcissus* (3rd ed.), 1895. *The Romantic Nineties*, 1925.

LEHMANN, A. G., *The Symbolist Aesthetic in France: 1885–95*, 1950.

LOMBARDO, A., *La Poesia Inglese dall'Estetismo al Simbolismo*, Rome 1950.

MADSEN, S. T., *Sources of Art Nouveau*, New York 1955.

MALLOCK, W. M., *The New Republic*, 1877.

MARILLIER, H. C., *Dante Gabriel Rossetti, an Illustrated Memorial of His Art and Life*, 1899.

MELCHIORI, G., *The Whole Mystery of Art: Pattern into Poetry in the Work of W. B. Yeats*, 1960.

MERRITT, J. D. (ed.), *The Pre-Raphaelite Poem*, New York 1966.

MICHAUD, G., *Message Poétique du Symbolisme*, 4 vols., Paris 1947.

MILLAIS, JOHN EVERETT, *Catalogue for an exhibition of his work* organized by the Walker Art Gallery, Liverpool and the Royal Academy of Arts, London 1967.

MILLAIS, T. G., *The Life and Letters of Sir John Everett Millais*, 2 vols., 1899.

MIX, K. L., *A Study in Yellow. The Yellow Book and its Contributors*, Lawrence, Kansas 1960.

MOORE, GEORGE, *Flowers of Passion*, 1878.

Literature at Nurse or Circulating Morals, 1885.

A Drama in Muslin, 1886.

A Mere Accident, 1887.

Confessions of a Young Man, 1888.

Mike Fletcher, 1889.

Modern Painting, 1893.

Esther Waters, 1894.

Celibates, 1895.

Memoirs of my Dead Life, 1906.

Impressions and Opinions, 1913.

(ed.) *Pure Poetry, an anthology*, 1924.

MORRIS, WILLIAM, *Collected Works*, with introductions by his daughter, 24 vols., 1910–15.

The Oxford and Cambridge Magazine for 1856, 12 nos., 1856.

PADEN, W. D., '*La Pia dei' Tolomei* by Dante Gabriel Rossetti', *The Register of the University of Kansas Museum of Art*, II, no. i, 1958.

The Pageant, 2 vols., 1896 and 1897.

Paintings and Drawings of the Pre-Raphaelites and their Circle, a Catalogue of an exhibition at the Fogg Museum of Art, Harvard University, with an introduction by Agnes Mongan and a note on the method and materials of Pre-Raphaelite painters by Richard D. Buck, 1946.

PATER, WALTER, *The Renaissance*, 1888 (first published as *Studies in the History of the Renaissance*, 1873).

Marius the Epicurean, 2 vols., 1909 (first ed., 1885).

Imaginary Portraits, 1901 (first ed., 1887).

Appreciations, 1913 (first published in 1889 with an essay, later omitted, on 'Aesthetic Poetry').

Miscellaneous Studies, 1910 (first ed., 1895).

Plato and Platonism, 1893.

Gaston de Latour, an unfinished romance, 1896.

PETERS, ROBERT L., *The Crowns of Apollo. Swinburne's Principles of Literature and Art. A Study in Victorian Criticism and Aesthetics*, Detroit 1965.

PLARR, V., *In the Dorian Mood*, 1896.

POUND, EZRA, *Literary Essays*, ed. with introduction by T. S. Eliot, 1954.

PRAZ, MARIO, *The Romantic Agony*, Meridian Books, New York 1956.

READE, BRIAN, *Art Nouveau and Alphonse Mucha* (H.M. Stationery Office), 1963.

RHYMERS' CLUB, *The Book of the Rhymers' Club*, 1892.

The Second Book of the Rhymers' Club, 1894.

RIEWALD, J. G., *Sir Max Beerbohm, Man and Writer*, Brattleboro, Vermont 1953.

*ROSENBLATT, LOUISE, *L'Idée de l'Art pour l'Art dans la Littérature Anglaise pendant la Période Victorienne*, Paris 1931.

ROSSETTI, CHRISTINA, *Poetical Works*, 1904.

Commonplace, and other short stories, 1870.

Speaking Likenesses, 1874.

Maud, a story for girls, with an introduction by W. M. Rossetti, 1908.

Family Letters of Christina Rossetti, ed. W. M. Rossetti, 1908.

ROSSETTI, DANTE GABRIEL, *Collected Works*, 2 vols., 1886.

Letters of Dante Gabriel Rossetti, ed. O. Doughty and J. R. Wahl, 5 vols., 1965–8.

Dante Gabriel Rossetti. An analytical list of MSs. in the Duke University Library, with hitherto unpublished verse and prose, ed. P. F. Baum, Durham, North Carolina 1931.

The House of Life, ed. P. F. Baum, Cambridge, Mass. 1928.

ROSSETTI, WILLIAM, MICHAEL, *Dante Gabriel Rossetti as Designer and Writer*, 1889.

(ed.) *Pre-Raphaelite Diaries and Letters*, 1900.

(ed.) *Ruskin, Rossetti and Pre-Raphaelitism*, 1899.

(ed.) *Rossetti Papers 1862–1870*, 1903.

(with Swinburne) *Notes on the Royal Academy Exhibition*, 1868.

*ROY, G. ROSS, 'A Bibliography of French Symbolism in English-language publications to 1910', *Revue de littérature comparée*, 34, 1960.

RUSKIN, JOHN, *Collected Works*, ed. E. T. Cook and Alexander Wedderburn, 39 vols., 1903–12.

RYALS, CLYDE DE L., *Decadence in British Literature Before the 'Fin de Siècle'*, University of Pennsylvania dissertation, 1957.

*SALVAN, J. L. *Le Romantisme Français et l'Angleterre Victorienne*, Paris 1949.

The Savoy, 8 nos., 1896.

The Savoy. Nineties Experiment, ed. with an introduction by Stanley Weintraub, University Park, Pennsylvania and London 1966.

SCHMUTZLER, ROBERT, *Art Nouveau*, 1964.

SCOTT, WILLIAM BELL, *Autobiographical Notes*, ed. W. Minto, 2 vols., 1892.

SECKER, MARTIN (ed.), *The Eighteen-Nineties. A Period Anthology in Prose and Verse*, with an introduction by John Betjeman, 1948.

SENIOR, JOHN, *The Way Down and Out: The Occult in Symbolist Literature*, Ithaca, New York 1959.

SICKERT, WALTER, *A Free House!*, ed Osbert Sitwell, 1947.

SOLOMON, SIMEON, *A Vision of Love Revealed in Sleep*, 1871.

The Spirit Lamp, a weekly, later fortnightly, finally monthly, ed. Lord Alfred Douglas, 15 nos., Oxford 1892–3.

*STARKIE, ENID, *From Gautier to Eliot: The Influence of France on English Literature: 1851–1939*, 1960.

STREET, G. S., *Episodes*, 1895.

SWINBURNE, A. C., *Collected Works*, 20 vols., 1925–7.

Letters, ed. Cecil Y. Lang, 6 vols., New Haven 1959–62.

Swinburne's Poems, 6 vols., 1919.

Notes on Poems and Reviews, 1866.

Under the Microscope, 1872.

'Simeon Solomon: Notes on his "Vision of Love" and other studies', *The Bibelot*, 14, Maine 1908.

William Blake. A critical essay, 1868.

(with W. M. Rossetti) *Notes on the Royal Academy Exhibition*, 1868.

SYMONDS, JOHN ADDINGTON, *In the Key of Blue and other prose essays*, 1918.

SYMONS, A. J. A., (ed.). *An Anthology of Nineties Verse*, 1928.

SYMONS, ARTHUR, *Poems*, 2 vols., 1919.

The Symbolist Movement in Literature, Dutton Everyman Paperback, New York 1958 (1st edition, 1899).

Studies in Two Literatures, 1897.
Studies in Prose and Verse, 1904.
Studies in Seven Arts, 1906.
William Blake, 1907.
Figures of Several Centuries, 1916.
Dramatis Personae, 1925.
Studies in Strange Souls, 1929.
A Study of Walter Pater, 1932.
'Henley's Poetry', *Fortnightly*, August 1892.
'The Decadent Movement in Literature', *Harper's New Monthly Magazine*, November 1893.
'La Littérature anglaise en 1893', *Mercure de France*, January– April 1894.
*TEMPLE, RUTH Z., *The Critic's Alchemy: a study of the introduction of French Symbolism into England*, New York 1953.
THOMPSON, PAUL, *The Work of William Morris*, 1967.
TINDALL, W. Y., *Forces in Modern British Literature, 1865–1940*, Vintage Books, New York 1956.
*TURQUET-MILNES, G., *The Influence of Baudelaire in France and England*, 1913.
*UNDERWOOD, V. P., *Verlaine et l'Angleterre*, Paris 1956.
'Rimbaud et les Lettres Anglo-Saxonnes', *Revue de Littérature Comparée*, July–September, 1961.
WARD, ANTHONY, *Walter Pater. The Idea in Nature*, 1966.
WELBY, T. EARLE, *A Study of Swinburne*, 1926.
WELLEK, RENÉ, 'Walter Pater's Literary Theory and Criticism', *Victorian Studies*, I, 1957.
WEST, PAUL, 'A Note on the 1890's', *English*, Summer 1958.
WHISTLER, JAMES A. MCN., *The Gentle Art of Making Enemies*, 1953.
WILDE, OSCAR, *The Works of Oscar Wilde*, ed., with an introduction by G. F. Maine, 1949.
Essays, Criticisms and Reviews, 1901 (priv. printed).
Decorative Art In America, ed. R. B. Glaenzer, New York 1906.
The Letters of Oscar Wilde, ed. Rupert Hart Davis, 1962.
De Profundis, with an introduction by V. Holland, 1949.
WILSON, EDMUND, *Axel's Castle*, The Scribner Library, New York 1959.
WRATISLAW, THEODORE, *Algernon Charles Swinburne: A Study*, 1900.
YEATS, W. B., *Collected Poems*, 1955.
Collected Plays, 1953.

Autobiographies, 1956.
Letters, ed. Allen Wade, 1954.
Mythologies, 1959.
Essays and Introductions, 1961.
The Yellow Book, a quarterly, 13 vols., 1894–7.
The Yellow Book: Quintessence of the Nineties, ed. Stanley Weintraub,
    Anchor Books, New York 1964.

Index

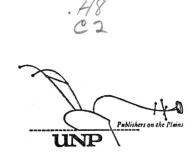

Publishers on the Plains

UNP

Published in the United States of America by
University of Nebraska Press, Lincoln 68508

Library of Congress Catalog Card No. 69–13334

Printed in Great Britain

THE
PRE-RAPHAELITE
IMAGINATION
1848-1900

JOHN DIXON HUNT

UNIVERSITY OF NEBRASKA PRESS

IN MEMORY OF MY

GRANDPARENTS:

Frank and Alice Dixon